THE LADIES' BOOK OF ETIQUETTES AND MANUAL OF POLITENESS

FLORENCE HARTLEY

Happy Hour Books

Published by:

HAPPY HOUR BOOKS

www.happyhoursbooks.com

email: happyhourbooks1@gmail.com

First published by Happy Hour Books 2024

Title : **The Ladies' Book of Etiquette and Manual of Politeness**

Paperback ISBN : 9789358486339

Hardback ISBN : 9789358487626

CHAPTER I

CONVERSATION

THE art of conversation consists in the exercise of two fine qualities. You must originate, and you must sympathize; you must possess at the same time the habit of communicating and of listening attentively. The union is rare but irresistible. None but an excessively ill-bred person will allow her attention to wander from the person with whom she is conversing; and especially she will never, while seeming to be entirely attentive to her companion, answer a remark or question made to another person, in another group. Unless the conversation is general among a party of friends, confine your remarks and attention entirely to the person with whom you are conversing. Steele says,

"I would establish one great general rule in conversation, which is this–that people should not talk to please themselves, but those who hear them. This would make them consider whether what they speak is worth hearing; whether there be either wit or sense in what they are about to say; and whether it be adapted to the time when, the place where, and the person to whom it is spoken."

Be careful in conversation to avoid topics which may be supposed to have any direct reference to events or circumstances which may be painful for your companion to hear discussed; you may unintentionally start a subject which annoys or troubles the friend with whom you may be conversing; in that case, do not stop abruptly, when you perceive that it causes pain, and, above all, do not make the matter worse by apologizing; turn to another subject as soon as possible, and pay no attention to the agitation your unfortunate remark may have excited. Many people will, for the sake of appearing witty or smart, wound the feelings of another deeply; avoid this; it is not only ill-bred, but cruel.

Remember that having all the talk sustained by one person is not conversation; do not engross all the attention yourself, by refusing to allow another person an opportunity to speak, and also avoid the other extreme of total silence, or answering only in monosyllables.

If your companion relates an incident or tells a story, be very careful not to interrupt her by questions, even if you do not clearly understand her; wait until she has finished her relation, and then ask any questions you may desire. There is nothing more annoying than to be so interrupted. I have heard a story told to an impertinent listener, which ran in this way:–

"I saw a fearful sight—-" "When?"

"I was about to tell you; last Monday, on the train—-" "What train?"

"The train from B—-. We were near the bridge—-" "What bridge?"

"I will tell you all about it, if you will only let me speak. I was coming from B—-"

"Last Monday, did you say?"

and so on. The story was interrupted at every sentence, and the relator condemned as a most tedious story-teller, when, had he been permitted to go forward, he would have made the incident interesting and short.

Never interrupt any one who is speaking. It is very ill-bred. If you see that a person to whom you wish to speak is being addressed by another person, never speak until she has heard and replied; until her conversation with that person is finished. No truly polite lady ever breaks in upon a conversation or interrupts another speaker.

Never, in speaking to a married lady, enquire for her husband, or, if a gentleman, ask for his wife. The elegant way is to call the absent party by their name; ask Mr. Smith how Mrs. Smith is, or enquire of Mrs. Jones for Mr. Jones, but never for "your husband" or "your wife." On the other hand, if you are married, never speak of your husband as your "lord," "husband," or "good man," avoid, also, unless amongst relatives, calling him by his Christian name.

If you wish others to respect him, show by speaking of him in respectful terms that you do so yourself. If either your own husband or your friend's is in the army or navy, or can claim the Dr., Prof., or any other prefix to his name, there is no impropriety in speaking of him as the colonel, doctor, or whatever his title may be.

It is a mark of ill-breeding to use French phrases or words, unless you are sure your companion is a French scholar, and, even then, it is best to avoid them. Above all, do not use any foreign word or phrase,

unless you have the language perfectly at your command. I heard a lady once use a Spanish quotation; she had mastered that one sentence alone; but a Cuban gentleman, delighted to meet an American who could converse with him in his own tongue, immediately addressed her in Spanish. Embarrassed and ashamed, she was obliged to confess that her knowledge of the language was confined to one quotation.

Never anticipate the point or joke of any anecdote told in your presence. If you have heard the story before, it may be new to others, and the narrator should always be allowed to finish it in his own words. To take any sentence from the mouth of another person, before he has time to utter it, is the height of ill-breeding. Avoid it carefully.

Never use the phrases, "What-d-ye call it,"

"Thingummy," "What's his name," or any such substitutes for a proper name or place. If you cannot recall the names you wish to use, it is better not to tell the story or incident connected with them. No lady of high breeding will ever use these substitutes in conversation.

Be careful always to speak in a distinct, clear voice; at the same time avoid talking too loudly, there is a happy medium between mumbling and screaming. Strive to attain it.

Overlook the deficiencies of others when conversing with them, as they may be the results of ignorance, and impossible to correct. Never pain another person by correcting, before others, a word or phrase mispronounced or ungrammatically constructed. If your intimacy will allow it, speak of the fault upon another occasion, kindly and privately, or let it pass. Do not be continually watching for faults, that you may display your own superior wisdom in correcting them. Let modesty and kind feeling govern your conversation, as other rules of life. If, on the other hand, your companion uses words or expressions which you cannot understand, do not affect knowledge, or be ashamed of your ignorance, but frankly ask for an explanation.

In conversing with professional gentlemen, never question them upon matters connected with their employment.

An author may communicate, voluntarily, information interesting to you, upon the subject of his works, but any questions from you would be extremely rude. If you meet a physician who is attending a friend, you may enquire for their progress, but do not expect him to give you a detailed account of the disease and his manner of treating it. The same rule applies to questioning lawyers about their clients, artists on their paintings, merchants or mechanics of their several branches of business. Professional or business men, when with ladies, generally wish for miscellaneous subjects of conversation, and, as their visits are for recreation, they will feel excessively annoyed if obliged to "talk shop." Still many men can converse on no other subject than their everyday employment. In this case listen politely, and show your interest. You will probably gain useful information in such conversation.

Never question the veracity of any statement made in general conversation. If you are certain a statement is false, and it is injurious to another person, who may be absent, you may quietly and courteously inform the speaker that he is mistaken, but if the falsehood is of no consequence, let it pass. If a statement appears monstrous, but you do not know that it is false, listen, but do not question its veracity.

It may be true, though it strikes you as improbable.

Never attempt to disparage an absent friend. It is the height of meanness. If others admire her, and you do not, let them have their opinion in peace; you will probably fail if you try to lower her in their esteem, and gain for yourself the character of an ill-natured, envious person.

In conversing with foreigners, if they speak slightly of the manners of your country, do not retort rudely, or resentfully. If their views are wrong, converse upon the subject, giving them frankly your views, but never retali-ate by telling them that some custom of their own country is worse. A gentleman or lady of true refinement will always give your words candid consideration, and admit that an American may possibly know the customs of her country better than they do, and if your opponent is not well-bred, your rudeness will not improve his manners. Let the conversation upon national subjects be candid, and at the same time courteous, and leave him to think that the ladies in America are well-bred, however much he may dislike some little national peculiarity.

Avoid, at all times, mentioning subjects or incidents that can in any way disgust your hearers. Many people will enter into the details of sicknesses which should be mentioned only when absolutely necessary, or describe the most revolting scenes before a room full of people, or even at a table.

Others speak of vermin, noxious plants, or instances of un-cleanliness. All such conversation or allusion is excessively ill-bred. It is not only annoying, but absolutely sickening to some, and a truly lady-like person will avoid all such topics.

I cannot too severely censure the habit of using sentences which admit a double meaning. It is not only ill-bred, but indelicate, and no person of true refinement will ever do it. If you are so unfortunate as to converse with one who uses such phrases, never by word, look, or sign show that you understand any meaning beyond the plain, outspoken language.

Avoid always any discussion upon religious topics, unless you are perfectly certain that your remarks cannot annoy or pain any one present. If you are tête-à-tête with a friend, and such a discussion arises, inquire about your companion's church and mention your own, so that you may yourself avoid unpleasant remarks, and caution him.

Never, when advancing an opinion, assert positively that a thing "is so," but give your opinion as an opinion. Say, "I think this is so," or "these are my views," but remember that your companion may be better informed upon the subject under discussion, or, where it is a mere matter of taste or feeling, do not expect that all the world will feel exactly as you do.

Never repeat to a person with whom you converse, any unpleasant speech you may have heard concerning her.

If you can give her pleasure by the repetition of a delicate compliment, or token of approval shown by a mutual friend, tell her the pleasant speech or incident, but do not hurt her feelings, or involve her in a quarrel by the repetition of ill-natured remarks.

Amongst well-bred persons, every conversation is considered in a measure confidential. A lady or gentleman tacitly confides in you when he (or she) tells you an incident which may cause trouble if repeated, and you violate a confidence as much in such a repetition, as if you were bound over to secrecy. Remember this.

Never criticise a companion's dress, or indeed make any remark whatsoever upon it. If a close friend, you may, if sincere, admire any article, but with a mere acquaintance let it pass unnoticed. If, however, any accident has happened to the dress, of which she is ignorant, tell her of it, and assist her in repairing the mischief.

To be able to converse really well, you must read much, treasure in your memory the pearls of what you read; you must have a quick comprehension, observe passing events, and listen attentively whenever there is any opportunity of acquiring knowledge. A quick tact is necessary, too, in conversation. To converse with an entirely uneducated person upon literature, interlarding your remarks with quotations, is ill-bred. It places them in an awkward situation, and does not add to your popularity. In conversing with persons of refinement and intelligence, do not endeavor to attract their admiration by pouring forth every item of your own information upon the subject under consideration, but listen as well as talk, and modestly follow their lead. I do not mean, to assent to any opinion they may advance, if you really differ in your own tastes, but do not be too ready to show your superior judgment or information. Avoid argument; it is not conversation, and frequently leads to ill feeling. If you are unfortunately drawn into an argument, keep your temper under perfect control, and if you find your adversary is getting too warm, endeavor to introduce some other topic.

Avoid any allusion to the age or personal defects of your companion, or any one who may be in the room, and be very careful in your language when speaking of a stranger to another person. I have heard a lady inquire of a gentleman, "who that frightful girl in blue could be," and receive the information that the lady in question was the gentleman's own sister.

Be careful, when traveling, not to wound the feelings of your friends in another country or city, by underrating their native place, or attempting to prove the superiority of your own home over theirs.

Very young girls are apt to suppose, from what they observe in older ones, that there is some particular manner to be put on, in talking to gentlemen, and, not knowing exactly what it is, they are embarrassed and reserved; others observe certain airs and looks, used by their elders in this intercourse, and try to imitate them, as a necessary part of company behaviours, and, so become affected, and lose that first of charms, simplicity, natural grace. To such, let me say, your companions are in error; it requires no peculiar manner, nothing to be put on, in order to converse with gentlemen, any more than with ladies; and the more pure and elevated your sentiments are, and the better cultivated your intellect is, the easier will you find it to converse pleasantly with all. One good rule can be always followed by young ladies; to converse with a lady friend as if there were gentlemen present, and to converse with a gentleman as if in the room with other ladies.

Avoid affectation; it is the sure test of a deceitful, vulgar mind. The best cure is to try to have those virtues which you would affect, and then they will appear naturally.

CHAPTER II

DRESS

"A LADY IS never so well dressed as when you cannot remember what she wears."

No truer remark than the above was ever made. Such an effect can only be produced where every part of the dress harmonizes entirely with the other parts, where each color or shade suits the wearer's style completely, and where there is perfect neatness in each detail. One glaring color, or conspicuous article, would entirely mar the beauty of such a dress. It is, unfortunately, too much the custom in America to wear any article, or shape in make, that is fashionable, without any regard to the style of the person purchasing goods. If it is the fashion it must be worn, though it may greatly exaggerate a slight personal defect, or conceal or mar what would otherwise be a beauty. It requires the exercise of some judgment to decide how far an individual may follow the dictates of fashion, in order to avoid the appearance of eccentricity, and yet wear what is peculiarly becoming to her own face or figure. Another fault of our fair countrywomen is their extravagance in dress. No better advice can be given to a young person than to dress always according to her circumstances. She will be more respected with a simple wardrobe, if it is known either that she is dependent upon her own exertions for support, or is saving a husband or father from unnecessary outlay, than if she wore the most costly fabrics, and by so doing incurred debt or burdened her relatives with heavy, unwarrantable expense. If neatness, consistency, and good taste, preside over the wardrobe of a lady, expensive fabrics will not be needed; for with the simplest materials, harmony of color, accurate fitting to the figure, and perfect neatness, she will always appear well dressed.

GENERAL RULES.

NEATNESS–This is the first of all rules to be observed with regard to dress. Perfect cleanliness and careful adjustment of each article in the dress are indispensable in a finished toilet. Let the hair be always smooth and becomingly arranged, each article exquisitely clean, neat collar and sleeves, and tidy shoes and stockings, and the simplest dress will appear well, while a torn or soiled collar, rough hair, or untidy feet will entirely ruin the effect of the most costly and elaborate dress. The many articles required in a lady's wardrobe make a neat arrangement of her drawers and closets necessary, and also require care in selecting and keeping goods in proper order. A fine collar or lace, if tumbled or soiled, will lose its beauty when contrasted with the same article in the coarsest material perfectly pure and smooth. Each article of dress, when taken off, should be placed carefully and smoothly in its proper place. Nice dresses should be hung up by a loop on the inside of the waistband, with the skirts turned inside out, and the body turned inside of the skirt. Cloaks should hang in smooth folds from a loop on the inside of the neck. Shawls should be always folded in the creases in which they were purchased. All fine articles, lace, embroidery, and handkerchiefs, should be placed by themselves in a drawer, always laid out smoothly, and kept from dust. Furs should be kept in a box, alone, and in summer carefully packed, with a quantity of lump camphor to protect from moths. The bonnet should always rest upon a stand in the band-box, as the shape and trimming will both be injured by letting it lie either on the face, sides, or crown.

ADAPTIVENESS–Let each dress worn by a lady be suitable to the occasion upon which she wears it. A toilet may be as offensive to good taste and propriety by being too elaborate, as by being slovenly. Never wear a dress which is out of place or out of season under the impression that "it will do for once," or "nobody will notice it." It is in as bad taste to receive your morning calls in an elaborate evening dress, as it would be to attend a ball in your morning wrapper.

HARMONY–To appear well dressed without harmony, both in color and materials, is impossible. When arranging any dress, whether for home, street, or evening, be careful that each color harmonizes well with the rest, and let no one article, by its glaring costliness, make all the rest appear mean. A costly lace worn over a thin, flimsy silk, will only make the dress appear poorer, not, as some suppose, hide its defects. A rich trimming looks as badly upon a cheap dress, as a mean one does upon an expensive fabric. Observe this rule always in purchasing goods. One costly article will entirely ruin the harmony in a dress, which, without it, though plain and inexpensive, would be becoming and beautiful.

Do not save on the dress or cloak to buy a more elaborate bonnet, but let the cost be well equalized and the effect will be good. A plain merino or dark silk, with a cloth cloak, will look much better than the most expensive velvet cloak over a cheap delaine dress.

FASHION–Do not be too submissive to the dictates of fashion; at the same time avoid oddity or eccentricity in your dress. There are some persons who will follow, in defiance of taste and judgment, the fashion to its most extreme point; this is a sure mark of vulgarity. Every new style of dress will admit of adaptation to individual cases, thus producing a pleasing, as well as fashionable effect. Not only good taste, but health is often sacrificed to the silly error of dressing in the extreme of fashion. Be careful to have your dress comfortable and becoming, and let the prevailing mode come into secondary consideration; avoiding, always, the other extreme of oddity or eccentricity in costume.

STYLE AND FORM OF DRESS–Be always careful when making up the various parts of your wardrobe, that each article fits you accurately. Not in the outside garments alone must this rule be followed, an ill-fitting pair of corsets, or wrinkles in any other article of the under-clothes, will make a dress set badly, even if it has been itself fitted with the utmost accuracy. A stocking which is too large, will make the boot uncomfortably tight, and too small will compress the foot, making the shoe loose and untidy. In a dress, no outlay upon the material will compensate for a badly fitting garment. A cheap calico made to fit the form accurately and easily, will give the wearer a more lady-like air than the richest silk which either wrinkles or is too tightly strained over the figure. Collars or sleeves, pinned over or tightly strained to meet, will entirely mar the effect of the prettiest dress.

ECONOMY–And by economy I do not mean mere cheap-ness. To buy a poor, flimsy fabric merely because the price is low, is extravagance, not economy; still worse if you buy articles because they are offered cheap, when you have no use for them. In purchasing goods for the wardrobe, let each material be the best of its kind. The same amount of sewing that is put into a good material, must be put into a poor one, and, as the latter will very soon wash or wear out, there must be another one to supply its place, purchased and made up, when, by buying a good article at first, this time and labor might have been saved. A good, strong material will be found cheapest in the end, though the actual expenditure of money may be larger at first.

COMFORT–Many ladies have to trace months of severe suffering to an improper disregard of comfort, in preparing their wardrobe, or in exposure after they are dressed. The most exquisite ball costume will never compensate for the injury done by tight lacing, the prettiest foot is dearly paid for by the pain a tight boot entails, and the most graceful effects will not prevent suffering from exposure to cold. A light ball dress and exquisite arrangement of the hair, too often make the wearer dare the inclemency of the coldest night, by wearing a light shawl or hood, to prevent crushing delicate lace or flowers. Make it a fixed rule to have the head, feet, and chest well protected when going to a party, even at the risk of a crushed flower or a stray curl. Many a fair head has been laid in a coffin, a victim to consumption, from rashly venturing out of a heated ball room, flushed and excited, with only a light protection against keen night air. The excitement of the occasion may prevent immediate discomfort in such cases, but it adds to the subsequent danger.

DETAILS–Be careful always that the details of your dress are perfectly finished in every point. The small articles of a wardrobe require constant care to keep in perfect order, yet they will wofully revenge themselves if neglected. Let the collar, handkerchief, boots, gloves, and belts be always whole, neat, and adapted to the dress. A lace collar will look as badly over a chintz dress, as a linen one would with velvet, though each may be perfect of its kind. Attention to these minor points are sure tests of taste in a lady's dress. A shabby or ill fitting boot or glove will ruin the most elaborate walking dress, while one of much planer make and coarser fabric will be becoming lady-like, if all the details are accurately fitted, clean, and we'll put on.

In arranging a dress for every occasion, be careful that there is no missing string, hook, or button, that the folds hang well, and that every part is even and properly adjusted.

Let the skirts hang smoothly, the outside ones being always about an inch longer than the under ones; let the dress set smoothly, carefully hooked or buttoned; let the collar fit neatly, and be fastened firmly and smoothly at the throat; let shoes and stockings be whole, clean, and fit nicely; let the hair be smooth and glossy, the skin pure, and the colors and fabric of your dress harmonize and be suitable for the occasion, and you will always appear both lady-like and well- dressed.

HOME DRESSES.

MORNING DRESS–The most suitable dress for breakfast, is a wrapper made to fit the figure loosely, and the material, excepting when the winter weather requires woolen goods, should be of chintz, gingham, brilliante, or muslin. A lady who has children, or one accustomed to perform for herself light household duties, will soon find the advantage of wearing materials that will wash. A large apron of domestic gingham, which can be taken off, if the wearer is called to see unexpected visiters, will protect the front of the dress, and save washing the wrapper too frequently. If a lady's domestic duties require her attention for several hours in the morning, whilst her list of acquaintances is large, and she has frequent morning calls, it is best to dress for callers before breakfast, and wear over this dress a loose sack and skirt of domestic gingham. This, while protecting the dress perfectly, can be taken off at a moment's notice if callers are announced. Married ladies often wear a cap in the morning, and lately, young girls have adopted the fashion. It is much better to let the hair be perfectly smooth, requiring no cap, which is often worn to conceal the lazy, slovenly arrangement of the hair. A few moments given to making the hair smooth and presentable without any covering, will not be wasted. Slippers of embroidered cloth are prettiest with a wrapper, and in summer black morocco is the most suitable for the house in the morning.

DRESS FOR MORNING VISITS–A lady should never receive her morning callers in a wrapper, unless they call at an unusually early hour, or some unexpected demand upon her time makes it impossible to change her dress after breakfast. On the other hand, an elaborate costume before dinner is in excessively bad taste. The dress should be made to fit the figure neatly, finished at the throat and wrists by an embroidered collar and cuffs, and, unless there is a necessity for it, in loss of the hair or age, there should be no cap or head dress worn. A wrapper made with handsome trimming, open over a pretty white skirt, may be worn with propriety; but the simple dress worn for breakfast, or in the exercise of domestic duties, is not suitable for the parlor when receiving visits of ceremony in the morning.

EVENING DRESS–The home evening dress should be varied according to circumstances. If no visitor is expected, the dress worn in the morning is suitable for the evening; but to receive visitors, it should be of lighter material, and a light head-dress may be worn.For young ladies, at home, ribbon or velvet are the most suitable materials for a head-dress. Flowers, unless they be natural ones in summer, are in very bad taste, excepting in cases where a party of invited guests are expected. Dark silk in winter, and thin material in summer, make the most suitable dresses for evening, and the reception of the chance-guests ladies in society may usually expect.

WALKING DRESSES–Walking dresses, to be in good taste, should be of quiet colors, and never conspicuous.

Browns, modes, and neutral tints, with black and white, make the prettiest dresses for the street. Above all, avoid wearing several bright colors. One may be worn with perfect propriety to take off the sombre effect of a dress of brown or black, but do not let it be too glaring, and wear but little of it. Let the boots be sufficiently strong and thick to protect the feet from damp or dust, and wear always neat, clean, nicely fitting gloves. The entire effect of the most tasteful costume will be ruined if attention is not paid to the details of dress. A soiled bonnet cap, untidy strings, or torn gloves and collar will utterly spoil the prettiest costume. There is no surer mark of vulgarity than over dressing or gay dressing in the street. Let the materials be of the costliest kind, if you will, but do not either wear the exaggerations of the fashion, or conspicuous colors. Let good taste dictate the limits where fashion may rule, and let the colors harmonize well, and be of such tints as will not attract attention.

FOR MORNING CALLS–The dress should be plain, and in winter furs and dark gloves may be worn.

FOR BRIDAL CALLS–The dress should be of light silk, the bonnet dressy, and either a rich shawl or light cloak; no furs, and light gloves. In summer, a lace or silk mantle and white gloves should be worn.

SHOPPING DRESSES–Should be of such material as will bear the crush of a crowded store without injury, and neither lace or delicate fabrics should ever be worn. A dress of merino in winter, with a cloth cloak and plain velvet or silk bonnet is the most suitable. In summer, a dress and cloak of plain mode-colored Lavella cloth, or any other cool but strong fabric, with a simply trimmed straw bonnet, is the best dress for a shopping excursion.

STORM DRESSES–A lady who is obliged to go out frequently in bad weather, will find it both a convenience and economy to have a storm dress. Both dress and cloak should be made of a woolen material, (varying of course with the season,) which will shed water. White skirts are entirely out of place, as, if the dress is held up, they will be in a few moments disgracefully dirty. A woolen skirt, made quite short, to clear the muddy streets, is the proper thing. Stout, thick-soled boots, and gloves of either silk, beaver-cloth, or lisle thread, are the most suitable. The bonnet should be either of straw or felt, simply trimmed; and, above all, carry a large umbrella. The little light umbrellas are very pretty, no doubt, but to be of any real protection in a storm, the umbrella should be large enough to protect the whole dress.

MARKETING–Here a dress of the most inexpensive kind is the best. There is no surer mark of vulgarity, than a costly dress in the market. A chintz is the best skirt to wear, and in winter a dark chintz skirt put on over a delaine dress, will protect it from baskets, and the unavoidable soils contracted in a market, while it looks perfectly well, and can be washed if required.

TRAVELING–Traveling dresses should be made always of some quiet color, perfectly plain, with a deep mantle or cloak of the same material. When traveling with a young babe, a dress of material that will wash is the best, but it should be dark and plain. A conspicuous traveling dress is in very bad taste, and jewelry or ornaments of any kind are entirely out of place. Let the dress be made of dark, plain material, with a simple straw or felt bonnet, trimmed with the same color as the dress, and a thick barege veil. An elastic string run through a tuck made in the middle of the veil, will allow one half to fall over the face, while the other half falls back, covering the bonnet, and protecting it from dust. If white collars and sleeves are worn, they should be of linen, perfectly plain. Strong boots and thick gloves are indispensable in traveling, and a heavy shawl should be carried, to meet any sudden change in the weather. Corsets and petticoats of dark linen are more suitable than white ones, as there is so much unavoidable dust and mud constantly meeting a traveler.

EVENING DRESSES–Must be governed by the number of guests you may expect to meet, and the character of the entertainment to which you are invited. For small social companies, a dark silk in winter, and a pretty lawn, barege, or white muslin in summer, are the most appropriate. A light head-dress of ribbon or velvet, or a plain cap, are the most suitable with this dress. For a larger party, low-necked, short-sleeved silk, light colored, or any of the thin goods made expressly for evening wear, with kid gloves, either of a color to match the dress or of white; black lace mittens are admissible, and flowers in the hair. A ball dress should be made of either very dressy silk, or light, thin material made over silk. It should be trimmed with lace, flowers, or ribbon, and made dressy. The coiffure should be elaborate, and match the dress, being either of ribbon, feather, or flowers. White kid gloves, trimmed to match the dress, and white or black satin slippers, with silk stockings, must be worn.

MOURNING–There is such a variety of opinion upon the subject of mourning, that it is extremely difficult to lay down any general rules upon the subject. Some wear very close black for a long period, for a distant relative; whilst others will wear dressy mourning for a short time in a case of death in the immediate family. There is no rule either for the depth of mourning, or the time when it may be laid aside, and I must confine my remarks to the different degrees of mourning.

For deep mourning, the dress should be of bombazine, Parramatta cloth, delaine, barege, or merino, made up over black lining. The only appropriate trimming is a deep fold, either of the same material or of crape. The shawl or cloak must be of plain black, without border or trimming, unless a fold of crape be put on the cloak; the bonnet should be of crape, made perfectly plain, with crape facings, unless the widow's cap be worn, and a deep crape veil should be thrown over both face and bonnet. Black crape collar and sleeves, and black boots and gloves. The next degree is to wear white collar and sleeves, a bow of crape upon the bonnet, and plain white lace facings, leaving off the crape veil, and substituting one of plain black net. A little later, black silk without any gloss, trimmed with crape, may be worn, and delaine or bombazine, with a trimming of broad, plain ribbon, or a bias fold of silk. The next stage admits a silk bonnet trimmed with crape, and lead color, dark purple, or white figures on the dress. From this the mourning passes into second mourning. Here a straw bonnet, trimmed with black ribbon or crape flowers, or a silk bonnet with black flowers on the outside, and white ones in the face, a black silk dress, and gray shawl or cloak, may be worn. Lead color, purple, lavender, and white, are all admissible in second mourning, and the dress may be lightened gradually, a white bonnet, shawl, and light purple or lavender dress, being the dress usually worn last, before the mourning is thrown aside entirely, and colors resumed. It is especially recommended to always buy the best materials when making up mourning. Crape and woolen goods of the finest quality are very expensive, but a cheaper article will wear miserably; there is no greater error in the economy than purchasing cheap mourning, for no goods are so inferior, or wear out and grow rusty so soon.

CHAPTER III

TRAVELING

THERE is no situation in which a lady is more exposed than when she travels, and there is no position where a dignified, lady-like deportment is more indispensable and more certain to command respect. If you travel under the escort of a gentleman, give him as little trouble as possible; at the same time, do not interfere with the arrangements he may make for your comfort. It is best, when starting upon your journey, to hand your escort a sufficient sum of money to cover all your expenses, retaining your pocket book in case you should wish to use it. Have a strong pocket made in your upper petticoat, and in that carry your money, only reserving in your dress pocket a small sum for incidental expenses. In your traveling satchel carry an oil skin bag, containing your sponge, tooth and nail brushes, and some soap; have also a calico bag, with hair brush and comb, some pins, hair pins, a small mirror, and some towels. In this satchel carry also some crackers, or sandwiches, if you will be long enough upon the road to need a luncheon.

In your carpet bag, carry a large shawl, and if you will travel by night, or stop where it will be inconvenient to open your trunks, carry your night clothes, and what clean linen you may require, in the carpet bag. It is best to have your name and address engraved upon the plate of your carpet bag, and to sew a white card, with your name and the address to which you are traveling, in clear, plain letters upon it. If you carry a novel or any other reading, it is best to carry the book in your satchel, and not open the carpet bag until you are ready for the night. If you are to pass the night in the cars, carry a warm woolen or silk hood, that you may take off your bonnet at night. No one can sleep comfortably in a bonnet. Carry also, in this case, a large shawl to wrap round your feet.

One rule to be always observed in traveling is punctuality. Rise early enough to have ample time for arranging everything needful for the day's journey. If you sleep upon the boat, or at a hotel, always give directions to the servant to wake you at an hour sufficiently early to allow ample time for preparation. It is better to be all ready twenty minutes too soon, than five minutes late, or even late enough to be annoyed and heated by hurrying at the last moment.

A lady will always dress plainly when traveling. A gay dress, or finery of any sort, when in a boat, stage, or car, lays a woman open to the most severe misconstruction. Wear neutral tints, and have the material made up plainly and substantially, but carefully avoid any article of dress that is glaring or conspicuous. Above all, never wear jewelry, (unless it be your watch,) or flowers; they are both in excessively bad taste. A quiet, unpretending dress, and dignified demeanor, will insure for a lady's respect, though she travels alone from Maine to Florida.

If you are obliged to pass the night upon a steamboat secure, if possible, a stateroom. You will find the luxury of being alone, able to retire and rise without witnesses, fully compensates for the extra charge. Before you retire, find out the position and number of the stateroom occupied by your escort, in case you wish to find him during the night. In times of terror, from accident or danger, such care will be found invaluable.

You may not be able to obtain a stateroom upon all occasions when traveling, and must then sleep in the ladies' cabin. It is best, in this case, to take off the dress only, merely loosening the stays and skirts, and, unless you are sick, you may sit up to read until quite late. Never allow your escort to accompany you into the cabin. The saloon is always open to both ladies and gentlemen, and the cabin is for ladies alone. Many ladies are sufficiently ill-bred to ask a husband or brother into the cabin, and keep him there talking for an hour or two, totally overlooking the fact that by doing so she may be keeping others, suffering, perhaps, with sickness, from removing their dresses to lie down. Such conduct is not only excessively ill-bred, but intensely selfish.

There is scarcely any situation in which a lady can be placed, more admirably adapted to test her good breeding, than in the sleeping cabin of a steam-boat. If you are so unfortunate as to suffer from sea- sickness, your chances for usefulness are limited, and patience is your only resource. In this case, never leave home without a straw- covered bottle of brandy, and another of camphor, in your carpet-bag. If you are not sick, be very careful not to keep the chambermaid from those who are suffering; should you require her services, dismiss her as soon as possible. As acquaintances, formed during a journey, are not recognized afterwards, unless mutually agreeable, do not refuse either a pleasant word or any little offer of service from your companions; and, on the other hand, be ready to aid them, if in your power. In every case, selfishness is the root of all ill-breeding, and it is never more conspicuously displayed than in traveling. A courteous manner, and graceful offer of service are valued highly when offered, and the giver loses nothing by her civility.

When in the car if you find the exertion of talking painful, say so frankly; your escort cannot be offended. Do not continually pester either your companion or the conductor with questions, such as "Where are we now?" "When shall we arrive?" If you are wearied, this impatience will only make the journey still more tedious. Try to occupy yourself with looking at the country through which you are passing, or with a book.

If you are traveling without any escort, speak to the conductor before you start, requesting him to attend to you whilst in the car or boat under his control. Sit quietly in the cars when they reach the depot until the first bustle is over, and then engage a porter to procure for you a hack, and get your baggage. If upon a boat, let one of the servants perform this office, being careful to fee him for it.

Make an engagement with the hackman, to take you only in his hack, and enquire his charge before starting. In this way you avoid unpleasant company during your drive, and overcharge at the end of it.

If you expect a friend to meet you at the end of your journey, sit near the door of the steam-boat saloon, or in the ladies' room at the car depot, that he may find you easily.

There are many little civilities which a true gentleman will offer to a lady traveling alone, which she may accept, even from an entire stranger, with perfect propriety; but, while careful to thank him courteously, whether you accept or decline his attentions, avoid any advance towards acquaintanceship. If he sits near you and seems disposed to be impertinent, or obtrusive in his attentions or conversation, lower your veil and turn from him, either looking from the window or reading. A dignified, modest reserve is the surest way to repel impertinence. If you find yourself, during your journey, in any awkward or embarrassing situation, you may, without impropriety, request the assistance of a gentleman, even a stranger, and he will, probably, perform the service requested, receive your thanks, and then relieve you of his presence. Never, upon any account, or under any provocation, return rudeness by rudeness. Nothing will rebuke incivility in another so surely as perfect courtesy in your own manner. Many will be shamed into apology, who would annoy you for hours, if you encouraged them by acts of rudeness on your own part.

In traveling alone, choose, if possible, a seat next to another lady, or near an elderly gentleman. If your neighbor seems disposed to shorten the time by conversing, do not be too hasty in checking him. Such acquaintances end with the journey, and a lady can always so deport herself that she may beguile the time pleasantly, without, in the least, compromising her dignity.

Any slight attention, or an apology made for crushing or incommoding you, is best acknowledged by a courteous bow, in silence.

CHAPTER IV

HOW TO BEHAVE AT A HOTEL

In America, where the mania for traveling extends through all classes, from the highest to the lowest, a few hints upon deportation at a hotel will not be amiss, and these hints are especially addressed to ladies traveling alone.

When you arrive at the hotel, enquire at once for the pro-prietor. Tell him your name and address, and ask him to conduct you to a good room, naming the length of time you purpose occupying it. You may also request him to wait upon you to the table, and allot you a seat. As the hours for meals, at a large hotel, are very numerous, it is best to mention the time when you wish to breakfast, dine, or sup. If you stay more than one day at the hotel, do not tax the pro-prietor with the duty of escorting you to the table more than once. Request one of the waiters always to meet you as you enter, and wait upon you to your seat. This saves the embarrassment of crossing the room entirely unattended, while it shows others that you are a resident at the house. The waiter will then take your order for the dishes you wish.

Give this order in a low tone, and do not harass the man by contradicting yourself several times; decide what you want before you ask for it, and then give your order quietly but distinctly. Use, always, the butter-knife, salt-spoon, and sugar-tongs, though you may be entirely alone in the use of them. The attention to the small details of table etiquette is one of the surest marks of good breeding. If any trifling civility is offered by the gentleman beside you, or opposite to you, thank him civilly, if you either accept or decline it.

Thank the waiter for any extra attention he may offer.

Remember that a lady-like deportment is always modest and quiet. If you meet a friend at table, and converse, let it be in a tone of voice sufficiently loud for him to hear, but not loud enough to reach ears for which the remarks are not intended. A boisterous, loud voice, loud laughter, and bold deportment, at a hotel, are sure signs of vulgar breeding.

When you have finished your meal, cross the room quietly; if you go into the parlor, do not attract attention by a hasty entrance, or forward manner, but take the seat you may select, quietly.

The acquaintances made in a hotel may be dropped afterwards, if desirable, without rudeness, and a pleasant greeting to other ladies whom you may recognize from meeting them in the entries or at table, is courteous and well-bred; be careful, however, not to force attentions where you see they are not agreeably received.

A lady's dress, when alone at a hotel, should be of the most modest kind. At breakfast let her wear a close, morning dress, and never, even at supper, appear alone at the table with bare arms or neck. If she comes in late from the opera or a party, in full dress, she should not come into the supper-room, unless her escort accompanies her. A traveling or walking-dress can be worn with perfect propriety, at any meal at a hotel, as it is usually travelers who are the guests at the table.

After breakfast, pass an hour or two in the parlor, unless you are going out, whilst the chambermaid puts your room in order. You should, before leaving the room, lock your trunk, and be careful not to leave money or trinkets lying about. When you go out, lock your door, and give the key to the servant to hand to the clerk of the office, who will give it to you when you return. You may do this, even if you leave the room in disorder, as the chambermaids all carry duplicate keys, and can easily enter your room in your absence to arrange it. The door should not be left open, as dishonest persons, passing along the entry, could enter without fear of being questioned.

If you see that another lady, though she may be an entire stranger, is losing her collar, or needs attention called to any disorder in her dress, speak to her in a low tone, and offer to assist her in remedying the difficulty.

Be careful always in opening a door or raising a window in a public parlor, that you are not incommoding any one else.

Never sit down to the piano uninvited, unless you are alone in the parlor. Do not take any book you may find in the room away from it.

It is best always to carry writing materials with you, but if this is not convenient, you can always obtain them at the office.In a strange city it is best to provide yourself with a small map and guide book, that you may be able to find your way from the hotel to any given point, without troubling any one for directions.

If you wish for a carriage, ring, and let the waiter order one for you.When leaving a hotel, if you have been there for several days, give the waiter at table, and the chambermaid, a fee, as your unprotected situation will probably call for many services out of their regular routine of duties.

On leaving, ring, order your bill, pay it, state the time at which you wish to leave, and the train you will take to leave the city. Request a man to be sent, to carry your baggage to the hack; and if you require your next meal at an unusual hour, to be ready for your journey, order it then.

CHAPTER V

EVENING PARTIES ETIQUETTE FOR THE HOSTESS

THE most fashionable as well as pleasant way in the present day, to entertain guests, is to invite them to evening parties, which vary in size from the "company,""sociable," "soirée," to the party, par excellence, which is but one step from the ball.

The entertainment upon such occasions, may vary with the taste of the hostess, or the caprice of her guests. Some prefer dancing, some music, some conversation. Small parties called together for dramatic or poetical readings are now fashionable, and very delightful.

In writing an invitation for a small party, it is kind, as well as polite, to specify the number of guests invited, that your friends may dress to suit the occasion. To be either too much, or too little dressed at such times is embarrassing.

For large parties, the usual formula is: Miss S—- 's compliments to Miss G—-, and requests the pleasure of her company for Wednesday, March 8th, at 8 o'clock.

Such an invitation, addressed either to an intimate friend or mere acquaintance, will signify full dress.

If your party is a musical soirée, or your friends meet for reading or conversation alone, say so in your invitation, as–Miss S—- requests the pleasure of Miss G—-'s company, on Thursday evening next, at 8 o'clock, to meet the members of the musical club, to which Miss S—- belongs; or,Miss S—- expects a few friends, on Monday evening next, at 8 o'clock, to take part in some dramatic readings, and would be happy to have Miss G—- join the party.

Always date your note of invitation, and put your address in one corner.Having dispatched these notes, the next step is to prepare to receive your guests. If the number invited is large, and you hire waiters, give them notice several days beforehand, and engage them to come in the morning. Give them full directions for the supper, appoint one to open the door, another to show the guests to the dressing rooms, and a third to wait in the gentleman's dressing-room, to attend to them, if their services are required.

If you use your own plate, glass, and china, show the waiters where to find them, as well as the table cloths, napkins, and other things they may require. If you hire the service from the confectioner's or restaurateur's where you order your supper, you have only to show your waiters where to spread supper, and tell them the hour.

You will have to place at least four rooms at the disposal of your guests–the supper room, and two dressing-rooms, beside the drawing- room.

In the morning, see that the fires in your rooms are in good order; and in the drawing-room, it is best to have it so arranged that the heat can be lessened towards evening, as the crowd, and dancing, will make it excessively uncomfortable if the rooms are too warm. See that the lights are in good order, and if you propose to have music instead of dancing, or to use your piano for dancing music, have it put in good tune in the morning. If you intend to dance, and do not wish to take up the carpets, you will find it economical, as well as much pleasanter, to cover them with coarse white muslin or linen; be sure it is fastened down smoothly, firmly, and drawn tightly over the carpets.

Do not remove all the chairs from the parlor; or, if this is necessary, leave some in the hall, for those who wish to rest after dancing.

In the dining-room, unless it will accommodate all your guests at once, have a silk cord so fastened that, when the room is full, it can be drawn across the door-way; those following the guests already in the room, will then return to the parlor, and wait their turn. A still better way, is to set the supper table twice, inviting the married and elderly people to go into the first table, and then, after it is ready for the second time, let the young folks go up.

Two dressing-rooms must be ready; one for the ladies, and the other for the gentlemen. Have both these rooms comfortably heated, and well lighted. Nothing can be more disagreeable than cold, ill-lighted rooms to dress in, particularly if your guests come in half-frozen by the cold of a winter's night, or still worse, damp from a stormy one.

Be sure that there is plenty of water, soap and towels on the washstand, two or three brushes and combs on the bureau, two mirrors, one large and one small, and a pin cushion, well filled with large and small pins.

In the ladies' room, have one, or if your party is large, two women to wait upon your guests; to remove their cloaks, overshoes, and hoods, and assist them in smoothing their dresses or hair. After each guest removes her shawl and hood, let one of the maids roll all the things she lays aside into a bundle, and put it where she can easily find it. It is an admirable plan, and prevents much confusion, to pin to each bundle, a card, or strip of paper, (previously prepared,) with the name of the person to whom it belongs written clearly and distinctly upon it.

Upon the bureau in the ladies' room, have a supply of hair-pins, and a workbox furnished with everything requisite to repair any accident that may happen to the dress of a guest. It is well, also, to have Eau de Cologne, hartshorn, and salts, in case of sudden faintness.

In the gentlemen's room, place a clothes brush and boot-jack. It is best to send out your invitations by your own servant, or one hired for that purpose especially. It is ill-bred to send invitations either by the dispatch, or through the post-office; and besides being discourteous, you risk offending your friends, as these modes of delivery are proverbially uncertain.

Be dressed and ready to receive your guests in good season, as some, in their desire to be punctual, may come before the time appointed. It is better to be ready too soon, than too late, as your guests will feel painfully embarrassed if you are not ready to receive them.

For the early part of the evening, take a position in your parlor, near or opposite to the door, that each guest may find you easily. It is not necessary to remain all the evening nailed to this one spot, but stay near it until your guests have all or nearly all assembled. Late comers will of course expect to find you entertaining your guests.

As each guest or party enter the room, advance a few steps to meet them, speaking first to the lady, or if there are several ladies, to the eldest, then to the younger ones, and finally to the gentlemen. If the new comers are acquainted with those already in the room, they will leave you, after a few words of greeting, to join their friends; but if they are strangers to the city, or making their first visit to your house, introduce them to a friend who is well acquainted in your circle, who will entertain them till you can again join them and introduce them to others.

Do not leave the room during the evening. To see a hostess fidgeting, constantly going in and out, argues ill for her tact in arranging the house for company. With well-trained waiters, you need give yourself any uneasiness about the arrangements outside of the parlors.

The perfection of good breeding in a hostess, is perfect ease of manner; for the time she should appear to have no thought or care beyond the pleasure of her guests.

Have a waiter in the hall to open the front door, and another at the head of the first flight of stairs, to point out to the ladies and gentlemen their respective dressing-rooms.

Never try to outshine your guests in dress. It is vulgar in the extreme. A hostess should be dressed as simply as is consistent with the occasion, wearing, if she will, the richest fabrics, exquisitely made, but avoiding any display of jewels or gay colors, such as will be, probably, more conspicuous than those worn by her guests.

Remember, from the moment your first guest enters the parlor, you must forget yourself entirely to make the evening pleasant for others. Your duties will call you from one group to another, and require constant watchfulness that no one guest is slighted. Be careful that none of the company are left to mope alone from being unacquainted with other guests. Introduce gentlemen to ladies, and gentlemen to gentlemen, ladies to ladies.

It requires much skill and tact to make a party for conversation only, go off pleasantly. You must invite only such guests as will mutually please, and you must be careful about introductions. If you have a literary lion upon your list, it is well to invite other lions to meet him or her, that the attention may not be constantly concentrated upon one person. Where you see a couple conversing slowly and wearily, stir them up with a few sprightly words, and introduce a new person, either to make a trio, or, as a substitute in the duet, carrying off the other one of the couple to find a more congenial companion elsewhere. Never interrupt an earnest or apparently interesting conversation. Neither party will thank you, even if you propose the most delightful substitute.

If your party meet for reading, have a table with the books in the centre of the apartment, that will divide the room, those reading being on one side, the listeners on the other.

Be careful here not to endeavor to shine above your guests, leaving to them the most prominent places, and taking, cheerfully, a subordinate place. On the other hand, if you are urged to display any talent you may possess in this way, remember your only desire is to please your guests, and if they are really desirous to listen to you, comply, gracefully and promptly, with their wishes.

If you have dancing, and have not engaged a band, it is best to hire a pianist for the evening to play dancing music.

You will find it exceedingly wearisome to play yourself all the evening, and it is ill-bred to ask any guest to play for others to dance. This victimizing of some obliging guest is only too common, but no true lady will ever be guilty of such rudeness. If there are several members of the family able and willing to play, let them divide this duty amongst them, or, if you wish to play yourself, do so. If any guest, in this case, offers to relieve you, accept their kindness for one dance only. Young people, who enjoy dancing, but who also play well, will often stay on the piano-stool all the evening, because their own good-nature will not allow them to complain, and their hostess wilfully, or through negligence, permits the tax.

See that your guests are well provided with partners, introducing every gentleman and lady who dances, to one who will dance well with them. Be careful that none sit still through your negligence in providing partners.

Do not dance yourself, when, by so doing, you are preventing a guest from enjoying that pleasure. If a lady is wanted to make up a set, then dance, or if, late in the evening, you have but few lady dancers left, but do not interfere with the pleasure in others. If invited, say that you do not wish to take the place of a guest upon the floor, and introduce the gentleman who invites you to some lady friend who dances.

It is very pleasant in a dancing party to have ices alone, handed round at about ten o'clock, having supper set two or three hours later. They are very refreshing, when it would be too early to have the more substantial supper announced.

It is very customary now, even in large parties, to have no refreshments but ice-cream, lemonade, and cake, or, in summer, fruit, cake, and ices. It is less troublesome, as well as less expensive, than a hot supper, and the custom will be a good one to adopt permanently.

One word of warning to all hostesses. You can never know, when you place wine or brandy before your guests, whom you may be tempting to utter ruin. Better, far better, to have a reputation as strict, or mean, than by your example, or the temptation you offer, to have the sin upon your soul of having put poison before those who partook of your hospitality. It is not necessary; hospitality and gen-erosity do not require it, and you will have the approval of all who truly love you for your good qualities, if you reso-lutely refuse to have either wine or any other intoxicating liquor upon your supper-table.

If the evening of your party is stormy, let a waiter stand in the vestibule with a large umbrella, to meet the ladies at the carriage door, and protect them whilst crossing the pave-ment and steps.

When your guests take leave of you, it will be in the drawing-room, and let that farewell be final. Do not accompany them to the dressing- room, and never stop them in the hall for a last word. Many ladies do not like to display their "sortie du soirée" before a crowded room, and you will be keeping their escort waiting. Say farewell in the parlor, and do not repeat it.

If your party is mixed, that is, conversation, dancing, and music are all mingled, remember it is your place to invite a guest to sing or play, and be careful not to offend any amateur performers by forgetting to invite them to favor the company. If they decline, never urge the matter. If the refusal proceeds from unwillingness or inability on that occasion, it is rude to insist; and if they refuse for the sake of being urged, they will be justly punished by a disappointment. If you have guests who, performing badly, will expect an invitation to play, sacrifice their desire to the good of the others, pass them by. It is torture to listen to bad music.

Do not ask a guest to sing or play more than once. This is her fair share, and you have no right to tax her too severely to entertain your other guests. If, however, the performance is so pleasing that others ask for a repetition, then you too may request it, thanking the performer for the pleasure given.

CHAPTER VI

EVENING PARTIES ETIQUETTE FOR THE GUEST

UPON receiving an invitation for an evening party, answer it immediately, that your hostess may know for how many guests she must provide. If, after accepting an invitation, any unforeseen event prevents your keeping the engagement, write a second note, containing your regrets.

The usual form is:– Miss G—- accepts with pleasure Miss S—-'s polite invitation for Monday next; or, Miss G—- regrets that a prior engagement will prevent her accepting Miss S—-'s kind invitation for Monday evening.

Punctuality is a mark of politeness, if your invitation states the hour at which your hostess will be ready to welcome you. Do not be more than half an hour later than the time named, but if unavoidably detained, make no apology when you meet your hostess; it will be in bad taste to speak of your want of punctuality.

When you arrive at your friend's house, do not stop to speak to any one in the hall, or upon the stairs, but go immediately to the dressing room. The gentleman who accompanies you will go to the door of the lady's room, leave you, to remove his own hat and overcoat, and then return to the door to wait for you.

In the dressing-room, do not push forward to the mirror if you see that others are before you there. Wait for your turn, then perform the needful arrangements of your toilette quickly, and re-join your escort as soon as possible. If you meet friends in the lady's-room, do not stop there to chat; you keep your escort waiting, and your friends will join you in the parlor a few moments later.

Avoid all confidential communications or private remarks in the dressing-room. You may be overheard, and give pain or cause annoyance by your untimely conversation.

When you enter the parlor, go immediately to your hostess, and speak to her; if the gentleman attending you is a stranger to the lady of the house, introduce him, and then join the other guests, as by delaying, to converse too long with your hostess, you may prevent her speaking to others who have arrived later than yourself.

If you have no escort, you may with perfect propriety send for the master of the house, to wait upon you from the dressing-room to the parlor, and as soon as you have spoken to the hostess, thank your host and release him, as the same attention may be required by others. Again, when alone, if you meet a friend in the dressing-room, you may ask the privilege of entering the parlor with her and her escort; or, if she also is alone, there is no impropriety in two ladies going into the room unattended by a gentleman.

While you maintain a cheerful deportment, avoid loud talking and laughing, and still more carefully avoid any action or gesture that may attract attention and make you conspicuous.

When dressing for a party, while you show that you honor the occasion by a tasteful dress, avoid glaring colors, or any conspicuous ornament or style of costume.

Avoid long tête-à-tête conversations; they are in bad taste, and to hold confidential communication, especially with gentlemen, is still worse.

Do not make any display of affection for even your dearest friend; kissing in public, or embracing, are in bad taste.Walking with arms encircling waists, or such demonstrative tokens of love, are marks of low breeding.

Avoid crossing the room alone, and never run, even if you feel embarrassed, and wish to cross quickly.If you are a musician, and certain that you will confer pleasure by a display of your talents, do not make a show of reluctance when invited to play or sing. Comply gracefully, and after one piece, leave the instrument. Be careful to avoid the appearance of wishing to be invited, and, above all, never hint that this would be agreeable. If your hostess has requested you to bring your notes, and you are dependent upon them, bring them, and quietly place them on the music stand, or, still better, send them in the afternoon. It is a better plan, if you are called upon frequently to contribute in this way to the evening's amusement, to learn a few pieces so as to play them perfectly well without notes.

Never attempt any piece before company, unless you are certain that you can play it without mistake or hesitation.

When you have finished your song or piece, rise instantly from the piano stool, as your hostess may wish to invite another guest to take the place. If you have a reason for declining to play, do so decidedly when first invited, and do not change your decision.

If your hostess or any of the family play for the guests to dance, it is both polite and kind to offer to relieve them; and if truly polite themselves, they will not take advantage of the offer, to over tax your good nature.

When others are playing or singing, listen quietly and attentively; to laugh or talk loudly when there is music in the room, is rude, both toward the performer and your hostess.

If you are conversing at the time the music begins, and you find that your companion is not disposed to listen to the performer at the harp or piano, converse in a low tone, and take a position at some distance from the instrument.

If the rooms are not large enough for all the guests to dance at one time, do not dance every set, even if invited. It is ill-bred and selfish.

When you go up to supper, do not accept anything from any gentleman but the one who has escorted you from the parlor. If others offer you, as they probably will, any refreshment, say that Mr. —- (naming your escort) has gone to get you what you desire. He has a right to be offended, if, after telling him what you wish for, he returns to find you already supplied. It is quite as rude to offer what he brings to another lady. Her escort is probably on the same errand from which yours has just returned. It may seem trivial and childish to warn a lady against putting cakes or bon-bons in her pocket at supper, yet it is often done by those who would deeply resent the accusation of rudeness or meanness. It is not only ill-bred, but it gives rise, if seen, to suspicions that you are so little accustomed to society, or so starved at home, that you are ignorant of the forms of etiquette, or are forced to the theft by positive hunger.

If you are obliged to leave the company at an earlier hour than the other guests, say so to your hostess in a low tone, when you have an opportunity, and then stay a short time in the room, and slip out unperceived. By a formal leave-taking, you may lead others to suppose the hour later than it is in reality, and thus deprive your hostess of other guests, who, but for your example, would have remained longer.

French leave is preferable to a formal leave-taking upon such occasions.If you remain until the usual hour for breaking up, go to your hostess before you leave the room, express the pleasure you have enjoyed, and bid her farewell.

Within the next week, you should call upon your hostess, if it is the first party you have attended at her house. If she is an intimate friend, the call should be made within a fortnight.

CHAPTER VII

VISITING ETIQUETTE FOR THE HOSTESS

WHEN you write to invite a friend to visit you, name a time when it will be convenient and agreeable for you to receive her, and if she accepts your invitation, so arrange your duties and engagements that they will not interfere with your devoting the principal part of your time to the entertainment of your guest. If you have certain duties which must be performed daily, say so frankly when she first arrives, and see that during the time you are so occupied she has work, reading, music, or some other employment, to pass the time away pleasantly.

Have a room prepared especially for her use, and let her occupy it alone. Many persons have a dislike to any one sleeping with them, and will be kept awake by a companion in the room or bed. Above all, do not put a child to sleep in the chamber with your guest.

The day before your friend arrives, have her room swept, dusted, and aired; put clean, fresh linen upon the bed, see that the curtains are in good order, the locks in perfect repair, and the closet or wardrobe and bureau empty for her clothes. Have upon the bureau a pin cushion well filled, hair pins, brush and comb, and two mirrors, one large, and one small for the hand, as she may wish to smooth her hair, without unpacking her own toilet articles. Upon the washstand, have two pitchers full of water, a cup, tumbler, soap-dish and soap, basin, brush-dish, and a sponge, wash rag, and plenty of clean towels.

Have both a feather bed and a mattress upon the bedstead, that she may place whichever she prefers uppermost.

Two sheets, a blanket, quilt, and counterpane, should be on the bed, and there should be two extra blankets in the room, should she require more covering in the night.

On the mantel piece, place a few books that she may read, if she wishes, before sleeping. Have upon the mantel piece a box of matches, and if the room is not lighted by gas, have also a supply of candles in a box, and a candlestick.

If the room is not heated by a furnace, be careful that the fire is made every morning before she rises, and keep a good supply of fuel in the room.

Besides the larger chairs, have a low one, to use while changing the shoes or washing the feet.

Upon the table, place a full supply of writing materials, as your guest may wish to send word of her safe arrival before unpacking her own writing-desk. Put two or three postage stamps upon this table.

Be sure that bells, locks, hinges, and windows, are all in perfect order.

Before your guest arrives, go to her room. If it is in winter, have a good fire, hot water on the washstand, and see that the windows are tightly closed, and the room cheerful with sunshine, or plenty of candle or gas light. If in summer, draw the curtains, bow the shutters, open the windows, and have a fan upon the table. It is well to have a bath ready, should your guest desire that refreshment after the dust and heat of traveling.

When the time arrives at which you may expect your guest, send a carriage to the station to meet her, and, if possible, go yourself, or send some member of the family to welcome her there. After her baggage is on the carriage, drive immediately to the house, and be certain all is ready there for her comfort.

As soon as she is at your house, have her trunks carried immediately to her own room, and lead her there yourself.

Then, after warmly assuring her how welcome she is, leave her alone to change her dress, bathe, or lie down if she wishes. If her journey has been a long one, and it is not the usual hour for your next meal, have a substantial repast ready for her about half an hour after her arrival, with tea or coffee.

If she arrives late at night, after she has removed her bonnet and bathed her face, invite her to partake of a substantial supper, and then pity her weariness and lead the way to her room. She may politely assert that she can still sit up and talk, but be careful you do not keep her up too long; and do not waken her in the morning. After the first day, she will, of course, desire to breakfast at your usual hour, but if she has had a long, fatiguing journey, she will be glad to sleep late the first day. Be careful that she has a hot breakfast ready when she does rise, and take a seat at the table to wait upon her.

After the chambermaid has arranged the guest-chamber in the morning, go in yourself and see that all is in order, and comfortable, and that there is plenty of fresh water and towels, the bed properly made, and the room dusted. Then do not go in again through the day, unless invited. If you are constantly running in, to put a chair back, open or shut the windows, or arrange the furniture, you will entirely destroy the pleasantest part of your guest's visit, by reminding her that she is not at home, and must not take liberties, even in her own room. It looks, too, as if you were afraid to trust her, and thought she would injure the furniture.

If you have children, forbid them to enter the room your friend occupies, unless she invites them to do so, or they are sent there with a message.

If your household duties will occupy your time for some hours in the morning, introduce your guest to the piano, book-case, or picture- folio, and place all at her service.

When your duties are finished, either join her in her own room, or invite her to sit with you, and work, chatting, meanwhile, together. If you keep your own carriage, place it at her disposal as soon as she arrives.

If she is a stranger in the city, accompany her to the points of interest she may wish to visit, and also offer to show her where to find the best goods, should she wish to do any shopping.

Enquire of your visitor if there is any particular habit she may wish to indulge in, such as rising late, retiring early, lying down in the daytime, or any other habit that your family do not usually follow. If there is, arrange it so that she may enjoy her peculiarity in comfort. If there is any dish which is distasteful to her, avoid placing it upon the table during her visit, and if she mentions, in conversation, any favorite dish, have it frequently placed before her.

If she is accustomed to eat just before retiring, and your family do not take supper, see that something is sent to her room every night.

If your friend has intimate friends in the same city, beside yourself, it is an act of kindly courtesy to invite them to dinner, tea, or to pass a day, and when calls are made, and you see that it would be pleasant, invite the caller to remain to dinner or tea.

Never accept any invitation, either to a party, ball, or public entertainment, that does not include your guest. In answering the invitation give that as your reason for declining, when another note will be sent enclosing an invitation for her. If the invitation is from an intimate friend, say, in answering it, that your guest is with you, and that she will accompany you.

It is a mistaken idea to suppose that hospitality and courtesy require constant attention to a guest. There are times when she may prefer to be alone, either to write letters, to read, or practice. Some ladies follow a guest from one room to another, never leaving them alone for a single instant, when they would enjoy an hour or two in the library or at the piano, but do not like to say so.

The best rule is to make your guest feel that she is heartily welcome, and perfectly at home.

When she is ready to leave you, see that her trunks are strapped in time by the servants, have a carriage ready to take her to the station, have the breakfast or dinner at an hour that will suit her, prepare a luncheon for her to carry, and let some gentleman in the family escort her to the wharf, check her trunks, and procure her tickets.

If your guest is in mourning, decline any invitations to parties or places of amusement whilst she is with you. Show her by such little attentions that you sympathize in her recent affliction, and that the pleasure of her society, and the love you bear her, make such sacrifices of gayety trifling, compared with the sweet duty of comforting her.

CHAPTER VIII

VISITING ETIQUETTE FOR THE GUEST

As first rule with regard to paying a visit, the best ones, never to accept a general invitation. Instances are very common where women (I cannot say ladies) have, upon a slight acquaintance, and a "When you are in C—- I should be very happy to have you visit me," actually gone to C—-from their own home, and, with bag and baggage, quartered themselves upon the hospitality of their newly made friend, for weeks at a time.

Even where there is a long-standing friendship it is not well to visit uninvited. It is impossible for you, in another city, to know exactly when it will be convenient for your friend to have you visit her, unless she tells you, and that will, of course, be a special invitation.

If your friends are really desirous to have you pay them a visit, they will name a time when it will be convenient and agreeable to have you come, and you may accept the invitation with the certainty that you will not incommode them.

Self-proposed visits are still worse. You, in a manner, force an invitation from your friend when you tell her that you can come at a certain time, unless you have previously arranged to let her know when you can be her guest. In that case, your own time is understood to be the most agreeable for her.

If, whilst traveling, you pass through a town where you have friends whom you wish to visit, and who would be hurt if you omitted to do so, go first to a hotel, and either call or send word that you are there. Then, it is optional with them to extend their hospitality or not. Do not be offended if it is not done. The love for you may be undiminished, and the desire to entertain you very great, yet family reasons may render such an invitation as you expect, impossible.

Your friend may have engagements or duties at the time, that would prevent her making the visit pleasant for you, and wish to postpone the invitation until she can entertain you as she wishes.

To drive, trunks and all, in such a case, to your friend's house, without a word of warning, is unkind, as well as ill-bred. You force her to invite you to stay, when it may be inconvenient, and, even if she is really glad to see you, and wishes you to make a prolonged visit, you may feel certain she would have preferred to know you were coming. If she really loves you, her natural desire would be to have everything ready to give you a comfortable reception, and not have to leave you, perhaps with your traveling costume on, for an hour or two, while she prepares a room for you. It is not enough to say, at such a time, "Don't mind me," or, "Treat me as one of the family." However much her politeness or love may conceal annoyance, be sure, in her secret heart she does mind you, and remember you are not one of her private family.

To take the liberty of going to the house of a mere acquaintance, for a night or two, while traveling, without invitation, is making a convenience of them, and wears the appearance of wishing to save the customary hotel-bill, so, while it is extremely ill-bred and impertinent, it is also excessively mean.

In case of relationship, or long intimate friendship, an unexpected visit may be pardoned and give pleasure, but it is better to avoid it, as the pleasure will surely be increased if your relative or friend has time to prepare for your reception as her love will prompt, and arrange her duties and engagements to really enjoy your company.

When you receive an invitation by letter to visit a friend, answer it immediately, thanking her for her proffered hospitality, and say decidedly then whether you can accept or decline.

If you accept the invitation, state in your letter by what train, and at what hour you will arrive, that she may meet you, and let nothing but positive necessity keep you from being punctually at the time and place appointed. To linger by the way, for mere pleasure, and make her come several times to meet you, is unkind, as well as ill-bred. If you are unavoidably detained, write to her, state the reason that will prevent your keeping the appointment, and name another time when you can come.

It is well in answering a letter of invitation, to state the limits of your visit, and then to keep them. If she is unwilling to let you go, and you are tempted to stay, that very fact promises well for the pleasure of a second visit. It is better to leave while all will regret you, than to linger on until you have worn out your welcome.

Inquire, as soon as possible after your arrival, what are the regular habits of the family; the hours for rising, for meals, and for retiring, and then be punctual in your attendance. Many ladies are very ceremonious about waiting for a guest, and by delay in your room, or inattention to the time, when you are out, you will keep the whole family waiting.

If you do not wake early enough for the usual breakfast hour, request the chambermaid to knock at your door in time for you to be ready to go down with the family. Before you leave your room in the morning, take the clothes off your bed, throw the upper bed over the foot-board, and then open all the windows (unless it storms), that room and bed may be thoroughly aired before you sit there again.

After breakfast, ask your hostess if you can be of any assistance to her in the household duties. If she declines your services, do not follow her from room to room whilst she is thus engaged, but take your work, books, or music to the sitting room or parlor, until your own room is ready for you. By thus proving that you can occupy yourself pleasantly, while she is away, you make it less annoying to her to feel the obligation to leave you.

As soon as you see that she is ready to sew and chat, leave your book, or, if in your own room, come to the sitting room, where she is, and work with her. It is polite and kind, if you see that she has a large supply of family sewing, to offer to assist her, but if she positively declines your aid, then have some work of your own on hand, that you may sew with her. Many pleasant mornings may be spent while visiting, by one lady reading aloud whilst the other sews, alternating the work.

It is a pretty compliment to repay the hospitality of your hostess, by working whilst with her upon some piece of fancy work, a chair cover, sofa cushion, or pair of ottomans, presenting them to her when finished, as a keepsake. They will be duly appreciated, and remind her constantly of the pleasures of your visit.

If you pass the morning out of the house, remember your time is hers, and have no engagement to interfere with the plans she has laid for entertaining you. Observe this rule during your whole visit, and do not act independent of her plans. By constantly forming engagements without her knowledge, going out without her, or staying in when she has made some excursion or party for your pleasure, you insult her, by intimating that her house is no more to you than a hotel, to sleep and eat in, while your pleasures lie elsewhere.

After dinner, retire for an hour to your own room, that your hostess may lie down if she is accustomed to do so.

If the hours kept are later than you have been accustomed to, or if the gayety of the family keeps you out at party or opera, it is best to sleep after dinner, even if you do not always do it. To give signs of weariness in the evening will be excessively rude, implying want of enjoyment, and making your hostess feel hurt and annoyed.

If you have shopping to do, find out where the best stores are, and then go to them alone, unless your hostess will accompany you upon similar business of her own. Do not tax her good nature to go, merely for the sake of aiding you as guide. If one of the children in the family is familiar with the stores and streets, ask her to accompany you, and be careful to acknowledge the kindness by buying something especially for the child whilst she is out with you, if it is only some cakes or bonbons. Choose an hour when you are certain your hostess has made no other engagement for you, or while she is busy in her domestic duties, for these shopping excursions. Offer, when you are going, to attend to any shopping she may want, and ask if there is any commission you can execute for her while you are out.

While on a visit to one friend, do not accept too many invitations from others, and avoid spending too much time in paying calls where your hostess is not acquainted. You owe the greater portion of your time and society to the lady whose hospitality you are accepting, and it is best to decline invitations from other houses, unless they inclose one for your hostess also.

Avoid paying any visits in a family not upon good terms with your hostess. If such a family are very dear friends of your own, or you can claim an acquaintance, pleasant upon both sides, with them, write, and state candidly the reason why you cannot visit them, and they will appreciate your delicacy.

If, while on a visit to one friend, you receive an invitation to spend some time with another friend in the same place, accept it for the period which you have named as the termination of your first visit. You insult your hostess by shortening your visit to her to accept another invitation, and quite as much of an insult is it, to take the time from the first visit to go to pay another, and then return to your first hostess, unless such an arrangement has been made immediately upon your arrival.

Never invite any friend who may call upon you to stay to dinner or tea; you will be taking a most unwarrantable liberty in so doing. This is the right of your hostess, and if, by her silence, she tacitly declines extending this courtesy, you will be guilty of impertinence in usurping her privilege.

Never take any one who calls upon you into any room but the parlor, unless invited to do so by your hostess. You have, of course, the entrée of other rooms, but you have no right to extend this privilege to others.

If you have many gentlemen visitors, check too frequent calls, and make no appointments with them. If they show you any such attention as to offer to drive you to places of interest, or visit with you picture galleries or public places, always consult your hostess before accepting such civilities, and decline them if she has made other engagements for you. If you receive an invitation to visit any place of public amusement, decline it, unless one of the family with whom you are staying is also invited. In that case you may accept.

If the gentleman who invites you is a stranger to the family, introduce him to your hostess, or mention her name in conversation. He will then, if he really desires you to accept his proffered attention, include her in the invitation.

When visiting in a family where the members are in mourning, decline all invitations to parties or places of public amusement. It is an insult to them to leave them to join in pleasure from which their recent affliction excludes them.

Your visit at such a time will be prompted by sympathy in their trouble, and for the time it is thoughtful and delicate to make their sorrows yours.

If sudden sickness or family trouble come to your friend whilst you are with her, unless you can really be useful, shorten your visit. In time of trouble families generally like to be alone, all in all to each other; and a visitor is felt a constant restraint.

If death comes while you are with your friend, endeavor to take from her as much of the care as you can, a really sympathizing friend is an inexpressible comfort at such a time, as the trying details which must be taken in charge by someone, will be less trying to her than to a member of the family. Do the necessary shopping for your friend, and relieve her of as much family care as you can. Let her feel that you are really glad that you are near her in her affliction, and repay the hospitality she offered in her season of joy by showing her that her sorrow makes her still more dear, and that, while you can enjoy the gayety of her house, you will not flee from its mourning. When your presence can be of no further service, then leave her.

Put out you're washing and ironing when on a visit. It is annoying and ill-bred to throw your soiled clothes into the family wash.

Take with you, from home, all the writing and sewing materials you may require while paying your visit. It is annoying to be constantly requested by a visitor to lend her scissors, pins, needles, or paper; no lady should be without her own portfolio and work-box.

Be very careful not to injure any article of furniture in your sleeping apartment, and if, unfortunately, anything suffers from your carelessness, have the accident repaired, or the article replaced, at your own expense.

When your visit is over, give a present to each of the servants, varying its value, according to the length of your visit or the services you may have required. You will add to the pleasure by presenting such gifts yourself, with a few pleasant words.

Never compare the house you may be visiting with your own, or any other you may visit. Avoid also speaking of any house where you may have been a guest in terms of over-praise, giving glowing pictures of its splendor. Your hostess may imagine you are drawing comparisons unfavorable to your present residence. Also avoid speaking unfavorably of any former visit, as your hostess will naturally conclude that her turn for censure will come as soon as your visit is over.

If any family secret comes to your knowledge while you are on a visit in that family, remember the hospitality extended to you binds you to the most inviolable secrecy. It is mean, contemptible, rude, and ill-bred to make your entertainers regret their hospitality by betraying any such confidence; for it is as sacred a confidence as if you were bound over to silence in the most solemn manner.

After paying a visit, you should write to your hostess as soon as you reach home again; thank her in this letter for her hospitality, speak warmly of the enjoyment you have had in your recent visit, and mention by name every member of the family, desiring to be remembered to all.

CHAPTER IX

MORNING RECEPTIONS OR CALLS ETIQUETTE FOR THE HOSTESS

IF your circle of visiting acquaintance is very large, while at the same time your time is fully occupied, or your home duties make it inconvenient to dress every morning to receive visitors, it is a good plan to set aside one morning in the week for a reception day.

Upon your own visiting cards, below the name, put the day when it will be proper to return the visit, thus: MRS. JAMES HUNTER.

AT HOME WEDNESDAYS. No. 1718 C—- St._Your friends will, unless there is some special reason for a call in the interval, pay their visit upon the day named.

Let nothing, but the most imperative duty, call you out upon your reception day. Your callers are, in a measure, invited guests, and it will be an insulting mark of rudeness to be out when they call. Neither can you be excused, except in case of sickness.

Having appointed the day when you will be at home to see your friends, you must, for that day, prepare to give your time wholly to them. The usual hours for morning receptions are from twelve to three, and you should be dressed, and ready for callers, at least half an hour before that time.

To come in, flushed from a hurried toilette, to meet your first callers, is unbecoming as well as rude.

Your dress should be handsome, but not showy. A silk or cashmere wrapper, richly trimmed, over an embroidered skirt, with a pretty cap, or the hair neatly arranged without head-dress, is a becoming and appropriate dress. Still better is a rich but plain silk, made high in the neck, with long sleeves. Wear a handsomely embroidered, or lace collar, and sleeves, and a rather dressy cap, or, still better, the hair alone, prettily arranged.

As each visitor arrives, rise, and advance part of the way to meet her. If gentlemen, rise, but do not advance.

It is not customary now to introduce callers at these morning receptions, though you can do so with perfect propriety where you know such an introduction will be agreeable to both parties.

In introducing a gentleman to a lady, address her first, as–"Miss Jones, permit me to introduce Mr. Lee;" and, when introducing a young lady to a matron, you introduce the younger one to the elder, as–"Mrs. Green, allow me to introduce to you my friend, Miss Brown."

In introducing strangers in the city it is well to name the place of their residence, as–Mr. James of Germany, or, Mr. Brown of New York, or, if they have recently returned from abroad, it is well to say so, as, Mr. Lee, lately from India; this is useful in starting conversation.

Be careful, when introducing your friends, to pronounce the name of each one clearly and distinctly, that there may be no mistake or necessity for repetition.

It is a good plan, if your receptions are usually largely attended, to have books and pictures on the centre table, and scattered about your parlors. You must, of course, converse with each caller, but many will remain in the room for a long time, and these trifles are excellent pastimes, and serve as subjects for conversation.

It requires much tact to know when to introduce friends, when to take refuge under the shield fashion offers, and not make them acquainted with each other. It is a positive cru-elty to force a talented, witty person to converse with one who is ignorant and dull, as they will, of course, be obliged to do, if introduced.

A well-bred lady, who is receiving several visitors at a time, pays equal attention to all, and attempts, as much as possible, to generalize the conversation, turning to all in succession. The last arrival, however, receives a little more attention at first, than the others.

If it is not agreeable to you to set aside a day for the especial reception of callers, and you have a large circle of acquaintances, be ready to receive them each day that you are at home.

If you are engaged, let the servant say so when she opens the door, and do not send down that message after your friend has been admitted. If she is told when she arrives that you are engaged, she will understand that you are denied to all callers, but if that message comes after she has sent up her card, she may draw the inference that you will not see her, though you may see other friends.

Never keep a caller waiting whilst you make an elaborate toilette. If you are not ready for visitors, it is best to enter the parlor in your wrapper, apologizing for it, than to keep your friend waiting whilst you change your dress.

If a stranger calls, bringing a letter of introduction, and sends the letter, you may read it before going down stairs, but if they wait till you are in the parlor before presenting the letter, merely glance at the signature and at the name of your caller; do not read the letter through, unless it is very short, or you are requested by the bearer to do so.

If you have a friend staying with you, invite her to join you in the parlor when you have callers, and introduce her to your friends.

If you wish to invite a caller to a luncheon or dinner, give the invitation as soon as you have exchanged greetings, not after she has been seated for some time. In the latter case it appears like an afterthought, not, as in the former, as if from a real desire to have the pleasure of her company.

If you have but one caller at a time, rise when she does, and accompany her to the vestibule; but, if there are several in the room, rise when each one does, but only accompany them to the parlor door; there take leave of them, and return to those who still remain seated.

If, after affliction, your friends call before you are able to see them, do not fear to give offence by declining to receive them. They will respect your sorrow, and the call is made more to show their sympathy than from a desire to converse with you.

Visits of condolence, paid between the death of one of your family and the day of the funeral, you may always excuse yourself from, with perfect propriety. They are made in kindness, and show interest, but if you decline seeing such callers, there is no offence given.

In parting from a gentleman caller, rise when he does, and remain standing until he leaves the room, but do not go towards the door.

When a gentleman calls in the morning, he will not remove his outside coat, and will hold his hat in his hand.

Never offer to take the latter, and do not invite him to remove his coat. Take no notice of either one or the other.

If strangers in the city call upon you, enquire at what hotel they are staying, and how long they will be there, that you may return their call before they leave town.

CHAPTER X

MORNING RECEPTIONS OR CALLS ETIQUETTE FOR THE CALLER

THE usual hours for paying morning calls are between eleven and two, or twelve and three, and all calls of ceremony should be made between these hours.

Never, in paying a ceremonious call, stay more than twenty minutes, or less than ten. If your hostess has several other visitors at the same time that you are in her parlor, make your visit short, that she may have more attention to bestow upon others.

After you have received an invitation to a party, call within a week or fortnight after the evening, whether you have accepted or declined the invitation. If you have declined on account of mourning, the excuse extends also to the call.

When the servant answers your ring, hand in your card.

If your friend is out or engaged, leave the card, and if she is in, send it up. Never call without cards. You may offend your friend, as she may never hear of your call, if she is out at the time, and you trust to the memory of the servant.

If your friend is at home, after sending your card up to her by the servant, go into the parlor to wait for her. Sit down quietly, and do not leave your seat until you rise to meet her as she enters the room. To walk about the parlor, examining the ornaments and pictures, is ill-bred. It is still more unlade-like to sit down and turn over to read the cards in her card basket. If she keeps you waiting for a long time, you may take a book from the center-table to pass the interval.

Never, while waiting in a friend's parlor, go to the piano and play till she comes. This is a breach of good-breeding often committed, and nothing can be more ill-bred. You may be disturbing an invalid unawares, or you may prevent your friend, if she has children, from coming down stairs at all, by waking the baby.

If you are a stranger in the city, and bring a letter of introduction to your hostess, send this letter up the stairs with your card, that she may read it, and know how to welcome you when she comes down stairs.

In this case, write upon the card the name of the hotel at which you are staying, and mention in the course of conversation, how long you will be in the city.

If you have a visitor, and desire to introduce her to your friends, you may invite her to accompany you when paying calls.

In making a call for condolence, it is sufficient to leave a card with your enquiries for the health of your friend, and offers of service. The same if calling upon invalids, if they are too ill to see you.

In visits of congratulation, go in, and be hearty in your expressions of interest and sympathy. Pay visits, both of condolence and congratulation, within a week after the event which calls for them occurs.

It is proper, when you have already made your call of the usual length, and another caller is announced, to rise and leave, not immediately, as if you shunned the new arrival, but after a moment or two. Never out-sit two or three parties of visitors, unless you have private business with your hostess which cannot be postponed. Many denounce the system of morning calls as silly, frivolous, and a waste of time. They are wrong. It may be carried to an excess, and so admit of these objections, but in moderation the custom is a good and pleasant one. You have then an opportunity of making friends of mere acquaintances, and you can, in a pleasant chat with a friend at home, have more real enjoyment in her society than in a dozen meetings in large companies, with all the formality and restraint of a party thrown around you. There are many subjects of conversation which are pleasant in a parlor, tête-à-tête with a friend, which you would not care to discuss in a crowded saloon, or in the street. Personal inquiries, private affairs can be cozily chatted over.

In paying your visits of condolence, show, by your own quiet gravity, that you sympathize in the recent affliction of your friend. Though you may endeavor to comfort and cheer her, you must avoid a gay or careless air, as it will be an insult at such a time. Avoid any allusion to the past that may be trying for her to hear or answer, yet do not ignore the subject entirely, as that appears like a want of interest in it. Though you may feel happy, avoid parading your own joyousness at such a time; whatever your own feeling may be, respect the sorrow of another.

Never sit gazing curiously around the room when paying a call, as if taking a mental inventory of the furniture. It is excessively rude. It is still worse to appear to notice any disorder or irregularity that may occur.

If, while paying a call, you perceive that any unforeseen matter in the family, calls for the attention of the lady of the house, leave instantly, no matter how short your call has been. Your friend may not appear to notice the screams of a child, a noise in the kitchen, or the cry from the nursery that the fire board has caught fire, but you may be sure she does hear it, and though too well-bred to speak of it, will heartily rejoice to say good-bye.

Do not take a child with you to pay calls, until it is old enough to behave quietly and with propriety.

To have a troublesome child constantly touching the parlor ornaments, balancing itself on the back of a chair, leaning from a window, or performing any of the thousand tricks in which children excel, is an annoyance, both to yourself and your hostess.

Make no remark upon the temperature of the room, or its arrangement, when you enter it. Never open or shut a window or door without asking permission, and unless really suffering from excessive heat or cold, refrain from asking leave to take this liberty.

If you are invited to go upstairs to your friend's private apartment, you will, of course, accept the invitation, but never go upstairs uninvited. When you reach her door, if the servant has not preceded and announced you, knock, and await her invitation to enter. Then, once in, take no notice of the room, but go instantly to your friend. If she is sewing, do not speak of the nature of her work, but request her to continue, as if you were not present.

In cases of long-standing friendship, you will not, of course, stand upon the ceremony of waiting for each and every one of your calls to be returned before paying another, but be careful that you are not too lavish of your visits. The most cordial welcome may be worn threadbare, if it is called into use too often.

If you are visiting an invalid, or one confined by physical infirmity to one apartment, while you are cheerful and ready to impart all the news that will interest them, do not, by too glowing descriptions of out-door pleasures, make them feel more keenly their own deprivations. It is well, when making such calls, to converse upon literature, or such general subjects as will not remind them of them misfortune.

In cases where, from long illness or other infirmity, a gentleman friend is confined entirely to his room, you may, with perfect propriety, call upon him. It is both polite and kind to do so, as otherwise he would be deprived entirely of the society of his lady friends. Many thus unfortunately situated, from study and reading while so shut out from the world, become the most delightful companions.

If, when you make a call, you unfortunately intrude upon an early dinner hour, do not go in, but leave your card, and say that you will call again.

If you call upon two ladies who are boarding at the same house, do not send up your card to both at the same time.

If one is out, send a card to her room, and then send up for the other. If the first one is in, wait till she comes down, and then chat as long as a call usually lasts. When you rise as if to take leave, accompany your friend to the parlor door, then tell her that you are going to send it to your other friend. She will bid you good-morning, and go to her own room; ring the bell after she leaves you, and send your card by the waiter to your other friend.

In calling at a hotel, enter by the ladies' door, and send your card to the room of your friend by the waiter. It is well, if you are calling upon an entire stranger, to choose a seat, and tell the waiter to say to the lady exactly where she will find you. She will probably enter with your card in her hand; then rise, greet her by name, and introduce yourself.

If you speak to another stranger upon the same errand as the one you expect, the error will be instantly perceived by the difference in name. If a stranger, bringing a letter of introduction, sends the letter with her card, instead of calling, courtesy requires you to make the first call, immediately; the same day that you receive the letter, if possible, if not, the day after.

CHAPTER XI

DINNER COMPANY

ETIQUETTE FOR THE HOSTESS

In issuing invitations for a large dinner party, the usual form is– Mr. and Mrs. G—- request the favor of Mr. and Mrs. L—-'s company to dinner, on Wednesday, March 8th, at —- o'clock.

If your husband is giving a party to gentlemen only, he will have a card printed or written for the occasion, but your duties as hostess, if he wishes you to preside, will still be as arduous as if your own friends were included in the invitation.

The directions given in the chapter on "Evening parties" for the arrangement of the parlor and the dressing-rooms, will apply here equally well, but the dining-room (in this case the centre of attraction) requires still more careful attention. Any fault here will mar your own comfort and the pleasure of your guests, and must be carefully avoided.

Send out your invitations by a servant, or man hired for the purpose; do not trust them to dispatch or penny post.

Be careful in selecting the guests for a dinner party. Remember that conversation will be the sole entertainment for several hours, and if your guests are not well chosen, your dinner, no matter how perfect or costly the viands, will prove a failure. The most agreeable dinners are those whose numbers will allow all the guests to join in a common conversation, and where the host has spirit and intelligence to take the lead, and start a new subject when the interest in the old one begins to flag. Dinners where the guests depend entirely upon the person next them for conversation, are apt to be stupid, as it requires marvelous tact to pair off all the couples, so that everyone will be entertaining in tête-à-tête conversation.

To give a good dinner, your means, room, and establishment must all be taken into consideration when you are preparing for a dinner company. If you invite a large number, you must increase your establishment for the occasion, as to sit down to a dinner badly served, with a scarcity of waiters, is tiresome, and shows little tact or grace on the part of the hostess.

One cook cannot prepare dinner properly for more than ten persons, and three waiters will find ample employment in waiting upon the same number. More than this number will require a table too large for general, easy conversation, and throw your company into couples or trios, for entertainment.

Have your table spread in a room that will accommodate all the guests comfortably, at the same time avoid putting a small social party in a large room, where they will appear lost in the space around them. Let the room be comfortably warmed, and if your dinner is late, have the apartments well lighted. If you sit down by daylight, but will remain in the room until after dark, have the shutters closed and the lights lit, before the dinner is announced, as nothing can be more awkward than to do this in the middle of the meal.

The shape of a table is a point of more importance than some people think. If you wish your dinner to be social–not a mere collection of tête-à-têtes–the table should be of a shape which will make it easy for each guest to address any one at the table. The long parallelogram, with the host at one end and the hostess at the other, is stiff, too broad, too long, and isolates the givers of the feast from the guests.

The round table, if large enough to accommodate many guests, has too large a diameter each way for easy conversation. The best table is the oval, and the host and hostess should sit in the middle of each side, facing each other.

The dining room, even in the heat of summer, should be carpeted, to deaden the noise of the servants' feet. The chairs should be easy, without arms, and with tall, slanting backs. It adds much to the comfort, if each person is provided with a foot-stool.

You must have, besides the waiters, one servant to carve, and he must be an adept. No dish should be carved upon the table, and that no guest shall wait too long for his meat, you must engage a rapid and dexterous carver.

For a party of ten, two waiters, and the carver, are amply sufficient. If you have too many servants, they will only interfere with each other, and stand staring at the guests.

Give your orders before dinner, and through the meal never speak to the servants. Your whole attention must be given to the guests. Even if you see that matters are going wrong, do not let your annoyance appear, but gracefully ignore the painful facts. Let each servant have his regular position at the table. One should take the guests at the right of the hostess, and the left of the host; the other the guests on the other side. They should wear light, noiseless shoes, and white gloves, and each one carry a folded napkin over his right arm.

The main point in the arrangement of the table itself, is to secure beauty, without interfering with conversation. The table cover and napkins must be of snowy damask, the glass clear as crystal, and taste must preside over each detail.

Let nothing high be placed on the table, that will effectively separate the guests from each other. There should be, first, a handsome center piece, and this may be of glass, silver, or China, and not too high or large, and must be elegant as a work of art, or it is better omitted altogether. Preserves or fruit stands, tastefully decorated, with the fruit on fresh, green leaves, and flowers mingled with them, form exquisite centerpieces. A pyramid of flowers, or tasty vase or basket, forms, too, a beautiful ornament for the center of the table. In addition to this, the French scatter vases of flowers all over the table, at the corners and in the center. Some place a small, fragrant bouquet before the plate of each guest. Nothing can be more beautiful than this arrangement. Glasses of celery, dishes of clear, transparent jellies or preserves, exquisite little glass plates of pickles should stand in order on the table.

Place before each guest, the plate, knife, fork, spoon, four wine-glasses of various sizes, the goblet for water, napkin, small salt cellar, salt spoon, and roll of bread. Place none of the meats or vegetables upon the large table. These should all be served at a side-table, each guest selecting his own, to be handed by the servants. The first course is soup. As this is not meant to destroy the appetite for other viands, it should be light, not too rich or thick. Let the servant hand one ladle full to each person. If you have more than one kind, he must first inquire which each guest prefers.

If you have wines, let them be handed round after the soup.

Next comes the fish. If you have large fish, let a slice, cut smoothly, not made into a hash by awkward carving, be placed upon the plate of the guest, with a slice of egg, and drawn butter. If the fish are small, one should be placed upon each plate.

Then come the patties of oysters, minced veal, or lobster; or, instead of these, you may have poultry or game.

Next the roast. With the meats have vegetables served on a separate plate, that the guest may take as much as he wishes with meat. You will, of course, have a variety of vegetables, but scarcely any guest will choose more than two.

The pastry and puddings come next in order, and these, too, are better served from a side table. Between the pastry and the dessert, have salad and cheese placed before each guest.

If you eat dessert in the same room that you dine in, it should be placed upon the table (with the exception of the ices) before the guests are seated, and this comes after the pastry has been discussed. It should consist of fruit and ices.

A pleasanter and more elegant way, is to have the fruit and ices spread in a separate room, and leave the dining room after the pastry has been eaten. The change of position, the absence of the meat flavor in the atmosphere, make the dessert much more delightful than if it is eaten in the same room as the dinner. In summer especially, the change to a cool, fresh room, where the ices and fruits are tastefully spread, and flowers are scattered profusely about the room, delights every sense.

Coffee follows the dessert, and when this enters, if your guests are gentlemen only, your duty is at an end. You may then rise, leave the room, and need not re-appear. If you have lady guests, you give the signal for rising after coffee, and lead the way to the parlor, where, in a few moments, the gentlemen will again join you.

Suppose your guests were invited, servants instructed, every arrangement made, and the important day arrived. The next point to consider is the reception of your guests. Be dressed in good season, as many seem to consider an invitation to dinner as one to pass the day, and come early. Take a position in your drawing-room, where each guest will find you easily, and remain near it, until every guest has arrived.

As each one enters, advance to meet him, and extend your hand.

Have plenty of chairs ready in the drawing-room, as an invitation to dinner by no means argues a "stand up" party.

As you have already arranged every detail, your duty as hostess consists in receiving your guests gracefully, conversing and looking as charmingly as possible. Flowers in the drawing-room are as great a proof of taste as in the dining room.

As the time just before dinner is very apt to be tiresome, you should bring forward all the armor against stupidity that you possess. Display upon tables arranged conveniently about the room, curiosities, handsome books, pho-tographs, engravings, stereoscopes, medallions, any works of art you may own, and have the ottomans, sofas, and chairs so placed that your guests can move easily about the room, or rooms.

The severest test of good breeding in a lady, is in the position of hostess, receiving dinner guests. Your guests may arrive all at once, yet you must make each one feel that he or she is the object of your individual attention, and none must be hurt by neglect. They may arrive very early, yet your duty is to make the time fly until dinner is announced. They may come late, and risk the ruin of your choicest dishes, yet you must not, upon pain of a breach of etiquette, show the least annoyance. If you know that the whole kitchen is in arms at the delay, you must conceal the anguish, as the Spartan boy did his pangs, to turn a cheerful, smiling face upon the tardy guests.

When dinner is announced, you will lead the way to the dining-room upon the arm of one of your gentlemen guests, having paired off the company in couples. The host comes in last with a lady upon his arm.

You may indicate to each couple, as they enter the dining-room, the seats they are to occupy, standing until all are seated, or you may allow them to choose their own places.

The English fashion of placing a card upon each plate with the name of the person to take that seat upon it, is a good one. It enables the hostess to place those whom she is certain will be mutually entertaining, next each other. Place the gentleman who escorts you from the parlor at your right hand.

Having once taken your seat at the table, you have nothing to do with the dinner but to partake of it. Not a word, or even a glance, will a well-bred hostess bestow upon the servants, nor will she speak to the guests of the dishes. Their choice rests between themselves and the waiters, and you must take no notice of what they eat, how much, or how little. Nay, should they partake of one dish only, you must ignore the fact.

The greatest tact is displayed where the hostess makes each guest feel perfectly at ease. She will aid her husband both in leading and supporting the conversation, and will see that no guest is left in silence from want of attention.

Whilst she ignores every breach of etiquette her guests may commit, she must carefully observe every rule herself, and this she must do in an easy, natural manner, avoiding every appearance of restraint. Her deportment, she may be sure, is secretly watched and criticized by each guest, yet she must appear utterly unconscious that she is occupying any conspicuous position.

To watch the servants, or appear uneasy, lest something should go wrong, is excessively ill-bred, and if any accident does occur, you only make it worse by noticing it. To reprove or speak sharply to a servant before your guests, manifests a shocking want of good breeding.

The rules given above are only applicable to large dinner parties, and where the guests are few, and the host himself carves, these rules will not apply. In this case, as you will only require the services of your own household domestics, you must, of course, attend personally to the wants of your guests.

Dinner not being served from a side table, you must, while putting tasteful ornaments upon it, be careful not to crowd them, and leave room for the substantial dishes.

You must watch the plate of each guest, to see that it is well provided, and you will invite each one to partake of the various dishes.

Have a servant to pass the plates from you to each guest, and from the host to you, after he has put the meat upon them, that you may add gravy and vegetables before they are set before your visitors.

At these smaller dinner companies, avoid apologizing for anything, either in the viands or the arrangement of them.

You have provided the best your purse will allow, prepared as faultlessly as possible; you will only gain credit for mock modesty if you apologize for a well-prepared, well-spread dinner, and if there are faults, they will only be made more conspicuous if attention is drawn to them by an apology.

Ease of manner, quiet dignity, cheerful, intelligent conversation, and gentle, lady-like deportment, never appear more charming than when they adorn a lady at the head of her own table.

CHAPTER XII

DINNERCOMPANYETIQUE FOR THE GUEST

WHEN you receive an invitation to join a dinner-party, answer it immediately, as, by leaving your hostess in doubt whether you intend to accept or decline her hospitality, you make it impossible for her to decide how many she must prepare for. If you accept at first, and any unforeseen event keeps you from fulfilling your engagement, write a second note, that your hostess may not wait for dinner for you.

Such a note, if circumstances render it necessary to write it, may be sent with perfect propriety an hour before the time appointed for dinner, though, if you are aware that you cannot attend, earlier, you must send the information in good season.

You should enter the house of your hostess from a quarter to half an hour earlier than the time appointed for dining. Proceed at once to the dressing-room, and arrange your dress and hair, and then enter the drawing-room. By going to the house too early, you may hasten or interrupt the toilet arrangements of your hostess; while, by being late, you will establish a most disagreeable association in the minds of all present, as "the lady who kept dinner waiting at Mrs.L—-'s."

Immediately upon entering the parlor find your hostess, and speak to her first. It is very rude to stop to chat with other guests before greeting the lady of the house. You may bow to any one you know, in passing, but do not stop to speak. Having exchanged a few words with your hostess, turn to the other guests, unless you are the first arrival. In that case, converse with your host and hostess until others come in.

Be careful, if dinner is delayed by the tardiness of the guests, or from any other cause, that you do not show by your manner that you are aware of such delay. To look towards the door often, consult your watch, or give tokens of weariness, are all marks of ill-breeding. Your hostess will probably be sufficiently annoyed by the irregularity itself; do not add to her discomfort by allowing her to suppose that her guests perceive the deficiencies. Look over the books and pictures with an air of interest, converse cheerfully, and in every way appear as if dinner were a matter of secondary importance, (as, indeed, it should be,) compared with the pleasure of the society around you.

When the signal for dinner is given, your hostess will probably name your escort to the table. If he is a stranger, bow in acknowledgment of the introduction, take his arm, and fall into your place in the stream of guests passing from the parlor to the dining-room.

Take the seat pointed out by your hostess, or the waiter, as soon as it is offered. Each one will do this upon entering, and it prevents the confusion that will result if those first entering the room, remain standing until all the other guests come in.

When you take your seat, be careful that your chair does not stand upon the dress of the lady next you, as she may not rise at the same instant that you do, and so you risk tearing her dress.

Sit gracefully at the table; neither so close as to make your movements awkward, nor so far away as to drag your food over your dress before it reaches your mouth. It is well to carry in your pocket a small pincushion, and, having unfolded your napkin, to pin it at the belt. You may do this quietly, without its being perceived, and you will thus really save your dress. If the napkin is merely laid open upon your lap, it will be very apt to slip down, if your dress is of silk or satin, and you risk the chance of appearing again in the drawing- room with the front of your dress soiled or greased.

If, by the carelessness or awkwardness of your neighbors or the servants, you have a plate of soup, glass of wine, or any dish intended for your mouth, deposited upon your dress, do not spring up, or make any exclamation. You may wipe off the worst of the spot with your napkin, and then let it pass without further notice.

If an apology is made by the unlucky perpetrator of the accident, try to set him at his ease by your own lady-like composure. He will feel sorry and awkward enough, without reproach, sullenness, or cold looks from you.

Gloves and mittens are no longer worn at table, even at the largest dinner-parties.

To make remarks upon the guests or the dishes is excessively rude. If the conversation is general, speak loudly enough to be heard by those around you, but, at the same time, avoid raising your voice too much. If the company is very large, and you converse only with the person immediately beside you, speak in a distinct, but low tone, that you may not interrupt other couples, but carefully avoid whispering or a confidential air. Both are in excessively bad taste. To laugh in a suppressed way, has the appearance of laughing at those around you, and a loud, boisterous laugh is always unlady-like. Converse cheerfully, laugh quietly, but freely, if you will, and while you confine your attention entirely to your neighbor, still avoid any air of secrecy or mystery.

Never use an eye-glass, either to look at the persons around you or the articles upon the table.

Eat your soup quietly. To make any noise while eating it, is simply disgusting. Do not break bread into your soup.

Break off small pieces and put them into your mouth, if you will, but either bite it from the roll or break it up, and eat it from your soup- plate with a spoon.

In eating bread with meat, never dip it into the gravy on your plate, and then bite the end off. If you wish to eat it with gravy, break off a small piece, put it upon your plate, and then, with a fork, convey it to your mouth.

When helped to fish, remove, with knife and fork, all the bones, then lay down the knife, and, with a piece of bread in your left hand and a fork in your right, eat the flakes of fish.

Need I say that the knife is to cut your food with, and must never be used while eating? To put it in your mouth is a distinctive mark of low-breeding.

If you have selected what you will eat, keep the plate that is placed before you; never pass it to the persons next you, as they may have an entirely different choice of meat or vegetables.

Never attempt to touch any dish that is upon the table, but out of your reach, by stretching out your arms, leaning forward, or, still worse, standing up. Ask the waiter to hand it, if you wish for it; or, if the gentleman beside you can easily do so, you may ask him to pass it to you.

Do not press those near you to take more or other things than are upon their plate. This is the duty of the hostess, or, if the company is large, the servants will attend to it. For you to do so is officious and ill-bred.

When conversing let your knife and fork rest easily upon your plate, even if still in your hand. Avoid holding them upright. Keep your own knife, fork, and spoon solely for the articles upon your own plate. To use them for helping yourself to butter or salt, is rude in the extreme.

When you do not use the salt-spoon, sugar tongs, and butter-knife, you may be sure that those around you will conclude that you have never seen the articles, and do not know their use.

You need not fear to offend by refusing to take wine with a gentleman, even your host. If you decline gracefully, he will appreciate the delicacy which makes you refuse. If, however, you have no conscientious scruples, and are invited to take wine, bow, and merely raise the glass to your lips, then set it down again. You may thus acknowledge the courtesy, and yet avoid actually drinking the wine.

No lady should drink wine at dinner. Even if her head is strong enough to bear it, she will find her cheeks, soon after the indulgence, flushed, hot, and uncomfortable; and if the room is warm, and the dinner a long one, she will probably pay the penalty of her folly, by having a headache all the evening.

If offered any dish of which you do not wish to partake, decline it, but do not assign any reason. To object to the dish itself is an insult to your entertainers, and if you assert any reason for your own dislike it is ill-bred.

Do not bend too much forward over your food, and converse easily. To eat fast, or appear to be so engrossed as to be unable to converse, is ill-bred; and it makes those around you suspect that you are so little accustomed to dining well, that you fear to stop eating an instant, lest you should not get enough.

It is equally ill-bred to accept everything that is offered to you.

Never take more than two vegetables; do not take a second plate of soup, pastry, or pudding. Indeed, it is best to accept but one plate of any article.

Never use a spoon for anything but liquids, and never touch anything to eat, excepting bread, celery, or fruit, with your fingers.

In the intervals which must occur between the courses, do not appear to be conscious of the lapse of time. Wear a careless air when waiting, conversing cheerfully and pleasantly, and avoid looking round the room, as if wondering what the waiters are about.

Never eat every morsel that is upon your plate; and surely no lady will ever scrape her plate, or pass the bread round it, as if to save the servants the trouble of washing it.

Take such small mouthfuls that you can always be ready for conversation, but avoid playing with your food, or partaking of it with an affectation of delicate appetite. Your hostess may suppose you despise her fare, if you appear to be very selective, or eat too sparingly. If your state of health deprives you of appetite, it is bad enough for you to decline the invitation to dine out.

Never examine the food before you. You insult your hostess by such a proceeding, as it looks as if you feared to find something upon the plate that should not be there.

If you find a worm on opening a nut, or in any of the fruit, hand your plate quietly, and without remark, to the waiter, and request him to bring you a clean one. Do not let others perceive the movement, or the cause of it, if you can avoid doing so.

Never make a noise while eating. To munch or smack the lips are vulgar faults.

Sit quietly at table, avoid stiffness, but, at the same time, be careful that you do not annoy others by your restlessness.

Do not eat so fast as to be done long before others, nor so slowly as to keep them waiting.

When the finger-glasses are passed round, dip the ends of your fingers into them, and wipe them upon your napkin; then do not fold your napkin, but place it beside your plate upon the table.

To carry away fruit or bonbons from the table is a sign of low breeding. Rise with the other ladies when your hostess gives the signal. After returning to the parlor, remain in the house at least an hour after dinner is over. If you have another engagement in the evening, you may then take your leave, but not before. You will insult your hostess by leaving sooner, as it appears that you came only for the dinner, and that being over, your interest in the house, for the time, has ceased. It is only beggars who "eat and run!"

CHAPTER XIII

TABLE ETIQUETTE

IN order to appear perfectly well-bred at table when in company, or in public, as at a hotel, you must pay attention, three times a day, to the points of table etiquette. If you neglect these little details at home and in private, they will be performed awkwardly and with an air of restraint when you are in company. By making them habitual, they will become natural, and appear easily, and sit gracefully upon you.

Even when eating entirely alone, observe these little details, thus making the most finished and elegant manners perfectly familiar, and thus avoiding the stiff, awkward air you will wear if you keep your politeness only for company, when you will be constantly apprehensive of doing wrong.

At breakfast or tea, if your seat is at the head of the table, you must, before taking anything upon your own plate, fill a cup for each one of the family, and pass them round, being careful to suit each one in the preparation of the cup, that none may return to you for more tea, water, sugar, or milk. If you have a visitor, pass the cup with the tea or coffee alone in it, and hand with the cup the sugar bowl and cream pitcher, that these may be added in the quantity preferred.

After all the cups have been filled and passed round, you may take the bread, butter, and other food upon your own plate. Train your children, so that they will pass these things to you as soon as they see you are ready to receive them.

If you are yourself at the side of the table, pass the bread, butter, etc., to the lady at the head, when you see that she has sent the cups from the waiter before her, to those seated at the table.

If you occupy the place of head of the table, you must watch the cups, offer to fill them when empty, and also see that each one of the family is well helped to the other articles upon the table.

Avoid making any noise while eating, even if each meal is eaten in a solitary state. It is a disgusting habit, and one not easily cured if once contracted, to make any noise with the lips when eating.

Never put large pieces of food into your mouth. Eat slowly, and cut your food into small pieces before putting it into your mouth.

Use your fork, or spoon, never your knife, to put your food into your mouth. At dinner, hold in your left hand a piece of bread, and raise your meat or vegetables with the fork, holding the bread to prevent the pieces slipping from the plate.

If you are asked at the table what part of the meat you prefer, name your favorite piece, but do not give such information unless asked to do so. To point out any special part of a dish, and ask for it, is ill-bred. To answer, when asked to select a part, that "it is a matter of indifference," or, "I can eat any part," is annoying to the carver, as he cares less than yourself certainly, and would prefer to give you the piece you really like best.

Do not pour coffee or tea from your cup into your saucer, and do not blow either these or soup. Wait until they cool.

Use the butter-knife, salt-spoon, and sugar-tongs as scrupulously when alone, as if a room full of people were watching you. Otherwise, you may neglect to do so when the omission will mortify you.

Never put poultry or fish bones, or the stones of fruit, upon the table-cloth, but place them on the edge of your plate.

Do not begin to eat until others at the table are ready to commence too.Sit easily in your chair, neither too near the table, nor too far from it, and avoid such tricks as putting your arms on the table, leaning back lazily in your chair, or playing with your knife, fork, or spoon.

Never raise your voice, when speaking, any higher than is necessary. The clear articulation and distinct pronunciation of each word, will make a low tone more agreeable and more easily understood, than the loudest tone, if the speech is rapid or indistinct.

Never pass your plate with the knife or fork upon it, and when you pass your cup, put the spoon in the saucer.

Never pile up the food on your plate. It looks as if you feared it would all be gone before you could be helped again, and it will certainly make your attempts to cut the food awkward, if your plate is crowded.

If there is a delicacy upon the table, partake of it sparingly, and never help yourself to it a second time.

If you wish to cough, or use your handkerchief, rise from the table, and leave the room. If you have not time to do this, cover your mouth, and turn your head aside from the table, and perform the disagreeable necessity as rapidly and quietly as possible.

Avoid gesticulation at the table. Indeed, a well-bred lady will never gesticulate, but converse quietly, letting the expression and animation of her features give force to her words.

Never, when at the home table, leave it until the other members of the family are also ready to rise.

CHAPTER XIV

CONDUCT IN THE STREET

A lady's conduct is never so entirely at the mercy of critics, because never so public, as when she is in the street. Her dress, carriage, walk, will all be exposed to notice; every passer-by will look at her, if it is only for one glance; every unlazy-like action will be marked; and in no position will a dignified, lady-like deportment be more certain to command respect.

Let me start with you upon your promenade, my friend, and I will soon decide your place upon the list of well-bred ladies.

First, your dress. Not that scarlet shawl, with a green dress, I beg, and–oh! spare my nerves! –you are not so in-sane as to put on a bluebonnet. That's right. If you wish to wear the green dress, don a black shawl, and–that white bonnet will do very well. One rule you must lay down with regard to a walking dress. It must never be conspicuous.

Let the material be rich, if you will; the set of each garment faultless; have collar and sleeves snowy white, and wear neatly-fitting, whole, clean gloves and boots. Every detail may be scrupulously attended to, but let the whole effect be quiet and modest. Wear a little of one bright color, if you will, but not more than one. Let each part of the dress

harmonize with all the rest; avoid the extreme of fashion, and let the dress suit you. If you are short and plump, do not wear flounces, because they are fashionable, and avoid large plaids, even if they are the very latest style. If tall and slight, do not add to the length of your figure by long stripes, a little mantilla, and a caricature of a bonnet, with long, streaming ribbons. A large, round face will never look well, staring from a tiny, delicate bonnet; nor will a long, thin one stands the test much better. Wear what is becoming to yourself, and only bow to fashion enough to avoid eccentricity. To have everything in the extreme of fashion, is a sure mark of vulgarity.

Wear no jewelry in the street accepting your watch and brooch. Jewelry is only suited for a full evening dress, when all the other details unite to set it off. If it is real, it is too valuable to risk losing in the street, and if it is not real, no lady should wear it. Mock jewelry is utterly detestable.

What are you doing? Sucking the head of your parasol!

Have you not had breakfast? Take that piece of ivory from your mouth! To suck it is unlady-like, and let me tell you, excessively unbecoming. Rosy lips and pearly teeth can be put to a better use.

Why did you not dress before you came out? It is a mark of ill-breeding to draw your gloves on in the street. Now your bonnet-strings, and now–your collar! Pray arrange your dress before you leave the house! Nothing looks worse than to see a lady fussing over her dress in the street. Take a few more moments in your dressing- room, and arrange your dress so that you will not need to think of it again whilst you are out.

Do not walk so fast! you are not chasing anybody! Walk slowly, gracefully! Oh, do not drag one foot after the other as if you were fast asleep–set down the foot lightly, but at the same time firmly; now, carry your head up, not so; you hang it down as if you feared to look any one in the face!

Nay, that is the other extreme! Now you look like a drill major, on parade! So that is the medium. Erect, yet, at the same time, easy and elegant.

Now, my friend, do not swing your arms. You don't know what to do with them? Your parasol takes one hand; hold your dress up a little with the other. Not so! No lady should raise her dress above the ankle.

Take care!

don't drag your dress through that mud-puddle! Worse and worse! If you take hold of your dress on both sides, in that way, and drag it up so high, you will be set down as a raw country girl. So. Raise it just above the boot, all round, easily, letting it fall again in the old folds.

Don't shake it down; it will fall back on itself.

Stop! don't you see there is a carriage coming? Do you want to be thrown down by the horses? You can run across?

Very lady-like indeed! Surely nothing can be more ungraceful than to see a lady shuffle and run across a street. Wait until the way is clear and then walk slowly across.

Do not try to raise your skirts. It is better to soil them.

(You were very foolish to wear white skirts on this muddy day.) They are easily washed, and you cannot raise them all. You will surely be awkward in making the attempt, and probably fail, in spite of your efforts. True, they will be badly soiled, and you expose this when you raise the dress, but the state of the streets must be seen by all who see your share of the dirt, and they will apologize for your untidy appearance in a language distinctly understood.

Don't hold your parasol so close to your face, nor so low down. You cannot see your way clearly, and you will run against somebody. Always hold an umbrella or parasol so that it will clear your bonnet, and leave the space before your face open, so that you may see your way clearly.

If you are ever caught in a shower, and meet a gentleman friend who offers an umbrella, accept it, if he will accompany you to your destination; but do not deprive him of it, if he is not able to join you. Should he insist, return it to his house or store the instant you reach home, with a note of thanks. If a stranger offers you the same services, decline it positively, but courteously, at the same time thanking him.

Never stop to speak to a gentleman in the street. If you have anything important to say to him, allow him to join and walk with you, but do not stop. It is best to follow the same rule with regard to ladies, and either walk with them or invite them to walk with you, instead of stopping to talk.

A lady who desires to pay strict regard to etiquette, will not stop to gaze in at the shop windows. It looks counterfeit. If she is alone, it looks as if she were waiting for someone; and if she is not alone, she is victimizing someone else, to satisfy her curiosity.

Remember that in meeting your gentlemen friends it is your duty to speak first, therefore do not cut them by waiting to be recognized. Be sure, however, that they see you before you bow, or you place yourself in the awkward position of having your bow pass, unreturned.

You are not expected to recognize any friend on the opposite side of the street. Even if you see them, do not bow.

Avoid "cutting" anyone. It is a small way of showing spite, and lowers you more than your enemy. If you wish to avoid any further intercourse bow, coldly and gravely, but do not look at any one, to whom you are in the habit of bowing, and pass without bowing.

If you do this, they may flatter themselves that they were really unrecognized, but a distant, cold bow will show them that you speak from civility only, not from friendship.

In the street a lady takes the arm of a relative, her affianced lover, or husband, but of no other gentleman, unless the streets are slippery, or in the evening.

When a lady walks with two gentlemen, she should endeavor to divide her attention and remarks equally between them.

If you do stop in the street, draw near the walls, that you may not keep others from passing.

Loud talking and laughing in the street are excessively vulgar. Not only this, but they expose a lady to the most severe misconstruction. Let your conduct be modest and quiet.

If a gentleman, although a stranger, offers his hand to assist you in leaving a carriage, omnibus, or to aid you in crossing where it is wet or muddy, accept his civility, thank him, bow and pass on.

If you wish to take an omnibus or car, see that it is not already full. If it is, do not get in. You will annoy others, and be uncomfortable yourself.

It is best to carry change to pay car or omnibus fare, as you keep others waiting whilst the driver is making change, and it is apt to fall into the straw when passing from one hand to another.

If a gentleman gives you his seat, hands your fare, or offers you any such attention, thank him. It is not categorized, it is lady-like. If you do not speak, bow.

Be careful not to be alone in the streets after nightfall. It exposes you to insults. If you are obliged to go out, have a servant, or another lady, if you cannot procure the escort of a gentleman, which is, of course, the best.

Walk slowly, do not turn your head to the right or left, unless you wish to walk that way, and avoid any gesture or word that will attract attention.

Never look back! It is excessively ill-bred.

Make no remarks upon those who pass you, while there is even a possibility that they may hear you.

Never stare at any one, even if they have peculiarities, which make them objects of remark.

In taking your place in an omnibus or car, do so quietly, and then sit perfectly still. Do not change your place or move restlessly. Make room for others if you see that the opposite side is full.

If you walk with a gentleman, when he reaches your door invite him in, but if he declines, do not urge him. If you are returning from a ball or party, and the hour is a very late (or early) one, you are not bound in politeness to invite your escort to enter; the hour will be your apology for omitting the ceremony.

CHAPTER XV

LETTER WRITING

THERE is no branch of education called so universally into requisition as the art of letter writing; no station, high or low, where the necessity for correspondence is not felt; no person, young or old, who does not, at some time, write, cause to be written, and receive letters. From the President in his official capacity, with the busy pens of secretaries constantly employed in this branch of service, to the Irish laborer who, unable to guide a pen, writes, also by proxy, to his kinsfolks across the wide ocean; all, at some time, feel the desire to transmit some message, word of love, business, or sometimes enmity, by letter.

Yet, in spite of the universal need, and almost universal habit, there are really but very few persons who write a good letter; a letter that is, at the same time long enough to interest, yet not long enough to tire; sufficiently condensed to keep the attention, and not tedious, and yet detailed enough to afford satisfaction; that is correct in grammatical construction, properly punctuated, written in a clear, legible hand, with the date, address, signature, all in the proper place, no words whose letters stand in utter defiance to spelling-book rules; in short, a well-written letter.

Thousands, millions are sent from post to post every day.

The lightning speed of the telegraph takes its messages from city to city; the panting steamer carries from continent to continent its heavy mail-bags, laden with its weight of loving messages; the "iron horse" drags behind it, its measure of the many missives; while, in the far- distant Western wilds, the lumbering wagon bears its paper freight, with its pen eloquence, to cheer and comfort, or sadden and crush, the waiting emigrants, longing for news of home.

To some, who, with hearts desolated by the separation from the home circle, could read, with an eager interest, volumes of the most common-place, trivial incidents, if only connected with the loved ones there, will come pages, from the pen of the dearest relative, full of learning, wit, and wisdom, wholly uninteresting to the receiver.

Why is this? Not from any desire upon the part of the writer to display learning or talent, but because, writing a letter being to them a great undertaking, and the letter being destined to go a long distance, they look upon it as an event too unusual to be wasted in detailing the simple, every-day details of domestic life, and ransack memory and learning for a subject worthy of the long journey and unusual labor.

Others will have, from mere acquaintances, long, tedious details of uninteresting trivialities, and from the near relatives, short, dry epistles, which fall like stones upon the heart longing for little, affectionate expressions, and home memories.

From some letter writers, who are in the midst of scenes and events of the most absorbing interest, letters arrive, only a few lines long, without one allusion to the interesting matter lying so profusely around them; while others, with the scantiest of outward subjects, will, from their own teem-ing brain, write bewitching, absorbing epistles, read with eagerness, laid aside with the echo of Oliver Twist's petition in a sigh; the reader longing for "more."

It is, of course, impossible to lay down any distinct rule for the style of letter writing. Embracing, as it does, all subjects and all classes, all countries and associations, and every relation in which one person can stand to another, what would be an imperative rule in some cases, becomes positive absurdity in others. Every letter will vary from others written before, in either its subject, the person addressed, or the circumstances which make it necessary to write it.

Letter writing is, in fact, but conversation, carried on with the pen, when distance or circumstances prevent the easier method of exchanging ideas, by spoken words. Write, therefore, as you would speak, were the person to whom your letter is addressed is seated beside you. As amongst relatives and intimate friends you would converse with a familiar manner, and in easy language, so in your letters to such persons, let your style be simple, entirely devoid of effort.

Again, when introduced to a stranger, or conversing with one much older than yourself, your manner is respectful and dignified; so let the letters addressed to those on these terms with yourself, be written in a more ceremonious style, but at the same time avoid stiffness, and above all, pedantry.

A letter of advice to a child, would of course demand an entirely different style, from that written by a young lady to a friend or relative advanced in life; yet the general rule, "write as you would converse," applies to each and every case.

Neatness is an important requisite in a letter. To send a fair, clean sheet, with the words written in a clear, legible hand, will go a great way in ensuring a cordial welcome for your letter. Avoid erasures, as they spoil the beauty of your sheet. If it is necessary to correct a word, draw your pen through it, and write the word you wish to use as a substitute, above the one erased; do not scratch out the word and write another over it: it is untidy, and the second word is seldom legible. Another requisite for a good letter is a clear, concise style. Use language that will be easily understood, and avoid the parenthesis. Important passages in letters are often lost entirely, by the ambiguous manner in which they are worded, or rendered quite as unintelligible by the blots, erasures, or villainously bad hand-writing. A phrase may, by the addition or omission of one word, or by the alteration of one punctuation mark, convey to the reader an entirely different idea from that intended by the writer; so, while you write plainly, use good language, you must also write carefully, and punctuate properly.

If you are in doubt about the correct spelling of a word, do not trust by chance, hoping it may be right, but get a dictionary, and be certain that you have spelt it as it ought to be.

Simplicity is a great charm in letter-writing. What you send in a letter, is, as a general rule, intended for the perusal of one person only. Therefore to cumber your epistles with quotations, similes, flowery language, and a stilted, pedan-tic style, is in bad taste. You may use elegant language, yet use it easily. If you use a quotation, let it come into its place naturally, as if flowing in perfect harmony with your ideas, and let it be short. Long quotations in a letter are tiresome. Make no attempt at display in a correspondence. You will err as much in such an attempt, as if, when seated face to face with your correspondent, alone in your own apartment, you were to rise and converse with the gestures and language of a minister in his pulpit, or a lecturer upon his platform.

As everything, in style, depends upon the subject of the letter, and the person to whom it is addressed, some words follow, relating to some of the various kinds of correspondence:

BUSINESS LETTERS should be as brief as is consistent with the subject; clear, and to the point. Say all that is necessary, in plain, distinct language, and say no more. State, in forcible words, every point that it is desirable for your correspondent to be made acquainted with, that your designs and prospects upon the subject may be perfectly well understood. Write, in such a letter, of nothing but the business in hand; other matters will be out of place there. Nowhere is a confused style, or illegible writing, more unpardonable than in a business letter; nowhere a good style and hand are more important. Avoid flowery language, too many words, all pathos or wit, any display of talent or learning, and every merely personal matter, in a business letter.

LETTERS OF COMPLIMENT must be restricted, confined entirely to one subject. If passing between acquaintances, they should be written in a graceful, at the same time respectful, manner.

Avoid hackneyed expressions,commonplace quotations, and long, labored sentences, but while alluding to the subject in hand, as if warmly interested in it, at the same time endeavor to write in a style of simple, natural grace.

LETTERS OF CONGRATULATION demand a cheerful, pleasant style, and an appearance of great interest. They should be written from the heart, and the cordial, warm feelings there will prompt the proper language. Be careful, while offering to your friend the hearty congratulations her happy circumstances demand, that you do not let envy at her good fortune creep into your head, to make the pen utter complaining words at your own hard lot. Do not dampen her joy, by comparing her happiness with the misery of another. There are many clouds in the life of every one of us. While the sun shines clearly upon the events of your friend’s life let her enjoy the brightness and warmth, unshadowed by any words of yours. Give her, to the full, your sympathy in her rejoicing, cheerful words, warm congratulations, and bright hopes for the future. Should there be, at the time of her happiness, any sad event you wish to communicate to her, of which it is your duty to inform her, write it in another letter. If you must send it the same day, do so, but let the epistle wishing her joy, go alone, unclouded with the news of sorrow. At the same time, avoid exaggerated expressions of congratulation, lest you are suspected of a desire to be satirical, and avoid underlining any words. If the language is not forcible enough to convey your ideas, you will not make it better by underlining it. If you say to your friend upon her marriage, that you wish her "joy in her new relations, and hope she may be entirely happy in her domestic life," you make her doubt your wishes, and think you mean to ridicule her chances of such happiness.

LETTERS OF CONDOLENCE are exceedingly trying, both to read and to write. If the affliction which calls for them is one which touches you nearly, really grieving and distressing you, all written words must seem tame and cold, compared with the aching sympathy which dictates them.

It is hard with the eyes blinded by tears, and the hand shak-ing, to write calmly; and it is impossible to express upon paper all the burning thoughts and words that would pour forth, were you beside the friend whose sorrow is yours. If you do not feel the trial, your task is still more difficult, for no letters demand truth, spoken from the heart, more than letters of condolence. Do not treat the subject for grief too lightly. Write words of comfort if you will, but do not appear to consider the affliction as a trifle. Time may make it less severe, but the first blow of grief must be heavy, and a few words of sincere sympathy will outweigh pages of mere expressions of hope for comfort, or the careless lines that show the letter to be one of mere duty, not feeling.

Let your friend feel that her sorrow makes her dearer to you than ever before, and that her grief is yours. To treat the subject with levity, or to wander from it into witticisms or every-day chit-chat, is a wanton insult, unworthy of a lady and a friend. Do not magnify the event, or plunge the mourner into still deeper despondency by taking a despair-ing, gloomy view of the sorrow, under which she is bent.

Show her the silver lining of her cloud, try to soothe her grief, yet be willing to admit that it is a cloud, and that she has cause for grief. To throw out hints that the sorrow is sent as a punishment to an offender; to imply that neglect or imprudence on the part of the mourner is the cause of the calamity; to hold up the trial as an example of retribution, or a natural consequence of wrong doing, is cruel, and barbarous. Even if this is true, (indeed, if this is the case, it only aggravates the insult); avoid such retrospection. It is as if a surgeon, called in to a patient suffering from a fractured limb, sat down, inattentive to the suffering, to lecture his patient upon the carelessness which caused the accident.

One of the most touching letters of condolence ever written was sent by a literary lady, well known in the ranks of our American authoresses, to her sister, who had lost her youngest child. The words were few, merely:–

"SISTER DARLING:

"I cannot write what is in my heart for you to-day, it is too full. Filled with a double sorrow, for you, for my own grief.

Tears blind me, my pen trembles in my hand.

Oh, to be near you! to clasp you in my arms! to draw your head to my bosom, and weep with you!

Darling, God comfort you, I cannot. "S."

That was all. Yet the sorrowing mother said that no other letter, though she appreciated the kind motive that dictated all, yet none comforted her as did these few lines. Written from the heart, their simple eloquence touched the heart for which they were intended. Early stages of great grief reject comfort, but they long, with intense longing, for sympathy.

LETTERS WRITTEN TO GENTLEMEN should be ceremonious and dignified. If the acquaintance is slight, write in the third person, if there is a necessity for a letter. If a business letter, be respectful, yet not servile. It is better to avoid correspondence with gentlemen, particularly whilst you are young, as there are many objections to it. Still, if a friend of long standing solicits a correspondence, and your parents or husband approve and permit compliance with the request, it would be over-prudish to refuse. Write, however, such letters as, if they were printed in the newspapers, would cause you no annoyance. If the acquaintance admits of a frank, friendly style, be careful that your expressions of good will do not become too vehement, and avoid any confidential communications. When he begins to ask you to keep such and such passages secret, believe me, it is quite time to drop the correspondence.

LETTERS OF ENQUIRY, especially if they request a favor, should contain a few lines of compliment. If the letter is upon a private subject, such as enquiry with regard to the illness or misfortune of a friend, avoid making it too brief.

To write short, careless letters upon such subjects, is unfeeling, and they will surely be attributed to motives of obligation or duty, not to interest. Letters of enquiry, referring to family matters, should be delicately worded, and appear dictated by interest, not mere curiosity. If the enquiry refers to matters interesting only to yourself, enclose a postage-stamp for the reply. In answering such letters, if they refer to your own health or subjects interesting to yourself, thank the writer for the interest expressed, and answer in a satisfactory manner. If the answer interests your correspondent only, do not reply as if the inquiry annoyed you, but express some interest in the matter of the letter, and give as clear and satisfactory a reply as is in your power.

LETTERS OFFERING FAVORS–Be careful in writing to offer a favor, that you do not make your friend feel a heavy weight of obligation by over-rating your services. The kindness will be duly appreciated, and more highly valued if offered in a delicate manner. Too strong a sense of obligation is humiliating, so do not diminish the real value of the service by forcing the receiver to acknowledge a fictitious value. Let the recipient of your good will feel that it affords you as much pleasure to confer the favor as it will give her to receive it. A letter accompanying a present, should be short and gracefully worded. The affectionate spirit of such little epistles will double the value of the gift which they accompany. Never refer to a favor received, in such a letter, as that will give your gift the appearance of being payment for such favor, and make your letter of about as much value as a tradesman's received bill.

LETTERS OF THANKS for enquiries made, should be short, merely echoing the words of the letter they answer, and contain the answer to the question, with an acknowledgement of your correspondent's interest. If the letter is your own acknowledgement of a favor conferred, let the language be simple, but strong, grateful, and graceful.

Fancy that you are clasping the hand of the kind friend who has been generous or thoughtful for you, and then write, even as you would speak. Never hint that you deem such a favor an obligation to be returned at the first opportunity; although this may really be the case, it is extremely indelicate to say so. In your letter gracefully acknowledge the obligation, and if, at a later day, you can return the favor, then let actions, not words, prove your grateful recollection of the favor conferred upon you. If your letter is written to acknowledge the reception of a present, speak of the beauty or usefulness of the gift, and of the pleasant associations with her name it will always recall.

LETTERS OF RECOMMENDATION should be truthful, polite, and carefully considered. Such letters may be business letters, or they may be given to servants, and they must be given only when really deserved. Do not be hasty in giving them; remember that you are, in some measure responsible for the bearer; therefore, never sacrifice truth and frankness, to a mistaken idea of kindness or politeness.

LETTERS OF INTRODUCTION must be left unsealed.

They must not contain any allusion to the personal qualities of the bearer, as such allusion would be about as sure a proof of ill-breeding as if you sat beside your friend, and ran over the list of the virtues and talents possessed by her.

The fact that the person bearing the letter is your friend, will be all sufficient reason for cordial reception by the friend to whom the letter is addressed. The best form is:–

PHILADELPHIA, June 18th, 18–. MY DEAR MARY:

This letter will be handed to you by Mrs. C., to whom I am pleased to introduce you, certain that the acquaintance thus formed, between two friends of mine, of so long standing and so much beloved, will be pleasant to both parties.

Any attention that you may find it in your power to extend to Mrs. C. whilst she is in your city, will be highly appreciated, and gratefully acknowledged, by

Your sincere friend, A—-.

LETTERS OF ADVICE should not be written unsolicited.

They will, in all probability, even when requested, be un-palatable, and should never be sent unless they can really be of service. Write them with frankness and sincerity. To write after an act has been committed, and is irrevocable, is folly, and it is also unkind. You may inform your friend that, "had you been consulted, a different course from the one taken would have been recommended," and you may really believe this, yet it will probably be false. Seeing the unfavorable result of the wrong course will enable you fully to appreciate the wisdom of the right one, but, had you been consulted when the matter was doubtful, you would probably have been as puzzled as your friend to judge the proper mode of action. You should word a letter of advice delicately, stating your opinion frankly and freely, but giving it as an opinion, not as a positive law. If the advice is not taken, do not feel offended, as others, more experienced than yourself upon the point in question, may have also been consulted. Let no selfish motive govern such a letter. Think only of the good or evil that result from your friend, and while you may write warmly and earnestly, let the motive be a really disinterested one.

LETTERS OF EXCUSE should be frank and graceful.

They must be written promptly, as soon as the occasion that calls for them admits. If delayed, they become insulting. If such a letter is called forth by an act of negligence on your own part, apologize for it frankly, and show by your tone that you sincerely desire to regain the confidence your carelessness has periled. If you have been obliged by positive inability to neglect the fulfilment of any promise you have given, or any commission you have undertaken, then state the reason for your delay, and solicit the indulgence of your friend. Do not write in such stiff, formal language that the apology will seem forced from you, but offer your excuse frankly, as if with a sincere desire to atone for an act of negligence, or remove a ground of offence.

LETTERS OF INTELLIGENCE are generally the answer to letters of enquiry, or the statement of certain incidents or facts, interesting both to the writer and reader of the letter.

Be careful in writing such a letter that you have all the facts in exact accordance with the truth. Remember that every word is set down against you, if one item of your information prove to be false; and do not allow personal opinion or prejudice to dictate a single sentence. Never repeat anything gathered from mere hearsay, and be careful, in such a letter, that you violate no confidence, nor force yourself upon the private affairs of any one. Do not let scandal or a mere love of gossip dictate a letter of intelligence. If your news is painful, state it as delicately as possible, and add a few lines expressive of sympathy. If it is your pleasant task to communicate a joyful event, make your letter cheerful and gay. If you have written any such letter, and, after sending it, find you have made any error in a statement, write, and correct the mistake immediately. It may be a trivial error, yet there is no false or mistaken news so trifling as to make a correction unnecessary.

INVITATIONS are generally written in the third person, and this form is used where the acquaintance is very slight, for formal notes, and cards of compliment. The form is proper upon such occasions, but should be used only in the most ceremonious correspondence. If this style is adopted by a person who has been accustomed to write in a more familiar one to you, take it as a hint, that the correspondence has, for some reason, become disagreeable, and had better cease.

AUTOGRAPH LETTERS should be very short; merely acknowledging the compliment paid by the request for the signature, and a few words expressing the pleasure you feel in granting the favor. If you write to ask for an autograph, always inclose a postage stamp for the answer.

Date every letter you write accurately, and avoid postscripts.

Politeness, kindness, both demand that every letter you receive must be answered. Nothing can give more pleasure in a correspondence, than prompt replies. Matters of much importance often rest upon the reply to a letter, and therefore this duty should never be delayed. In answering friendly letters, it will be found much easier to write what is kind and interesting, if you sit down to the task as soon as you read your friend's letter. Always mention the date of the letter to which your own is a reply.

Never write on a half sheet of paper. Paper is cheap, and a half sheet looks both mean and slovenly. If you do not write but three lines, still send the whole sheet of paper. Perfectly plain paper, thick, smooth, and white, is the most elegant.

When in mourning, use paper and envelopes with a black edge. Never use the gilt edged, or fancy bordered paper; it looks vulgar, and is in bad taste. You may, if you will, have your initials stamped at the top of the sheet, and on the seal of the envelope, but do not have any fancy ornaments in the corners, or on the back of the envelope.

You will be guilty of a great breach of politeness, if you answer either a note or letter upon the half sheet of the paper sent by your correspondent, even though it may be left blank.

Never write, even the shortest note, in pencil. It looks careless, and is rude.

Never write a letter carelessly. It may be addressed to your most intimate friend, or your nearest relative, but you can never be sure that the eye for which it is intended, will be the only one that sees it. I do not mean by this, that the epistle should be in a formal, studied style, but that it must be correct in its grammatical construction, properly punctuated, with every word spelt according to rule.

Even in the most familiar epistles, observe the proper rules for composition; you would not in conversing, even with your own family, use incorrect grammar, or impertinent language; therefore avoid saying upon paper what you would not say with your tongue.

Notes written in the third person, must be continued throughout in the same person; they are frequently very mysterious from the confusion of pronouns, yet it is a style of correspondence much used and very proper upon many occasions. For compliment, inquiry where there is no intimacy between the parties, from superiors to inferiors, the form is elegant and proper. If you receive a note written in the third person, reply in the same form, but do not reply thus to a more familiar note or letter, as it is insulting, and implies offence taken. If you wish to repel undue familiarity or impertinence in your correspondent, then reply to the epistle in the most formal language, and in the third person.

It is an extraordinary fact, that persons who have received a good education, and who use their pens frequently, will often, in writing notes, commence in the third person and then use the second or first personal pronoun, and finish by a signature; thus–

Miss Claire's compliments to Mr. James, and wishes to know whether you have finished reading my copy of "Jane Eyre," as if Mr.James had finished it, I would like to lend it to another friend. Sincerely yours,

ELLA CLAIRE.

The errors in the above are too glaring to need comment, yet, with only the alteration of names, it is a copy, verbatim, of a note written by a well educated girl.

Never sign a note written in the third person, if you begin the note with your own name. It is admissible, if the note is worded in this way:–Will Mr. James return by bearer, the copy of "Jane Eyre" he borrowed, if he has finished reading it, and oblige his sincere friend, ELLA CLAIRE.

If you use a quotation, never omit to put it in quotation marks, otherwise your correspondent may, however unjustly, accuse you of a desire to pass off the idea and words of another, for your own.

Avoid postscripts. Above all, never send an inquiry or compliment in a postscript. To write a long letter, upon various subjects, and in the postscript desire to be remembered to your friend's family, or inquire for their welfare, instead of a compliment, becomes insulting. It is better, if you have not time to write again and place such inquiries above your signature, to omit them entirely. Nobody likes to see their name mentioned as an afterthought.

Punctuate your letters carefully. The want of a mark of punctuation, or the incorrect placing of it, will make the most woful confusion. I give an instance of the utter absurdity produced by the alteration of punctuation marks, turning a sensible paragraph to the most arrant nonsense:

"Cæsar entered; on his head his helmet; on his feet armed sandals; upon his brow there was a cloud; in his right hand his faithful sword; in his eye an angry glare; saying nothing, he sat down."

By using precisely the same words, merely altering the position of the punctuation marks, we have–

"Caesar entered on his head; his helmet on his feet; armed sandals upon his brow; there was a cloud in his right hand; his faithful sword in his eye; an angry glare saying nothing; he sat down."

Be careful, then, to punctuate properly, that you may convey to the reader the exact sense of what is in your mind.

If you receive an impertinent letter, treat it with contempt; do not answer it.

Never answer a letter by proxy, when you are able to write yourself. It is a mark of respect and love, to answer, in your own hand, all letters addressed to you. If you are obliged to write to a friend to refuse to grant a favor asked, you will lessen the pain of refusal by wording your letter delicately. Loving words, if it is a near friend, respectful, kind ones if a mere acquaintance, will make the disagreeable contents of the letter more bearable. Try to make the manner smooth and soften the hardness of the matter.

Every letter must embrace the following particulars: 1st. The date. 2d. The complimentary address. 3d. The body of the letter. 4th. The complimentary closing. 5th. The signature. 6th.

The address.

There are two ways of putting the date, and the address. The first is to place them at the top of the sheet, the other is to place them after the signature.

When at the top, you write the name of your residence, or that of the city in which you reside, with the day of the month and the year, at the right hand of the first line of the sheet.

Then, at the left hand of the next line, write the address, then the complimentary address below the name; thus–_Q WILLOW GROVE, NEWYORK, June 27th, 1859.

MRS. E. C. HOWELL,

My dear Madam,

I received your letter, etc.

At the end of the letter, on the right hand of the sheet, put the complimentary closing, and then the signature; thus–

I remain, my dear madam, With much respect,

Yours sincerely,

S. E. LAW.

If you place the date and address after the signature, put it at the left of the sheet; thus–

I remain, my dear Madam, With much respect,

Yours sincerely,

S. E. LAW.

MRS. E. C. HOWELL.

June 27th, 1859.

For a long letter, it is better to put the date and address at the top of the page. For a letter of only a few lines, which ends on the first page, the second form is best. In a letter written to a person in the same city, you need not put the address under the signature; if not, write it–

S. E. LAW,

WILLOW GROVE, NEW YORK.

In writing to a dear friend or relative, where there is no formality required, you may omit the name at the top of the letter; put the date and address thus–

WILLOW GROVE, NEW YORK

June 27th, 1859. DEAR ANNA:

I write, etc.

It is best, however, to put the full name at the bottom of the last page, in case the letter is mislaid without the envelope; thus–

E. C. LAW.

MISS ANNA WRIGHT.

If you use an envelope, and this custom is now universal, fold your letter neatly to fit into it; then direct on the envelope. Put first the name, then the name of the person to whose care the letter must be directed, then the street, the city, and State. If the town is small, put also the county.

This is the form:–

MISS ANNA WRIGHT,

Care of Mr. John C. Wright, No. 40, Lexington street, Greensburg– Lee County.

Mass.

If the city is a large one, New York, Philadelphia, Baltimore, or any of the principal cities of the Union, you may omit the name of the county. If your letter is to go abroad, add the name of the country: as, England, or France, in full, under that of the city.

The name of the state is usually abbreviated, and for the use of my readers, I give the names of the United States with their abbreviations:

Maine, Me. New Hampshire, N. H. Vermont, Vt. Mas-sachusetts, Mass. Rhode Island, R. I. Connecticut, Conn.New York, N. Y. New Jersey, N. J. Pennsylvania, Pa., or, Penn. Delaware, Del. Maryland, Md. Virginia, Va. North Carolina, N. C. South Carolina, S. C. Georgia, Ga., or, Geo.Alabama, Ala. Mississippi, Miss. Missouri, Mo. Louisiana, La. Tennessee, Tenn. Kentucky, Ky. Indiana, Ind. Ohio, O. Michigan, Mich. Illinois, Ill. Wisconsin, Wis. Arkansas, Ark. Texas, Tex. Iowa, Io. Florida, Flo. Oregon, O. Cali-fornia, Cal. Minnesota, Minn. District of Columbia, D. C.

If you are writing from another country to America, put United States of America after the name of the state.

On the upper right hand corner of your envelope, put your postage- stamp.

If you send a letter by private hand, write the name of the bearer in the lower left hand corner, thus: MRS. E. A. HOWELL,

Clinton Place, Boston.

Mr. G. G. Lane.

In directing to any one who can claim any prefix, or addition, to his proper name do not omit to put that "republican title." For a clergyman, Rev. for Reverend is put before the name, thus:–

REV. JAMES C. DAY.

For a bishop:

RIGHT REVEREND E. BANKS.

For a physician:

DR. JAMES CURTIS.

or,

JAMES CURTIS, M.D.

For a member of Congress:

ON. E. C. DELTA.

For an officer in the navy:

CAPT. HENRY LEE, U. S. N.

For an officer in the army:

COL. EDWARD HOLMES, U. S. A.

For a professor:

PROF. E. L. JAMES.

If the honorary addition, LL.D., A. M., or any such title belongs to your correspondent, add it to his name on the envelope, thus:–

J. L. PETERS, LL.D.

If you seal with wax, it is best to put a drop under the turn-over, and fasten this down firmly before you drop the wax that is to receive the impression.

Cards of compliment are usually written in the third person. I give a few of the most common and proper forms.

For a party:Miss Lee's compliments to Mr.Bates, for Wednesday evening,Nov. 18th, at 8 o'clock.

Addressed to a lady:Miss Lee requests the pleasure of Miss Howard's company on Wednesday evening, Nov. 18th, at 8 o'clock.

For a ball, the above form, with the word Dancing, in the left hand corner.

Invitations to dinner or tea specify the entertainment thus: Mrs. Garret's compliments to Mr. and Mrs.Howard, and requests the pleasure of their company to dine (or take tea) on Wednesday, Nov. 6th, at 6 o'clock.

The form for answering, is:– Miss Howard accepts with pleasure Miss Lee's polite invitation for Wednesday evening. or, Miss Howard regrets that a prior engagement will prevent her accepting Miss Lee's polite invitation for Wednesday evening. Mr. and Mrs. Howard's compliments to Mrs.Garret, and accept with pleasure her kind invitation for Wednesday. or,Mrs. Howard regrets that the severe illness of Mr. Howard will render it impossible for either herself or Mr. Howard to join Mrs. Garret's party on Wednesday next.

Upon visiting cards, left when the caller is about to leave the city, the letters p. p. c. are put in the left hand corner, they are the abbreviation of the French words, pour prendre congé, or may, with equal propriety, stand for presents parting compliments. Another form, p. d. a., pour dire adieu, may be used.

No accomplishment within the scope of human knowledge is so beautiful in all its features as that of epistolary correspondence. Though distance, absence, and circumstances may separate the holiest alliances of friendship, or those who are bound together by the still stronger ties of affection, yet the power of interchanging thoughts, words, feelings, and sentiments, through the medium of letters, adds a sweetness to the pain of separation, renovating to life, and adding to happiness.

The wide ocean may roll between those who have passed the social years of youth together, or the snow-capped Alps may rise in sublime grandeur, separating early associates; still young remembrances may be called up, and the par-adise of memory made to bloom afresh with unwithered flowers of holy recollection.

Though we see not eye to eye and face to face, where the soft music of a loved voice may fall with its richness upon the ear, yet the very soul and emotions of the mind may be poured forth in such melody as to touch the heart "that's far away," and melt down the liveliest eye into tears of ecstatic rapture.

Without the ability to practice the refined art of epistolary correspondence, men would become cold and discordant: an isolated compound of misanthropy. They would fall off in forsaken fragments from the great bond of union which now adorns and beautifies all society. Absence, distance, and time would cut the silken cords of parental, brotherly, and even connubial affection. Early circumstances would be lost in forgetfulness, and the virtues of reciprocal friendship "waste their sweetness on the desert air."

Since, then, the art and practice of letter-writing is productive of so much refined and social happiness, a laudable indulgence in it must ever be commendable. While it elevates the noble faculties of the mind, it also chastens the disposition, and improves those intellectual powers which would otherwise remain dormant and useless.

Notwithstanding the various beauties and pleasures attendant upon the accomplishment, yet there are many who have given it but a slight portion of their attention, and have, therefore, cause to blush at their own ignorance when necessity demands its practice. There is no better mode by which to test the acquirements of either a young lady or gentleman than from their letters.

Letters are among the most useful forms of composition.

There are few persons, who can read or write at all, who do not frequently have occasion to write them; and an elegant letter is much more rare than an elegant specimen of any other kind of writing.

The more rational and elevated the topics are, on which you write, the less will you care for your letters being seen, or for paragraphs being read out of them; and where there is no need of any secrecy, it is best not to bind your friend by promises, but to leave it to her discretion.

CHAPTER XVI

POLITE DEPORTMENT, AND GOOD HABITS

LORD Chesterfield says, "Good sense and good nature suggest civility in general; but in good breeding there are a thousand little delicacies which are established only by custom."

It is the knowledge and practice of such "little delicacies" which constitutes the greatest charm of society.

Manner may be, and, in most cases, probably is, the cloak of the heart; this cloak may be used to cover defects, but is it not better so to conceal these defects, than to flaunt and parade them in the eyes of all whom we may meet?

Many persons plead a love of truth as an apology for rough manners, as if truth was never gentle and kind, but always harsh, morose, and forbidding. Surely good manners and a good conscience are no more inconsistent with each other than beauty and innocence, which are strikingly akin, and always look the better for companionship.

Roughness and honesty are indeed sometimes found together in the same person, but he is a poor judge of human nature who takes ill-manners to be a guarantee of probity of character. Some persons object to politeness, that its language is unmeaning and false. But this is easily answered.

A lie is not locked up in a phrase, but must exist, if at all, in the mind of the speaker. In the ordinary compliments of civilized life, there is no intention to deceive, and consequently no falsehood.

Polite language is pleasant to the ear, and soothing to the heart, while rough words are just the reverse; and if not the product of ill temper, are very apt to produce it. The plainest of truths, let it be remembered, can be conveyed in civil speech, while the most malignant lies may find utterance, and often do, in the language of the fish market.

Many ladies say, "Oh, I am perfectly frank and outspoken; I never stop to mince words," or, "there is no affectation about me; all my actions are perfectly natural," and, upon the ground of frankness, will insult and wound by rude language, and defend awkwardness and ill- breeding by the plea of "natural manners."

If nature has not invested you with all the virtues which may be desirable in a lady, do not make your faults more conspicuous by thrusting them forward upon all occasions, and at all times. "Assume a virtue if you have it not," and you will, in time, by imitation, acquire it.

By endeavoring to appear generous, disinterested, self-sacrificing, and amiable, the opposite passions will be brought into subjection, first in the manner, afterwards in the heart. It is not the desire to deceive, but the desire to please, which will dictate such a course. When you hear one, who pretends to be a lady, boast that she is rough, capricious, and gluttonous, you may feel sure that she has never tried to conquer these faults, or she would be ashamed, not proud, of them.

The way to make yourself pleasing to others, is to show that you care for them. The whole world is like the miller at Mansfield, "who cared for nobody–no, not he–because nobody cared for him." And the whole world will serve you so, if you give them the same cause. Let every one, therefore, see that you do care for them, by showing them, what Sterne so happily calls, "the small, sweet courtesies of life,"

those courtesies in which there is no parade; whose voice is too still to tease, and which manifest themselves by tender and affectionate looks, and little, kind acts of attention, giving others the preference in every little enjoyment at the table, in the field, walking, sitting, or standing.

Thus the first rule for a graceful manner is unselfish consideration of others.

By endeavoring to acquire the habit of politeness, it will soon become familiar, and sit on you with ease, if not with elegance. Let it never be forgotten, that genuine politeness is a great fosterer of family love; it allays accidental irrita-tion, by preventing harsh retorts and rude contradictions; it softens the boisterous, stimulates the indolent, suppresses selfishness, and by forming a habit of consideration for others, harmonizes the whole. Politeness begets politeness, and brothers may be easily won by it, to leave off the rude ways they bring home from school or college. Sisters ought never to receive any little attention without thanking them for it, never to ask a favor of them but in courteous terms, never to reply to their questions in monosyllables, and they will soon be ashamed to do such things themselves. Both precept and example ought to be laid under contribution, to convince them that no one can have really good manners abroad, who is not habitually polite at home.

If you wish to be a well-bred lady, you must carry your good manners everywhere with you. It is not a thing that can be laid aside and put on at pleasure. True politeness is uniform disinterestedness in trifles, accompanied by the calm self-possession which belongs to a noble simplicity of purpose; and this must be the effect of a Christian spirit running through all you do, or say, or think; and, unless you cultivate it and exercise it, upon all occasions and towards all persons, it will never be a part of yourself.

It is not an art to be paraded upon public occasions, and neglected in every-day duties; nor should it, like a ball-dress, be carefully laid aside at home, trimmed, ornamented, and worn only when out. Let it come into every thought, and it will show forth in every action. Let it be the rule in the homeliest duties, and then it will set easily when in public, not in a stiff manner, like a garment seldom worn.

I wish it were possible to convince every woman that politeness is a most excellent good quality; that it is a necessary ingredient in social comfort, and a capital assistant to actual prosperity. Like most good things, however, the word politeness is often misunderstood and misapplied; and before urging the practical use of that which it represents, it may be necessary to say what it means, and what it does not mean.

Politeness is not hypocrisy:–cold-heartedness, or unkindness in disguise. There are persons who can smile upon a victim, and talk smoothly, while they injure, deceive, or betray. And they will take credit to themselves, that all has been done with the utmost politeness; that every tone, look, and action, has been in perfect keeping with the rules of good breeding. "The words of their mouth are smoother than butter, but war is in their heart: their words are softer than oil, yet they are drawn swords." Perish for ever and ever such spurious politeness as this!

Politeness is not servility. If it were so, a Russian serf would be a model of politeness. It is very possible for persons to be very cringing and obsequious, without a single atom of politeness; and it often happens that men of the most sturdy independence of character, are essentially polite in all their words, actions, and feelings. It were well for this to be fully understood, for many people will abstain from acts of real politeness, and even of common civility, for fear of damaging their fancied independence.

True politeness, as I understand it, is kindness and courtesy of feeling brought into every-day exercise. It comprehends hearty good will towards everybody, thorough and constant good-humor, an easy deportment, and obliging manners. Every person who cultivates such feelings, and takes no pains to conceal them, will necessarily be polite, though she may not exactly know it; while, on the other hand, a woman essentially morose and selfish, whatever may be her pretensions, must be very far from truly polite.

It is very true there are those whose position in society compels them to observe certain rules of etiquette which pass for politeness. They bow or courtesy with a decent grace; shake hands with the precise degree of vigor which the circumstances of the case require; speak just at the right time, and in the required manner, and smile with elegant propriety. Not a tone, look, or gesture, is out of place; not a habit indulged which etiquette forbids; and yet, there will be wanting, after all, the secret charm of sincerity and heart kindness, which those outward signs are intended to represent; and, wanting which, we have only the form, without the essence, of politeness.

Let me recommend, therefore, far beyond all the rules ever penned by teachers of etiquette, the cultivation of kind and loving feelings. Throw your whole soul into the lesson, and you will advance rapidly towards the perfection of politeness, for "out of the abundance of the heart the mouth speaketh," and the movements of your form and the words you utter will follow faithfully the hidden springs of action within.

There cannot be genuine good breeding to any happy degree, where there is not self-respect. It is that which imparts ease and confidence to our manners, and impels us, for our own sake, as well as for the sake of others, to behave becomingly as intelligent beings.

It is a want of true politeness that introduces the discord and confusion which too often make our homes unhappy.

A little consideration for the feelings of those whom we are bound to love and cherish, and a little sacrifice of our own wills, would, in multitudes of instances, make all the difference between alienation and growing affection. The principle of genuine politeness would accomplish this; and what a pity it is that those whose only spring of rational enjoyment is to be found at home, should miss that enjoyment by a disregard of little things, which, after all, make up the sum of human existence!

What a large amount of actual discomfort in domestic life would be prevented, if all children were trained, both by precept and example, to the practice of common politeness!

If they were taught to speak respectfully to parents, and brothers, and sisters, to friends, neighbors, and strangers, what bawlings, and snarlings would be stilled! If their be-havior within doors, and especially at the table, were regulated by a few of the common rules of good breeding, how much natural and proper disgust would be spared! If courtesy of demeanor, towards all whom they meet in field or highway, were instilled, how much more pleasant would be our town travels, and our rustic rambles! Every parent has a personal interest in this matter; and if every parent would but make the needful effort, a great degree of gross incivility, and consequent annoyance, would soon be swept away from our hearths and homes.

Whilst earnestly endeavoring to acquire true politeness, avoid that spurious imitation, affectation. It is to genuine politeness and good breeding, what the showy paste is to the pure diamond. It is the offspring of a sickly taste, a deceitful heart, and a sure proof of low breeding.

The certain test of affectation in any individual, is the looking, speaking, moving, or acting in any way different when in the presence of others, especially those whose opinion we regard and whose approbation we desire, from what we should do in solitude, or in the presence of those only whom we disregard, or who we think cannot injure or benefit us. The motive for resisting affectation is that it is both unsuccessful and sinful. It always involves a degree of hypocrisy, which is exceedingly offensive in the sight of God, which is generally detected even by men, and which, when detected, exposes its subject to contempt which could never have been excited by the mere absence of any quality or possession, as it is by the false assumption of what is not real. The best cure for affectation is the cultivation, on principle, of every good, virtuous, and amiable habit and feeling, not for the sake of being approved or admired, but because it is right in itself, and without considering what people will think of it. Thus a real character will be formed instead of a part being assumed, and admiration and love will be spontaneously bestowed where they are really deserved.

Artificial manners are easily seen through; and the result of such observations, however accomplished and beautiful the object may be, is contempt for such littleness.

Many ladies, moving, too, in good society, will affect a forward, bold manner, very disagreeable to persons of sense. They will tell of their wondrous feats, when engaged in pursuits only suited for men; they will converse in a loud, boisterous tone; laugh loudly; sing comic songs, or dashing bravuras in a style only fit for the stage or a gentleman's after-dinner party; they will lay wagers, give broad hints and then brag of their success in forcing invitations or presents; interlard their conversation with slang words or phrases suited only to the stable or bar-room, and this they think is a dashing, fascinating manner. It may be encouraged, admired, in their presence, by gentlemen, and imitated by younger ladies, but, be sure, it is looked upon with contempt, and disapproval by every one of good sense, and that to persons of real refinement it is absolutely disgusting.

Other ladies, taking quite as mistaken a view of real refinement, will affect the most childish timidity, converse only in whispers, move slowly as an invalid, faint at the shortest notice, and on the slightest provocation; be easily moved to tears, and profess never to eat, drink, or sleep.

This course is as absurd as the other, and much more troublesome, as everybody dreads the scene which will follow any shock to the dear creature's nerves, and will be careful to avoid any dangerous topics.

Self-respect, and a proper deference for our superiors in age or intellect, will be the best safeguards against either a cringing or insolent manner.

Without self-respect you will be apt to be both awkward and bashful; either of which faults are entirely inconsistent with a graceful manner. Be careful that while you have sufficient self-respect to make your manner easy, it does not become arrogance and so engender insolence. Avoid sarcasm; it will, unconsciously to yourself, degenerate into pertness, and often downright rudeness. Do not be afraid to speak candidly, but temper candor with courtesy, and never let wit run into that satire that will wound deeply, whilst it amuses only slightly.

Let your carriage be at once dignified and graceful. There are but few figures that will bear quick motion; with almost every one its effect is that of a jerk, a most awkward movement. Let the feet, in walking or dancing, be turned out slightly; when you are seated, rest them both on the floor or a footstool. To sit with the knees or feet crossed or doubled up, is awkward and unlady-like. Carry your arms, in walking, easily; never crossing them stiffly or swinging them beside you. When seated, if you are not sewing or knitting, keep your hands perfectly quiet. This, whilst one of the most difficult accomplishments to attain, is the surest mark of a lady. Do not fidget, playing with your rings, brooch, or any little article that may be near you; let your hands rest in an easy, natural position, perfectly quiet.

Never gesticulate when conversing; it looks theatrical, and is ill-bred; so are all contortions of the features, shrugging of shoulders, raising of the eyebrows, or hands.

When you open a conversation, do so with a slight bow and smile, but be careful not to simper, and not to smile too often, if the conversation becomes serious.

Never point. It is excessively ill-bred.

Avoid exclamations; they are in excessively bad taste, and are apt to be vulgar words. A lady may express as much polite surprise or concern by a few simple, earnest words, or in her manner, as she can by exclaiming "Good gracious!"

"Mercy!" or "Dear me!"

Remember that every part of your person and dress should be in perfect order before you leave the dressing-room, and avoid all such tricks as smoothing your hair with your hand, arranging your curls, pulling the waist of your dress down, or settling your collar or sleeves.

Avoid lounging attitudes, they are indelicate, except in your own private apartment. Nothing but ill health will excuse them before company, and a lady had better keep her room if she is too feeble to sit up in the drawing-room.

Let your deportment suit your age and figure; to see a tiny, fairy-like young girl, marching erect, stiff, and awkwardly, like a soldier on parade, is not more absurd than to see a middle-aged, portly woman, aping the romping, hoy-donnish manners of a school-girl.

Let the movements be easy and flexible, and accord with the style of the lady.

Let your demeanor be always marked by modesty and simplicity; as soon as you become forward or affected, you have lost your greatest charm of manner.

You should be quite as anxious to talk with propriety as you are to think, work, sing, paint, or write, according to the most correct rules.

Always select words calculated to convey an exact impression of your meaning.

Let your articulation be easy, clear, correct in accent, and suited in tone and emphasis to your discourse.

Avoid a muttering, mouthing, stuttering, droning, gut-total, nasal, or lisping, pronunciation.

Let your speech be neither too loud nor too low; but adjusted to the ear of your companion. Try to prevent the necessity of any person crying, "What? What?"

Avoid a loquacious propensity; you should never occupy more than your share of the time, or more than is agreeable to others.

Beware of such vulgar interpolations as "You know," "You see," "I'll tell you what."

Pay a strict regard to the rules of grammar, even in private conversation. If you do not understand these rules, learn them, whatever be your age or station.

Though you should always speak pleasantly, do not mix your conversation with loud bursts of laughter.

Never indulge in uncommon words, or in Latin and French phrases, but choose the best understood terms to express your meaning.

Above all, let your conversation be intellectual, graceful, chaste,discreet, edifying, and profitable.

CHAPTER XVII

CONDUCT IN CHURCH

IN entering a church of a different denomination from the one you have been in the habit of frequenting, ask the sexton to show you to a seat. It is the height of rudeness to enter a pew without invitation, as the owner may desire, if her family does not require all the seats, to invite her own personal friends to take the vacant places. If you are not perfectly familiar with the manner of conducting the worship, observe those around you, rise, kneel, and sit, as you see they do. It is a mark of disrespect for the pastor as well as irreverence for the Most High, to remain seated through the whole service, unless you are ill, or otherwise incapacitated from standing and kneeling.

Enter the sacred edifice slowly, reverentially, and take your seat quietly. It is not required of you to bow to any friend you may see in passing up the aisle, as you are supposed yourself to be, and suppose her to be entirely absorbed in thought proper for the occasion. To stare round the church, or if you are not alone, to whisper to your companion, is irreverent, indelicate, and rude. If your own feelings will not prompt you to silence and reverence, pay some regard to the feelings of others.

Be careful not to appear to notice those around you. If others are so rude as to talk or conduct improperly, fix your own mind upon the worship which you come to pay, and let the impertinence pass unheeded.

If there is another person in the same pew with yourself, who, more familiar with the service, hands you the book, or points out the place, acknowledge the civility by a silent bow; it is not necessary to speak.

In your own pew, extend this courtesy to a stranger who may come in beside you, and even if it is a gentleman you may, with perfect propriety, hand him a book, or, if there is but one, offer him a share of your own.

Endeavor always to be in your seat before the service commences, and after it is over do not hurry away, and, above all, do not begin your preparations for departure, by shutting up your book, or putting on any article of dress you have removed, before the benediction.

If you are invited to accompany a friend to church, be sure you are ready in good season, that you may not keep her waiting when she calls, or cause her to lose any part of the service by detaining her at your house. If you invite a friend to take a seat in your pew, call for her early, give her the most comfortable place, and be sure she has a prayer and hymn-book.

If you are invited to stand as god-mother to a friend's child, be at the house of the parents in season to accompany the family to church, and send, the day before, the gift you design for the babe. A silver cup is the usual present, with your little namesake's initials, or full name, engraved upon it.

In assisting at a wedding at church, if you are one of the bridesmaids, wear white, a white bonnet but no veil. If you occupy the first place, the bride's, it is in better taste to be married in a simple dress and bonnet, and don your full dress when you return home to receive your friends. In such ceremonies the wedding-party all meet in the vestry, and go to the altar together.

For further particulars, see chapter on Bridal Etiquette.

At a funeral, enter the church quietly, and, unless you belong to the mourners, wait until they leave the church before you rise from your seat. Never attempt to speak to any of the afflicted family. However heartfelt your sympathy, it will not be welcome at that time.

If, when entering a crowded church, a gentleman sees you and offers his seat, acknowledges his civility, whether accepted or declined, by a bow, and a whispered "thank you." Many, who claim the name of lady, and think they are well-bred, will accept such an act of politeness without making the slightest acknowledgement. If the service has commenced, do not speak; a courteous inclination of the head will convey your sense of obligation.

Remember, as an imperative, general rule, in whatever church you may be, whether at home or abroad, conform to the mode of worship whilst you are in that church. If you find, in these modes, forms which are disagreeable to you, or which shock your own ideas of religion, avoid a second visit, but do not insult the congregation, by showing your contempt or disapproval, whilst you are among them.

Silence, quiet attention, and a grave, reverential demeanor, mark the Christian lady in church.

CHAPTER XVIII

BALLROOMETIQUETFOR THE HOSTESS

When you have decided upon what evening you will give your ball, send out your invitations, a fortnight before the evening appointment. To ladies, word them:– Mrs. L—- requests the pleasure of Miss G—-'s company on Wednesday evening, Jan. 17th, at 9 o'clock. Dancing.

The favor of an early answer is requested. To gentlemen:–

Mrs. L—-'s compliments to Mr. R—- for Wednesday evening, Jan. 17th, at 9 o'clock.

Dancing.

The favor of an early answer is requested.

If you are unmarried, put your mother's name with your own upon the cards. If you have a father or grown-up brother, let the invitations to the gentlemen go in his name.

In making your list for a ball, do not set down all of your "dear five hundred friends." The middle-aged, (unless they come as chaperons,) the serious, and the sober-minded, will not accept your invitation, and the two last names may consider it insulting to be invited to such frivolous amusement.

By the way, I do not agree with the straight-laced people, who condemn all such amusements. I agree with Madame Pilau. When the curé of her parish told her he was writing a series of sermons against dancing, she said to him:

"You are talking of what you do not understand. You have never been to a ball, I have; and I assure you there is no sin in the manner worthy of mention or notice."

If you really wish for dancing, you will accommodate your guests to your rooms, inviting one third more than they will hold, as about that number generally disappoint a ball-giver. If you wish to have a rush of people, and do not mind heat, crowding, and discomfort, to insure an immense assembly, (a ball to be talked about for its size only,) then you may invite everybody who figures upon your visiting list.

Over one hundred is a "large ball," under that a "ball," unless there are less than fifty guests, when it is merely a "dance."

The directions given in chapter 5th for the arrangement of the dressing-rooms will apply here, but your parlor, or ball room, requires some attention. Have the carpets taken up two days before the evening of the ball, and the floor waxed. A smooth, polished floor is an absolute necessity for pleasant dancing. At one end of your ball room, have a space partitioned off for the musicians. Leave, for their use, plenty of room, as silence or discord will come from a crowded orchestra. If your house is double, and you use the rooms on each side, place the musicians in the hall.

Four pieces of music is enough for a private ball, unless your rooms are very large. For one room a piano, violin, and violoncello makes a good band.

You must have your rooms well ventilated if you wish to avoid fainting and discomfort.

To secure a really brilliant ball, pay considerable attention to the arrangement of your ball room. In Paris this arrangement consists in turning the room, for the evening, into a perfect garden. Every corner is filled with flowers.

Wreaths, bouquets, baskets, and flowering-plants in moss-covered pots. With brilliant light, and taste in the details of arranging them, this profusion of flowers produces an exquisitely beautiful effect, and harmonizes perfectly with the light dresses, cheerful faces, and gay music. The pleasure of your guests, as well as the beauty of the rooms, will be increased by the elegance of your arrangements; their beauty will be heightened by brilliant light, and by judicious management a scene of fairy-like illusion may be produced.

Not only in the ball room itself, but in the hall, supper-room, and dressing-rooms, place flowers. A fine effect is produced, by placing a screen, covered with green and flowers, before the space set apart for the musicians. To hear the music proceeding from behind this floral embankment, and yet have the scraping and puffing men invisible, adds very much to the illusion of the scene.

In the dressing-rooms have, at least, two servants for each. Let them take the cloaks and hoods, and put a numbered ticket upon each bundle, handing the duplicate number to the lady or gentleman owning it.

It is best to have the supper-room upon the same floor as the ball room. The light dresses, worn upon such occasions, suffer severely in passing up and down a crowded staircase.

Have a number of double cards written or printed with a list of the dances, arranged in order, upon one side, and a space for engagements upon the other. Attach a small pencil to each. Let a waiter stand at the entrance to the ballroom, and hand a card to each guest as they pass in.

The first strain of music must be a march; then follows a quadrille, then a waltz. Other dances follow in any order you prefer until the fourteenth, which should be the march which announces supper. If you throw open the supper-room, early, and the guests go out when they wish, the march may be omitted. Twenty-one to twenty-four dances are sufficient. Have an interval of ten minutes after each one.

The supper-room should be thrown open at midnight, and remain open until your last guest has departed. Let it be brilliantly lit, and have plenty of waiters in attendance.

There can be no rule laid down for supper. It may be hot or heavily iced. It may consist entirely of confectionery, or it may include the bill of fare for a hotel table. One rule you must observe; have abundance of everything. Other entertainments may be given upon economical principles, but a ball cannot. Light, attendance, supper, every detail must be carefully attended to, and a ball must be an expensive luxury.

At a ball-supper every one stands up. The waiters will hand refreshment from the tables to the gentlemen, who, in turn, wait upon the ladies.

You must bring forth your whole array of smiles, when you

perform the part of hostess in a ball room. As your guests will come dropping in at all hours, you must hover near the door to greet each one entering. There will be many strangers amongst the gentlemen. Miss G. will bring her fiancée. Miss L., her brother, just returned, after ten years' absence, from India. Miss R. introduces her cousin, in the city for a week. Miss M., as a belle, will, perhaps, take the liberty of telling some ten or twelve of her most devoted admirers where she may be seen on the evening of your ball, and, though strangers, they will, one after another, bow over your hand. To each and every one you must extend the amiable greeting due to an invited guest. If you are the only lady of the house, your duties will, indeed, be laborious. You must be everywhere at the same moment.

Not a guest must pass unwelcomed. You must introduce partners to all the wall-flowers. You must see that every set is made up before the music commences. Each guest must be introduced to a proper partner for every dance, and not one frown, one pettish word, one look of fatigue, one sigh of utter weariness must disturb your smiling serenity.

You must be ready to chat cheerfully with every bore who detains you, when crossing the room, to make up a set of quadrilles in a minute's time; listen patiently to the sighing lover, whose fair one is engaged fifty times during twenty dances; secure a good dancer for each longing belle; do the same for the beaux; yet you must never be hurried, worried, or fatigued.

If there are several ladies, a mother and two or three daughters, for instance, divide the duties. Let one receive the guests, another arrange the sets, a third introduce couples, and a fourth pair off the talkers. A brother or father will be a treasure in a ball room, as the standing of sets can be better managed by a gentleman than a lady.

None of the ladies who give the ball should dance until every fair guest has a partner.

One of your duties will be to see that no young ladies lose their supper for want of an escort to ask them to go out. You may give the hint to an intimate gentleman friend, if there is no brother or father to take the duty, introduce him to the disconsolate damsel, and send her off happily. If all the guests go to the supper-room when it is first thrown open, you must be the last to leave the ball room. For the hostess to take the lead to the supper-room, leaving her guests to pair off, and follow as they please, is in very bad taste.

If you announce supper by a march, many of your guests will remain in the ballroom, to promenade, avoid the crowd at the first table, and indulge in a tête-à-tête conversation.

These will afterwards go out, in pairs, when the first crush in the the refreshment-room is over.

If, by accident or negligence, you miss an introduction to any of your gentlemen guests, you may still speak to them if you wish. It is your privilege as hostess to introduce yourself, and invite any gentleman to dance with you, or offer to introduce him to a partner. In the latter case he ought to mention his name, but if he omits to do so, you may ask it.

There has been a custom introduced in some of our large cities lately, which is an admirable one for a private ball. It is to hire, for the evening, a public hall. This includes the dressing-room, supper- room, every comfort, and saves you from the thousand annoyances which are certain to follow a ball in a private house. You hire the hall and other rooms, the price including light, hire a band of music, and order a supper at a confectioners, hiring from his establishment all the china, glass, and silver you will want. In this case you must enclose in every invitation a ticket to admit your friend's party, to prevent loungers from the street coming in, uninvited.

You will, perhaps, find the actual outlay of money greater, when you thus hire your ball room, but you will save more than the difference in labor, annoyance, and the injury to your house. You secure a better room than any parlor, you have the floor waxed and polished without the trouble of taking up your carpets. You save all the dreadful labor of cleaning up the house the next day, as well as that of preparation.

You can, if you wish, invite a few friends to a late dinner with you, and all proceed to the ball room together. You must be the first to enter the room, the last to leave it, and every duty is the same as if you were at home; the ball room is, in fact, your own house, for the evening.

If you wish your guests to come in costume for a fancy ball, name the character of the entertainment in your invitation.

CHAPTER XIX

BALLROOMETIQUETTE FOR THE GUEST

As in every other case where hospitality is extended to you by invitation, you must send your answer as soon as possible, accepting or declining the civility.

In preparing a costume for a ball, choose something very light. Heavy, dark silks are out of place in a ball room, and black should be worn in no material but lace. For a married lady, rich silk of some light color, trimmed with flowers, lace, or tulle; white silk plain, or lace over satin, make an exquisite toilette. Jewels are perfectly appropriate; also feathers in the coiffure.

For the young lady, pure white or light colors should be worn, and the most appropriate dress is of some thin material made over silk, white, or the same color as the outer dress. Satin or velvet are entirely out of place on a young lady. Let the coiffure be of flowers or ribbons, never feathers, and but very little jewelry is becoming to an unmarried lady. All ladies must wear boots or slippers of satin, white, black, or the color of the dress. White is the most appropriate; black, the most coming to the foot. White kid gloves, full trimmed, a fine lace trimmed handkerchief, and a fan, are indispensable. Be very careful, when dressing for a ball, that the hair is firmly fastened, and the coiffure properly adjusted. Nothing is more annoying than to have the hair loosen or the head-dress fall off in a crowded ballroom.

Your first duty, upon entering the room, is to speak to your hostess.

After a few words of greeting, turn to the other guests.

At a private ball, no lady will refuse an introduction to a gentleman. It is an insult to her hostess, implying that her guests are not gentlemen. It is optional with the lady whether to continue or drop the acquaintance after the ball is over, but for that evening, however disagreeable, etiquette requires her to accept him for one dance, if she is disengaged, and her hostess requests it. At a public ball, it is safest to decline all introductions made by the master of ceremonies, though, as before, such acquaintances are not binding after the evening is over.

Be very careful how you refuse to dance with a gentleman. A prior engagement will, of course, excuse you, but if you plead fatigue, or really feel it, do not dance the set with another gentleman; it is most insulting, though sometimes done. On the other hand, be careful that you do not engage yourself twice for the same quadrille. In a polka or valse, you may do this, saying, "I will dance the second half with you, but have a prior engagement for the first." Then, after a few rounds with your first partner, say to him that you are engaged for the remainder of the dance, resume your seat, and your second partner will seek you.

Let your manner in a ball room be quiet. It looks very bad to see a lady endeavoring to attract attention by her boisterous manner, loud talking, or over-active dancing. Do not drag through dances as if you found them wearisome; it is an insult to your partner, but while you are cheerful and animated, be lady-like and dignified in your deportment.

At the end of each dance, your partner will offer his arm, and conduct you to a seat; then bow, and release him from further attendance, as he may be engaged for the next dance.

When invited to dance, hand your ball card to the gentleman, who will put his name in one of the vacant places.

If you wish to go to the supper-room, accept the invitation that will be made, after the dances whilst it is open, but do not remain there long. You may be keeping your escort from other engagements.

If you are accompanied by a gentleman, besides your father or brother, remember he has the right to the first dance, and also will expect to take you in to supper. Do not let anyone else interfere with his privilege.

If you wish, during the evening, to go to the dressing-room to arrange any part of your dress, request the gentleman with whom you are dancing to escort you there.

He will wait for you at the door, and take you back to the ball-room. Do not detain him any longer than is necessary.

Never leave the ball room, for any such purpose, alone, as there are always gentlemen near and round the door, and it looks very bad to see a lady, unattended, going through a crowd of gentlemen.

It is best at a ball, to dance only every other dance, as over-fatigue, and probably a flushed face, will follow too much dancing. Decline the intermediate ones, on the plea of fatigue, or fear of fatigue.

Never go into the supper-room with the same gentleman twice. You may go more than once, if you wish for an ice or glass of water, (surely no lady wants two or three suppers,) but do not tax the same gentleman more than once, even if he invites you after each dance.

No lady of taste will carry on a flirtation in a ball room, so as to attract remark. Be careful, unless you wish your name coupled with his, how you dance too often with the same gentleman.

If you are so unfortunate as, forgetting a prior engagement, to engage yourself to two gentlemen for the same dance, decline dancing it altogether, or you will surely offend one of them.

Never press forward to take the lead in a quadrille, and if others, not understanding the figures, make confusion, try to get through without remark. It is useless to attempt to teach them, as the music, and other sets, will finish the figure long before you can teach and dance it. Keep your temper, refrain from all remarks, and endeavor to make your partner forget, in your cheerful conversation, the annoyances of the dance.

There is much that is exhilarating in the atmosphere of a ball room. The light, music, company, and even dancing itself, are all conducive to high spirits; be careful that this flow of spirits does not lead you into hoydenism and rudeness. Guard your actions and your tongue, that you may leave the room as quietly and gracefully as you enter it.

Avoid confidential conversation in a ball room. It is out of season, and in excessively bad taste.

Be modest and reserved, but avoid bashfulness. It looks like a school-girl, and is invariably awkward.

Never allow your partner, though he may be your most intimate friend, to converse in a low tone, or in any way assume a confidential or lover-like air at a ball. It is in excessively bad taste, and gives annoyance frequently, as others suppose such low-toned remarks may refer to them.

Dance as others do. It has a very absurd look to take every step with dancing-school accuracy, and your partner will be the first one to notice it. A quadrille takes no more steps than a graceful walk. Never stand up to dance in a quadrille, unless you are perfectly familiar with the figures, depending upon your partner to lead you through. You will probably cause utter confusion in the set, annoy the others forming it, and make yourself appear absurd.

No young lady should go to a ball, without the protection of a married lady, or an elderly gentleman.

Never cross a ball room alone.

Never remain in a ball room until all the companies have left it, or even until the last set. It is ill-bred, and looks as if you were unaccustomed to such pleasures, and so desirous to prolong each one. Leave while there are still two or three sets to be danced. Do not accept any invitation for these late dances, as the gentleman who invites you may find out your absence too late to take another partner, and you will thus deprive him of the pleasure of dancing.

CHAPTER XX

PLACES OF AMUSEMENT

Do not accept an invitation to visit any place of public amusement, with a gentleman with whom you are but slightly acquainted, unless there is another lady also invited. You may, as a young lady, go with a relative or your fiancée, without a chaperon, but not otherwise.

Having received an invitation which it is proper for you to accept, write an answer immediately, appointing an hour for your escort to call for you, and be sure that you are ready for the good season. To arrive late is not only annoying to those near your seat, whom you disturb when you enter, but it is ill-bred; you will be supposed to be someone who is unable to come early, instead of appearing as a lady who is mistress of her own time.

If the evening is cloudy, or it rains, your escort will probably bring a carriage; and let me say a few words here about entering and leaving a carriage.

How to get in is difficult, but of less importance than getting out; because if you stumble in, no one sees you, but some one who may happen to be in the carriage; but how to get out is so important, that I will illustrate it by a short diplomatic anecdote:–

"The Princess of Hesse-Darmstadt," says MY. Mercy d'Argenteau, an ambassador of the last century, "having been desired by the Empress of Austria to bring her three daughters to court, in order that her Imperial Majesty might choose one of them for a wife to one of her sons, drove up in her coach to the palace gate. Scarcely had they entered the presence, when, before even speaking to them, the empress went up to the second daughter, and, taking her by the hand, said, 'I choose this young lady.' The mother, astonished at the suddenness of her choice, inquired what had caused it. 'I watched the young ladies get out of their carriage,' said the empress. 'Your eldest daughter stepped on her dress, and only saved herself from falling by an awkward scramble; the youngest jumped from the coach to the ground, without touching the steps; the second, just lifting her dress in front, so as she descended to show the point of her shoe, calmly stepped from the carriage to the ground, neither hurriedly nor stiffly, but with grand dignity: she is fit to be an empress; he eldest sister is too awkward, her youngest too wild."'

THE THEATRE–Here you must wear your bonnet, though you may throw aside your cloak or shawl, if you desire it. Your escort will pass to your seats first, and then turn and offer his hand to lead you to your own. Once seated, give your attention entirely to the actors whilst the curtain is up–to your companion when it is down.

Do not look round the house with your glass. A lady's deportment should be very modest in a theatre. Avoid carefully every motion, or gesture that will attract attention. To flirt a fan, converse in whispers, indulge in extravagant gestures of merriment or admiration, laugh loudly or clap your hands together, are all excessively vulgar and unlady-like.

Never turn your head to look at those seated behind you, or near you.

If you speak to your companion while the curtain is up, lower your voice, that you may not disturb others interested in the conversation on the stage.

THE OPERA–Here you should wear full dress, an opera cloak, and either a head-dress, or dressy bonnet of some thin material. Your gloves must be of kid, white, or some very light tint to suit your dress. Many dress for the opera as they would for the theatre; but the beauty of the house is much enhanced by each lady contributing her full dress toilette to the general effect.

If you go to the dressing-room, leave your hood and shawl in the care of the woman in waiting, whom you must fee when she returns them to you.

If you do not wish to go to the dressing-room, allow your escort to take off your shawl or cloak, and throw it over the back of the seat. As your opera cloak must be light enough to keep on all the evening, though you may throw it open, you must wear over it a heavier cloak or a shawl. Throw this off in the lobby, just before you enter your box. Your gloves you must keep on all evening.

Avoid handling the play bills, as the printing ink will soil your gloves in a few minutes, making your hands appear very badly for the rest of the evening.

You should be in your seat at the opera before the over-ture commences.

Never converse during the performance. Even the lowest toned remark will disturb a real lover of music, and these will be near you on all sides. Exclamations of admiration,

"Exquisite!" "Beautiful!" or "Lovely!" are in the worst taste. Show your appreciation by quiet attention to every note, and avoid every exclamation or gesture.

In our new opera houses there are rooms for the promenade, and between the acts your escort may invite you to walk there. You may accept the invitation with perfect propriety.

He will leave the box first and then offer his hand to you.

In the lobby take his arm, and keep it until you return to the box. If you have taken your cloak or shawl to your seat, leave them there during your promenade. Return to your seat when the gong sounds the recall, that you may not disturb others after the next act commences.

In walking up and down in the promenading saloon, you may pass and repass friends. Bow the first time you meet them, but not again.

If you meet your gentlemen friends there, bow, but do not stop to speak. They may join you for once round the room, then allow them to leave you. Your escort will feel justly offended if you allow any other gentlemen to engross your attention entirely when he has invited you to the entertainment.

CONCERTS–Here, as at the opera, you may wear a bonnet or not, as you will. Go early to the hall, unless you have secured a seat, and then, be in time for the first song. If you are unavoidably late, enter quietly, and take a seat near the door. It is very rude to push forward to the front of the hall, and either crowd those upon the benches, or force some gentleman to offer you his place. If the hall is so crowded that even the back seats are full, and a gentleman offers you his place, you should thank him before accepting it.

Again, I repeat, do not converse, or disturb those around you by exclamations or gesticulations.

LECTURES–Two ladies may attend a lecture, unaccompanied by a gentleman, without attracting attention.

The dress, bonnet, and cloak, worn in the street, should be worn in a lecture-room, as these are, by no means, occasions for full dress.

If you return at an early hour from any place of amusement, invite your escort into the house upon your arrival there, and lay aside your bonnet and shawl. If you keep them on, he will conclude that you expect him to shorten his visit. If it is late when you reach home, he will probably decline your invitation to enter. If, however, he accepts it, do not lay aside your shawl, and he will soon leave you.

If he asks permission to call in the morning, you must, unless prevented by an imperative engagement, remain at home to see him.

Upon your way home from the theatre, concert, or opera, speak warmly of the pleasure of the evening, and, at parting, thank him for that pleasure. Show by your manner that you have heartily enjoyed the entertainment you owe to his civility. If you are weary, do not allow him to see it. If disappointed, conceal that also. You will be able to find some good points in the performance; speak of these and ignore the bad ones.

If at the theatre, opera, or in a concert-room, you see an acquaintance, you are not expected to recognize her, unless near enough to speak. A lady must not bow to any one, even her own sister, across a theatre or concert-room.

CHAPTER XXI

ACCOMPLISHMENTS

IN the present age, when education is within the reach of all, both rich and poor, every lady will endeavor to become, not only well educated, but accomplished. It is not, as some will assert, a waste of time or money. Not only the fingers, voice, and figure are improved, but the heart and intellect will become refined, and the happiness greatly increased.

Take the young lady after a solid basis has been laid in her mind of the more important branches of education, and rear upon that basis the structure of lighter education–the accomplishments. To cultivate these, disregarding the more solid information, is to build your castle without any foundation, and make it, not only absurd, but unsteady. The pleasure of hearing from a lady a cavatina executed in the most finished manner, will be entirely destroyed, if her first spoken words after the performance are vulgar, or her sentence ungrammatical.

A lady without her piano, or her pencil, her library of French, German, or Italian authors, her fancy work and tasteful embroideries, is now rarely met with, and it is right that such arts should be universal. No woman is fitted for society until she dances well; for home, unless she is perfect mistress of needlework; for her own enjoyment, unless she has at least one accomplishment to occupy thoughts and fingers in her hours of leisure.

First upon the list of accomplishments, comes the art of conversing well. It is always ready. Circumstances in society will constantly throw you into positions where you can use no other accomplishment. You will not have a musical instrument within reach, singing would be out of place, your fancy work at home, on many occasions, and then you can exert your most fascinating as well as useful accomplishment, the art of conversing well.

Little culture, unfortunately, is bestowed upon this accomplishment, which, beyond all others, promotes the happiness of home, enlivens society, and improves the minds of both speaker and listener. How many excellent women are deficient in the power of expressing themselves well, or, indeed, of expressing themselves at all! How many minds "cream and mantle" from the want of energy to pour themselves out in words! On the other hand, how some, equally well-intentioned, drown the very senses in their torrent of remarks, which dashes, like a waterfall, into a sombre pool of ennui below!

One lady will enter society, well-dressed, well-looking, polite; she does not intend to chill it by her presence; yet her absence is a relief. She takes her place as if she considered it sufficient to dress and look well. She brings no stock to the community of ideas. Her eyes return no response to the discourse which is going on. When you have once glanced at her, she becomes a mere expletive in the company.

Another one will be found as a talker. She is like a ca-nary bird; when others begin to speak, she hurries in her remarks, in an accompaniment. Her voice must be uppermost; conversation becomes a contest who can speak the most rapidly. The timid and modest retire from the encounter–she has the field to herself. She goes on, without mercy; the voice of a syren would fatigue, if heard continually. Others revolt at the injustice of the monopoly, and the words fall on ears that would be deaf if they could.

These are extreme cases; there are many other minor errors. The higher qualities of conversation must undoubtedly be based upon the higher qualities of the mind; then it is, indeed, a privilege to commune with others.

To acquire the power of thus imparting the highest pleasure by conversational powers, attention must be paid to literature. I am supposing the solid foundation of a good education has already been laid, but by literature, I do not mean only that class which is taught at school.

Reading, at the present day, is too much confined to light

literature. I would not speak against this. The modern novels, and the poets of all ages, are good reading, but let them be taken in moderation, and varied by something more solid. Let them be the dessert to the more substantial dinner of history, travels, and works of a like nature.

Regardless of the strength and polish given to the mind by a thorough course of reading, there is another reason why a lady should devote some portion of her time to it; she cannot do without it. She may, lacking this, pass through life respectably, even elegantly; but she cannot take her part in a communing with superior minds; she may enjoy, in wondering, the radiance of their intelligence; but the wondering must be composed, in part, of amazement at her own folly, in not having herself sought out the treasure concealed in the fathomless depths of books. She cannot truly enjoy society, with this art neglected. She may, for a few brief years, be the ornament of the drawing-room; but it must be, like many other ornaments there, in still life; she can never be the companion of the intellectual; and the time is gone by, when women, with all their energies excited, will be contented to be the mere plaything of brother, husband, or father.

Still it is not to the erudite, nor to the imaginative only, that it is given to please in conversation.

The art of imparting our ideas easily and elegantly to others, may be improved by ourselves, if there are opportunities of mingling in good society, with little study. The mind must first be cultivated; but it should not abash those who are conscious of moderate talents, or imperfect cultivation, from taking a due part in conversation, on account of their inferiority. It is a very different thing to shine and to please; to shine in society is more frequently attempted than compassed: to please is in the power of all. The effort to shine, when fruitless, brings a certain disgrace, and engenders mortification; all good people are inclined to take the will for the deed, when they see a desire to please. A gentle, deferential, kind manner, will disarm even the most discerning from criticizing too severely the deficiencies of the inexperienced; confidence, disrespect of others, volubil-ity, eagerness to dispute, must irritate the self-love of others, and produce an averseness to acknowledge talent or information, where they may even happen to exist.

It is wiser and safer for a young lady, in general, to observe the good, old-fashioned rule of being addressed first; but then she must receive the address readily, meeting it half way, repaying it by enlarging a little upon the topic thus selected, and not sinking into a dull silence, the moment after a reply is given. Some young ladies start, as if thunderstruck, when spoken to, and stare as if the person who pays them that attention, had no right to awaken them from their reverie. Others look affronted, possibly from shyness, and begin a derogatory attack upon the beauty of their dress by twitching the front breadth– or move from side to side, in evident distress and consternation. Time remedies these defects; but there is one less curable and less endurable–that of pertness and flippancy–the loud remarks and exclamations–the look of self-sufficiency and confidence. But these offensive manifestations spring from some previous and deep-seated defects of character, and are only to be repelled by what, I fear, they will frequently encounter–the mortification of inspiring disgust.

Neither is the lengthy, prosy, didactic reply, consistent with the submission and simplicity of youth; egotism, and egotism once removed, that is, the bringing into the topic one's own family and relations, are also antidotes to the true spirit of conversation. In general, it is wiser, more in good taste, safer, more becoming, certainly more in accordance with good breeding, to avoid talking of persons. There are many snares in such topics; not merely the danger of ca-lumniating, but that of engendering a slippery conscience in matters of fact. A young girl, shy and inexperienced, states a circumstance; she feels her deficiency as a narrator, for the power of telling a story, is a power to be acquired only by practice. She is sometimes tempted to heighten the incidents a little, in order to get on a little better, and to make more of an impression. She must of course defend her positions, and then she perils the sanctity of truth. Besides, few things narrow the intellect more than dwelling on the peculiarities, natural or incidental, of that small coterie of persons who constitute our world.

It is, in general, a wise rule, and one which will tend much to insure your comfort through life, to avoid disclosures to others of family affairs. I do not mean to recommend reserve, or art; to friends and relations, too great frankness can hardly be practised; but, with acquaintance, the less our own circumstances are discussed, the happier, and the more dignified will our commerce with them continue. On the same principle, let the concerns of others be touched upon with delicacy, or, if possible, passed over in silence; more especially those details which relate to strictly personal or family affairs. Public deeds are, of course, public property.

But personal affairs are private; and there is a want of true good breeding, a want of consideration and deference, in speaking freely of them, even if your friend is unconscious of the liberty taken.

It seems paradoxical to observe that the art of listening well forms a part of the duty of conversation. To give up the whole of your attention to the person who addresses himself to you, is sometimes a heavy tax, but it is one which we must pay for the privileges of social life, and an early practice will render it an almost involuntary act of good breeding; whilst consideration for others will give this little sacrifice a merit and a charm.

To listen well is to make an unconscious advance in the power of conversing. In listening we perceive in what the interest, in what the failure of others consists; we become, too, aware of our own deficiencies, without having them taught through the medium of humiliation. We find ourselves often more ignorant than we could have supposed possible. We learn, by a very moderate attention to the sort of topics which please, to form a style of our own. The “art of conversation” is an unpleasant phrase. The power of conversing well is least agreeable when it assumes the character of an art.

In listening, a well-bred lady will gently sympathize with the speaker; or, if needs must be, differ, as gently. Much character is shown in the act of listening. Some people appear to be in a violent hurry whilst another speaks; they hasten on the person who addresses them, as one would urge on a horse–with incessant “Yes, yes, very good–indeed–proceed!” Others sit, in full stare, eyes fixed as those of an owl, upon the speaker. Others will receive every observation with a little hysterical giggle.

But all these vices of manners may be avoided by a gentle attention and a certain calm dignity of manners, based upon a reflective, cultivated mind.

Observation, reading, and study, will form the ground-work for good powers of conversation, and the more you read, study, and see, the more varied and interesting your topics will be.

A young lady should consider music as one branch of her education, inferior, in importance, to most of those studies which are pointed out to her, but attainable to a sufficient degree by the aid of time, perseverance, and a moderate degree of instruction. Begun early, and pursued steadily, there is ample leisure in youth for the attainment of a science, which confers more cheerfulness, and brings more pleasure than can readily be conceived.

A young lady should be able to play with taste, correctness, and readiness, upon the general principle that a well educated woman should do all things well. This, I should suppose, is in the power of most persons; and it may be attained without loss of health, of time, or any sacrifice of an important nature. She should consider it as an advantage, a power to be employed for the gratification of others, and to be indulged with moderation and good sense for her own resource, as a change of occupation.

Consider in this light, music is what Providence intended it to be–a social blessing. The whole creation is replete with music,–a benign Power has made the language of the feathered tribe harmony; let us not suppose that He condemns his other creatures to silence in the song.

Music has an influence peculiar to itself. It can allay the irritation of the mind; it cements families, and makes a home, which might sometimes be monotonous, a scene of pleasant excitement. Pursued as a recreation, it is gentle, rational, lady-like. Followed as a sole object, it loses its charm, because we perceive it is then over-rated. The young lady who comes modestly forward, when called upon as a performer, would cease to please, were she, for an instant, to assume the air and confidence of a professional musician. There is a certain style and manner–confined now to second-rate performers, for the highest and most esteemed dispense with it–there is an effort and a dash, which disgust in the lady who has bad taste enough to assume them.

And, whilst I am on this topic, let me remark that there is a great deal in the choice of music, in the selection of its character, its suitability to your feelings, style, and taste, and this especially with respect to vocal music.

There is no doubt that a good Italian style is the best for instruction, and that it produces the most careful and accomplished singers. Suppose a case. Your parents, most fair readers, have paid a high price to some excellent professor, to instruct you–and, with a fair ear, and a sufficient voice, you have been taught some of those elaborate songs which are most popular at the opera. A party is assembled–music is one of the diversions. Forth you step, and, with a just apprehension of the difficulties of your task, select one of those immortal compositions which the most eminent have made their study; you execute it wonderfully, only just falling a little short of all the song should be; only just provoking a comparison, in every mind, with a high standard, present in the memory of every cultivated musician near you. A cold approval, or a good-natured "bravo!" with, believe me, though you do not hear it, a thorough, and, often, expressed conviction that you had better have left the thing alone, follows the effort which has merely proclaimed the fact that, despite the time and money spent upon the cultivation of your voice, you are but a second- rate singer.

But, choose a wiser, less pretending, a less conspicuous path. Throw your knowledge into compositions of a less startling, less aspiring character. Try only what you can compass. Be wise enough not to proclaim your deficiencies, and the critics will go away disarmed, even if they are not charmed. But if there be any voice, any feeling, any science, the touching melody, made vocal by youth and taste, will obtain even a far higher degree of encomium than, perhaps, it actually merits. You will please–you will be asked to renew your efforts. People will not be afraid of cadenzas five minutes long, or of bravura, every note of which makes one hope it may be the last.

It is true that, to a person who loves music, the performance of one of the incomparable songs of Bellini, Rosini, Flotow, or Mozart, is an actual delight–but; when attempted by a young amateur, it should be, like many other delights, confined to the private circle, and not visited upon society in general.

Do not suppose that I mean to recommend poor music, or feeble, ephemeral compositions. What is good need not, of necessity, be always difficult. Ballad music is rich in songs adapted for the private performer–and there are many, in Italian, of great beauty, which, though they would not be selected for a concert-room, or for brilliant display, are adapted for ladies.

Music is the greatest, best substitute for conversation. It has many merits, in this light. It can never provoke angry retorts; it can never make enemies; it can injure no one's character by slander; and in playing and singing one can commit no indiscretion.

Music is a most excellent amusement, and, in society, an indispensable one. It aids conversation by occasionally interrupting it for a short period, to be renewed with a new impetus. It makes the most delightful recreation for the home circle, varying the toil and trouble of the father's or husband's working day, by the pleasures of the evening made by music's power to glide smoothly and swiftly.

There are but few persons who are entirely without a love for music, even if they do not understand it. They will be borne along upon the waves of a sweet melody to high, pure thoughts, often to delicious memories.

The piano is, at the present day, the most popular instrument in society. The harp has ceased to be fashionable, though it is sometimes heard. The latter is a most beautiful accompaniment for the voice, but requires a large room, as, in a small one, it will sound stringy and harsh.

The guitar, while it makes a very pleasant accompaniment for the voice, has also the advantage of being easily carried from place to place.

It requires as much judgment to select proper instrumental pieces for a parlor performance, as you would display in a choice of songs. Page after page of black, closely printed notes, will drive those who see them from the piano. They may be executed in the most finished style, but they are not suited to general society. In their place, for practice, or for a musical soirée, where everyone puts forth her best musical powers, they are appropriate, and will give pleasure, but they are not suited for a mixed party. When asked to play, choose, if you will, a brilliant, showy piece, but let it be short. It is better still to make no attempt at display, but simply try to please, selecting the music your own judgment tells you is best suited to your audience.

Avoid the loud, thumping style, and also the over-solemn style.

Be sure, before you accept any invitation to play, that you know perfectly the piece you undertake. It is better to play the simplest airs in a finished, faultless manner, than to play imperfectly the most brilliant variations.

Avoid movement at the piano. Swinging the body to and fro, moving the head, rolling the eyes, raising the hands too much, are all bad tricks, and should be carefully abstained from.

With respect to drawing, modeling, or any pursuits of the same nature, so much depends on taste and opportunity, and they are so little the accomplishments of society that they require but few of those restrictions which music, in its use and abuse, demands. Drawing, like music, should be cultivated early. Its advantages are the habits of perseverance and occupation, which it induces; and the additional delight which it gives to the works, both of nature and of art. Like music, it gives independence–independence of society. The true lover of the arts has a superiority over the indifferent, and, if she is not better prepared for society, is much better fitted for retirement than those who are not so happily endowed with tastes, when in moderation, so innocent and beneficial.

There is no accomplishment more graceful, pleasing, healthy, and lady-like, than that of riding well. Avoiding, at the same time, timidity and the "fast" style, keeping within the bounds of elegant propriety, gracefully yielding to the guidance of your escort, and keeping your seat easily, yet steadily, are all points to be acquired.

To ride well is undoubtedly an admirable qualification for a lady, as she may be as feminine in the saddle as in the ball room or home circle. It is a mistaken idea to suppose that to become an accomplished horse-woman a lady must unsex herself. But she must have a reserve in her manner, that will prevent contamination from the intercourse which too much riding may lead to. To hunt, or follow the field sports, in a pursuit which is the track of blood, disgusts the true admirer of gentle breeding. And such diversions will certainly result in a coarseness of manner and expression, growing upon the fair equestrian slowly but surely. A harsh voice, loud tone, expressions suited only to manly lips, but unconsciously copied, will follow her devotion to the unfeminine pursuit.

Nothing is more revolting than a woman who catches the tone and expressions of men. To hear the slang of jockeys from female lips, is very offensive, yet ladies who mix in field sports are liable, nay, almost certain, to fall into a style of conversation which is ten times worse than the coarsest terms from the lips of a man. Instances there are, of the fairest of our sex, from a fondness for such diversions, and a habitual participation in such society, becoming hard, bold, and disgusting, even whilst retaining all their female loveliness of person.

A lady, unless she lives in the most retired parts of the country, should never ride alone, and even then she will be awkwardly placed, in case of an accident, without an escort. In the cities, not only is it unfeminine, but positively dangerous, for a lady to ride unaccompanied by a gentleman, or a man servant.

Although it is impossible, within the limits of this little volume, to give many hints upon riding, a few may not be amiss. Like many other accomplishments, a teacher is necessary, if you wish to attain perfection, and no written directions can make you a finished horse-woman, unless you have had tuition and practice.

In mounting you are desired, gentle Amazon, to spring gracefully into your saddle, with the slight assistance of a hand placed beneath the sole of the shoe, instead of scrambling uncouthly to your "wandering throne," as Miss Fan-shake wittily calls it, from a high chair, as is frequently done by those who have not been properly instructed. To mount in the orthodox manner, you should stand nearly close to the horse, level with the front of the saddle, and taking the reins slackly in your right hand, you should place that hand on the nearest pommel, to secure your balance in rising, and with your left hand gather up the front of the habit, so as to leave the feet clear. The gentleman should place himself firmly, near, but not so near to you as to impede your rising, and with the same view must hold his head well back, as should he lose his hat from a whisk of your habit the effect produced is not good. You should then present your left foot, and the gentleman placing one hand beneath its sole, and the other above, so as to possess a safe hold, should, with nice judgment, give just such assistance as will enable you easily, with a spring, to vault gracefully into the saddle. You will then arrange your right leg comfortably over the pommel, your cavalier will then place your left foot in the stirrup and arrange the flow of the habit-skirt, and all is complete. All this, though so seemingly simple and easy, requires some little practice to effect neatly and gracefully.

Secondly, when riding with a gentleman, remember that you are best placed on the left side; because in that position the graceful flow of your habit is seen to the greatest advantage, while it does not inconvenience the gentleman by getting entangled with his stirrup, nor does it receive the splashes of his horse.

But when you have a double attendance of cavaliers, if you be at all a timid rider, it may become discreet to" pack" you (forgive the homely phrase) between the two, since, in this position, you are the most thoroughly protected from your own horse's shying, or from other horses or vehicles approaching you too closely, being thus forced to take that part of the road to which the better judgment of your companions inevitably guides you. If you are an accomplished equestrian, you will prefer being outside, and (as has been said) to the left.

Sit erect in the middle of your saddle, turning your face full towards the head of your horse. Cling as closely as possible to the saddle, but avoid stooping forward, or using your hands to keep you in your seat. Nervous motions on horseback are not only ungraceful, but dangerous, as your horse will not make any allowance for the delicacy of your nerves, and may prove his objections to a jerking hand, or a twitching rein, in a most decided and disagreeable manner.

The riding-dress, or habit, is best made to fit the figure tightly, with tight sleeves. It may be open in the front, over a neatly fitting chemisette, or buttoned close to the throat, with a neat linen collar and cuffs. The loose sacque is ungraceful, but a basque is mostly on horseback.

Gauntlet gloves, of leather, are the most suitable, and must be loose enough to give your hand perfect freedom, yet not so loose as to interfere with its motions. Do not wear the skirt too long; it will be dangerous in case of accident, and it may prove annoying to your horse. Your habit must be made of a material sufficiently heavy to hang gracefully, and not move too much with the wind. For a winter habit, a warmly-lined basque, trimmed at the throat and hands with fur, is an elegant and appropriate dress, and a round cap of the same cloth as the habit, with a band, and pieces to cover the ears, of fur to match the dress trimmings, makes a handsome and appropriate dress.

In summer, your hat should be of fine straw, and slouched to shade the face; in winter, of felt, or, if you prefer, a close cap of cloth. The hat may be trimmed with feathers or knots of ribbon, and the shape should be one to protect the complexion, at the same time graceful and becoming.

Avoid any display in a riding dress. Choose a material of some dark or neutral tint, and never use showy trimmings.

Curls, or any flowing loose style of wearing the hair, will be found exceedingly troublesome on horseback. Arrange it neatly and compactly under your hat, for if a stray curl or lock annoys you, or is blown across your eyes by the wind, your hands will be too fully occupied to remedy the difficulty.

Your whip should be light and small, tasteful if you will, but not showy.

At the period for which these hints are intended, the Modern Languages should form a portion of acquisition.

As in music, an intelligent and assiduous girl may, I believe, acquire an adequate degree of proficiency in French, German, and Italian, without having been abroad, though a foreign tour will be of the greatest use in the acquisition of the accent and niceties of each tongue. With respect to French, it is no doubt essential to comfort to understand it; it is one of the attributes of a lady to speak it well; still, it is not indispensable to speak it so well that the American lady is mistaken for a Parisian. This, which but seldom happens, can only be acquired, in most cases, by a residence abroad. But French is thoroughly and grammatically taught in America. It is only the habit of speaking, the idioms and niceties, which cannot be acquired except by converse with a native.

There are hundreds of competent instructors in this country, French ladies and gentlemen amongst the number, who form classes for conversation and familiarizing their pupils with these very idioms. After availing herself of such advantages, a young lady will find that a very short residence abroad will improve and facilitate her French conversation.

Much, however, will depend upon how you use the opportunities within your reach. There are many opportunities of practice in large towns; and foreigners give all facilities, by their readiness to converse, their good-nature in listening, and in helping the beginner by kind hints. If a young lady, with simplicity, good breeding, and good taste, endeavors to speak whenever she has an opportunity, words will come as if by intuition. Do not think of by-standers and lookers-on; think only of the individual to whom you are addressing yourself. If possible, be not abashed by one or two errors at the first plunge–swim on till you have confidence. The effort, I grant, is great, and it may be obviated by a foreign education; but where this is impossible, the freedom acquired will more than repay the exertion.

In foreign literature, walk carefully, and if you have an older, wiser head than your own to point out the best paths, improve the advantage.

One cannot help deeming it a great era in education that German is cultivated as well as Italian and French, and that stores of literature are opened, to vary the delights of intellect, and to give freshness and interest to the studies of youth.

The rapture with which the works of Schiller are perused in the original, seems to repay the hours devoted to German; and I am sure the perusal of Tasso, or of the Aris-todemo of Monti, would reward the study of Italian, were not the acquisition of that exquisite language itself a source of poetic pleasure.

The modern French writers have increased an everlast-ing responsibility in corrupting the sources of amusement, open to the young readers, and it is remarkable that most of the distinguished French authors seem to have felt that they had erred, and to have retrieved in some of their works the tendencies of their other productions. Take for instance, Madame de Stael; her books cannot be judged altogether; the effect of some of her eloquent and almost incomparable writings varies to an extraordinary degree. Whilst "Del-phine" is unfit for the perusal of a modest woman, her "L'Allemagne" is finely written throughout, and her criti-cisms and analyses of German writers are full of instruction as well as interest. Still the works open to readers of French are numerous.

The tragedies of Corneille and Racine are forcible and finished, and should be read because it is classical. The "Alzire" of Voltaire and his "Zaire " with the dramas of Casimir de la Vigne are also worthy of perusal. It is not an inspiring kind of reading, but it is rich in sentiment, and perfectly unexceptionable in moral tone.

Although the skepticism of most German writers renders this literature dangerous to a young mind, there are fields of pure, noble writing open in that language. The works of Schiller, for example. His mind was originally noble, his heart good, his love to mankind, and his inquiry after truth were sincere. In early life, he wavered; and the besetting skepticism of the Germans dimmed, for a time, his perceptions of all that is most sublime, as well as true, in our finite knowledge. He was chastened–he suffered–he believed. He died an early but a bright instance that great genius may exist with true and humble piety, and that the mind is never so powerful as when illumined by divine light. His works are a magnificent library in themselves–and I could almost say, be content to learn German and to read Schiller. Some of his works are open to objection, his "Bride of Messina," portions of "The Robbers," are better omitted from your collection, but "Wallenstein" and "Maria Stuart" are noble and admirable productions. On this subject, and, indeed, on the whole of German literature, Madame de Stael is an excellent guide in her

"L'Allemagne," to which I refer the young German student, who is sincerely desirous of gleaning the good, and avoiding the evil in German compositions.

Italian literature furnishes a delightful theme for comment. It is singular that an enslaved, and, during many ages, a depraved and degraded people, should have possessed the purest poetry, the least exceptionable drama, in Europe. There is little to exclude, and much to recommend, in this beautiful language. The works of Tasso abound with high sentiment; the "Inferno" of Dante is a sublime picture of eternal retribution, softened with most touching pictures of human woe. Happy are those who have leisure to pursue extensively the acquisition of Italian literature, they may read and commit to memory without fear of an insidious meaning beneath the polished verse, or the prose which has all the charm of poetry.

Spanish literature will require the same judicious prun-ing which is necessary in French and German, but of all languages, it is the most musical for speech, and singing.

A lady in society must, if she would not grow utterly weary in company, know how to dance. It has been the practice among many excellent people to represent the ball room as a "pitfall covered with flowers;" a sheet of breaking ice; above, all gayety and motion; below, all darkness and danger. It may be that to some minds the ballroom may be replete with temptations; but there are minds which find temptations everywhere. The innocent may be innocent, nay, the pious may feel devout, even in a ball room.

There is nothing immoral or wrong in dancing; it is the tendency of youth to dance–it is the first effort of a child–the first natural recreation. It seems so natural that I confess I am always doubtful of the sincerity of those young ladies who profess to dislike the ballroom.

In the present day, you must understand how to move gracefully through quadrilles, to dance polka, Schottische, Varsovienne, and waltz. To these you may add a great variety of dances, each season, probably, bringing a new one.

"Dancing," says Mr. Sheldrake, "is one of the most healthy, as well as one of the most pleasing amusements that can be practised by the young. If it is learned from those who are well qualified to teach it, and practised, as it ought to be, consistently with the instructions given, it will contribute more to improve the health, as well as the form of the human frame, than any other exercise. For the dis-covery and promulgation of the true and correct principles according to which dancing should be taught, the world is indebted to France, a country which has long taken the lead in the elegant arts. In France, dancing was first raised to the dignity of a science, a royal academy being founded for the purpose of teaching and perfecting it, in the reign of Louis Quatorze. In this academy were trained many of the most distinguished dancers of both sexes." One of the most celebrated, Madame Simonet, gave the following account to Mr. Sheldrake of the mode of instruction pursued in the academy:–"All the pupils, before they were permitted to attempt to dance, were completely instructed in what were called the preparatory exercises; that is, a system of exercises, which endued all their limbs with strength, firmness, elasticity, and activity; when they had acquired these properties, they began to dance.

"In these preparatory exercises, the motions were of the most simple kind, the object being to teach the pupil, gradually and separately, all those movements which, when combined, and rapidly executed, constitute dancing." Madame Simonet thus described those elementary instructions, as gone through by herself:–"She successively learned to stand flat and firm upon both her feet, with her limbs quite straight, and the whole person perfectly upright, but not stiff; then to lift one foot from the ground, and to keep it so for some time without moving any part of her body; she then replaced that foot on the ground, and raised the other in the same manner. These simple actions were repeated till the pupils were quite familiar with them; they were then directed to keep the body quite erect, but not stiff, and bearing firmly upon one leg, to raise the other from the ground, gradually and slowly, by bending the upper joint of the limb, at the same time making the knee straight, and putting the toe to its proper extent, but no more. The foot, after it had been kept in this state for some time, was returned to the ground from whence it was taken, and the other foot treated in the same manner; when quite familiarized to these actions, they were directed to walk (march, as some people will call it) slowly, performing the same motions with the feet alternately." The exercises which followed these, were upon the turning out of the feet, the balancing of the body, and other attitudes, which need not be particularized.

Mr. Sheldrake gives several examples of persons trained upon these initiatory principles to the profession of dancing, who have lived in health to a great age. "This," says he, "is not the chance lot of a few; for I have, through life, been accustomed to see many persons of the same profession; I have communicated my own observations to many others, and all have agreed in remarking, that those who follow this profession have, very generally, excellent health, which very many of them carry into extreme old age. This indis-putable fact can only be accounted for by supposing that the preparatory exercises which these persons go through, are a modification of what I have called regulated muscular tension, or action, and the early and constant practice of which lays a firm foundation for that high health which accompanies them through life. It is upon the same principle that a soldier is never seen with spinal curvature, or other personal deformity, or a stage dancer of either sex with a deformed person; it is, perhaps, impossible that such things should exist, for the plain reason, that the exercises which they begin to practice early in life, and continue regularly through its whole course, render it impossible for them to become so.

"The inference to be drawn from these incontrovertible facts is, that if we, in very early life, teach young children to practice similar exercises, and follow them steadily afterwards, we shall confirm them in excellent health, and prevent the accession of those evils which so often cause deformity to the figure, and destruction to the constitution, at later periods of life. I do not propose to make every boy a soldier, or every girl a dancer upon the stage, but to adopt the principles, by the application of which those persons are trained to the successful practices of their several occupations, and so to modify them, that they may qualify other classes of society to follow their different pursuits with equal success; and I am not without hopes that this undertaking will contribute something towards producing this desirable effect."

Dancing is an exercise which has been practiced by mankind from the most remote ages. With the Egyptians, Assyrians, and Persians, the founders of the three great empires of the ancient world, dancing was the favorite exercise or accomplishment, and the practice was not less prevalent among their successors in power and importance, the Greeks and Romans. The Jews, also, we learn from Scrip-ture, were strongly attached to the exercise at all periods of their history.

At the present day, almost every person that exists, whether barbarous or civilized, has its own form of dancing. It is this universality of the exercise that makes dancing a subject of importance. Being so extensively practiced, it must be the instrument either of good or evil to the human race.

It is one of the most healthful and elegant amusements, and cannot be too highly recommended. Among a rude and dissolute people it may degenerate into something worthy of condemnation; but all the blessings we have are similarly liable to abuse, and it would be most unjust to condemn a cheerful domestic amusement, merely because it has, at times, been degraded by people of low, vulgar, immoral tastes. By all physicians, dancing, when pursued in moderation, is recommended as highly conducive to bodily health; and it may be truly said, that, allied with music, nothing is more conducive to mental health, more calculated to drive away melancholy, and put the whole temper into good humor.

Dancing is the poetry of motion. It must be performed with ease and grace, and always with a perfect regard for propriety of movement.

As an art it is taught by professed masters; and one of the leading rules given to the learner is to raise and lower herself gracefully on the elastic part of her feet, and to keep perfect time to the music. Dancing is really a simple and elegant gliding on the toes, which bend more or less to accommodate the steps, and prevent harsh, ungraceful motion.

The most popular dances of the present day are, first, the quadrille.

These are of French origin, comparatively tranquil in their character, and generally danced once or more in every party.

They are danced by four couples, one standing on each side of a square. There are many sets of quadrilles, the figures in each varying from the others. But there are five figures in each set. The plain, fancy, Lancers, Polka, Mazourka, and German, are among the most popular.

In plain quadrilles, a lady takes no steps, merely walking gracefully through the figures, but her feet must keep perfect time to the music, and she must know the changes of position perfectly.

A quadrille may be very properly described as a conversation dance, as there are long pauses between the figures, when the dancers must have a fund of small talk ready for their partners.

When moving in the figures, hold out your skirt a little with the right hand, merely to clear the ground, and prevent the possibility of treading upon it.

Next come the round dances, the Valse, Polka, Schottische, Varsovienne, and Redowa.

The Waltz is danced both à troistemps and deuxtemps. In the waltz, the position is the most important point. You may lean upon your partner's arm, and so carry your figure, that the prudish can find but little fault, but you can also make the dance a most immodest one. I cannot, within the limits of my book, go into a long argument as to the propriety of these round dances. Opinions differ, and I am not writing a sermon, but giving, as far as is in my power, hints to ladies in society. It is, therefore, enough for me to know that these dances are tolerated, and that, even were I so inclined, I could not exclude them.

To return to the position. Stand a little to the right of your partner, that, in clasping your waist, he may draw you upon his arm to his shoulder, not his breast; the last position is awkward. By observing the first, you have your head free; turn it a little towards the left shoulder; need I say, never lay it upon your partner's shoulder? Throw the head and shoulders a little back, not too much to be consistent with easy grace, place one hand upon your partner's shoulder, and the other in his disengaged hand. So, you are ready to start.

The waltz may be danced to very fast time, or to slow music. The last is the most graceful, and there is not so much danger of giddiness. Grace can only be gained by a perfect timing of the steps to the music, and also evenness of step.

It is, when properly timed with perfect step, and easy, gliding motion, the most graceful of dances. The Germans, who dance for the sake of dancing, will only allow a certain number of waltzers on the floor at one time, and these waltz in streams, all going down one side of the room and up the other, thus rendering collisions impossible.

An English writer, in a recent work published on etiquette, speaks of waltzing thus:–

"It is perhaps useless to recommend flat-foot waltzing in this country, where ladies allow themselves to be almost hugged by their partners, and where men think it necessary to lift a lady almost off the ground, but I am persuaded that if it were introduced, the outcry against the impropriety of waltzing would soon cease. Nothing can be more delicate than the way in which a German holds his partner.

It is impossible to dance on the flat foot unless the lady and gentleman are quite free of one another. His hand, therefore, goes no further round her waist than to the hooks and eyes of her dress, hers, no higher than to his elbow. Thus danced, the waltz is smooth, graceful, and delicate, and we could never in Germany complain of our daughter's languishing on a young man's shoulder. On the other hand, nothing is more graceless and absurd, than to see a man waltzing on the tips of his toes, lifting his partner off the ground, or twirling round and round with her like the figures on a street organ. The test of waltzing in time is to be able to stamp the time with the left foot. The waltz is of German origin, but where it is still danced in Germany in the original manner, (as, for instance, among the peasants of the Tyrol,) it is a very different dance. It is very slow and graceful; the feet are thrown out in a single long step, which Turvey drop, I presume, would call a jets. After a few turns, the partners waltz alone in the same step, the man keeping the time by striking together his iron-shod heels, until with a shout and clapping of hands he again clasps his partner and continues in the same slow measure with her."

The position for the polka, redowa, and other round dances, should be the same as that for the waltz, and for the steps, they can only be acquired from a dancing teacher, and are impossible to describe properly.

One of the most delightful accomplishments which a lady can possess, and one which is unfortunately but little cultivated, is the art of reading aloud well; reading with expression, taste, animation, and correctness; and this art once acquired, let her also be able to recite well.

Long lectures may be given upon elocution, but the advice can be condensed into two directions. First, be sure you pronounce, accent, and enunciate every word correctly; then, throw your whole soul into the words. Study your author carefully, so that you may know precisely what he means by each expression, and then try to bury your personal identity, to become, for the time, the character you represent.

One of the most delightful ways to spend a social evening is to devote it to dramatic literature. Invite only guests who read well, or who are really interested listeners, and select a play, or scenes from several plays, and cast the parts among your guests. All jealousy must be put aside, and to-night's Hamlet must condescend to direct Richard to "Stand by, my lord, and let the coffin pass," to-morrow.

After a few meetings, the peculiar talent of each reader will be recognized, and you can select your tragedy hero, comedy hero, queen, chambermaid, and other members of the force, with a view to the display of each one's best powers. Vary the entertainment by reciting monologues and di-alogues. A whole play will often be found tiresome; it is best to select several scenes, keeping up the thread of the plot, and introducing the best characters, and leave out what is mere interlude, and dispense with some of the subordinate characters.

Leave one end of the room entirely vacant for the readers.

You will find it more interesting to have the readers stand, and use some little motion; the words will flow more easily, the expressions come more forcibly if the appropriate gesture is made. Love scenes will, of course, require delicate handling, and embracing can be easily omitted; neither would I recommend the action of a dueling scene, or a murder, but merely to add gesture enough to give interest to both readers and audience.

You will find some little difficulty from bashfulness, and the "don't like to" people at first, but soon you will discover with delight how many of your friends possess the talent for reading well, and never knew it themselves.

You will do well to take a few lessons in elocution, but you need not fear to read if you have never made the accomplishment a study. With a correct knowledge of your own language, and a love for fine writing, you will soon read well.

Give to every part you undertake, the full effect intended by the writer. Do not throw all your energy, your whole soul, into a leading part at one time, and slight a subordinate character at another. If you have but five words to read, read them as they would be spoken were you the character you represent for the time. To hear a splendidly written, tragic burst of passion read in a weak, a whining voice, is no worse than to have a few simple words from a servant's lips delivered with the gesture and emphasis suited to a Medea or Lady Macbeth.

I shall be condemned by many serious and well-judging persons,if I say one word in favor of private theatricals; yet, as it appears to me, there are in these diversions some advantages which are not to be found to excuse the waltz, or the polka, or the ballet, or the hunting field. In private theatricals there is the possibility of some benefit. The study of the finest dramatists, especially of Shakespeare, is not likely to demoralize the mind, or to cool the enthusiasm for what is good. We can scarcely know too well those works which have tended more to form character than any collection of any kind whatsoever.

Shakespeare, Sheridan, Bulwer,–but I cannot go through the list of fine dramatic writers whose works elevate the mind and taste.

The plays of Sheridan, Knowles, and Bulwer, are, in most instances, well adapted for private representations–the most exquisite delineations of female character may be found in the dramatic library, and high, pure, manly thoughts, may be traced, line after line, to the same source.

Private theatricals should, however, be regulated with much judgment. I see no reason to severely restrict talent of this kind where it exists, any more than to crush a dawning taste for the other fine arts. What we have to do is to raise and direct it; never to let it occupy too much time, nor to become the business of life; never to let it infringe upon duties; never to allow it to lead us into an unreasonable, and, therefore, criminal expense. Our ancestors were content to strew their stage at the end of their halls with rushes, and to hang up the name of the scene, instead of a scene, before each act. The best preparations, which generally render private theatricals both laborious and expensive, add but little to the pleasure of the beholders, whose attention is fixed upon the actors, and who can always see far finer scenes at a minor theatre than at any private theatricals. Were we content with greater simplicity in our amusements, how much vain ostentation, heart-sickening expense, self-recrimination, and trouble, might be avoided!

As a valid objection to private theatricals, it has been urged that they are apt to encourage a taste for the green-room of the public theatre in young men and boys; in women the risk is less, for few women are ever known to go on the stage except from necessity. I own this objection to theatricals as the greatest that can be urged. It can only be answered in mitigation that, where there exists a taste of the kind, it is better that it should be indulged at home, instead of at the theatre, with the modest inmates of a well-governed house, instead of with professional actors. Like all other amusements, the abuse is probable, but the power of restraint rests within ourselves.

Under the same head as private theatricals may come dramatized charades and proverbs, so much in fashion at the present time. These last have some great advantages over the standard plays; they are better suited to a parlor; they do not provoke comparison between the young actors, and the favorite public idols; they require but little scenery and arrangement; they are short; and they do not require so many subordinate characters.

Impromptu charades and proverbs are delightful, and are the occasion for much merriment; the mistakes, the absurd contrasts between character and costume, the scenery–a deep, hanging wood, the court of Louis Quatorze or the deck of a man of war, being improvised at a moment's notice, only add to the merry enjoyment.

One rule you must observe if you join in these amusements: never to carry your gayety into romping. Merry and laughing you may be, yet never forget you are a lady. You may personate a newly-caught Irish chambermaid, use the broadest brogue, wear the commonest dress, throw yourself heartily and thoroughly into the part, losing your personal identity almost entirely, and yet you may retain that name-less charm, which will place you in the mind of each of the audience as a lady of refinement.

You must also be perfectly good-natured and self-sacrificing; ready to play the smallest parts with the same interest you would throw into the principal ones. Try to throw out all the good points in the parts taken by the other members of the company. If you play an insignificant part, play it well, with all the grace you can, make the most of it, but do not try to raise it to the first place. Yield gracefully the prominent position to those who claim it in the plot of the play, and never try by conspicuous dress or by play, to go beyond the position set down for you.

Another delightful accomplishment, and one which will aid you if you are studying drawing and painting, is that of arranging tableaux vaunts.

Mrs. Severn gives the following hints upon this subject:

"Perhaps there is no intellectual amusement in fashionable life, the nature of which is so little understood, as the tableau vivant;

it being generally considered as only a vehicle for display, whereas its real purpose is to arrange scientifically a combination of natural objects, so as to make a good picture according to the rules of art.

"A tableau vivant is literally what its name imports–a living picture composed of living persons; and, when skillfully arranged and seen at a proper distance, it produces all the effect of a real picture. It is said, that the first living picture was contrived by a profligate young German noble-man, who having, during the absence of his father, sold one of the celebrated pictures belonging to the old castle, which was an heir-loom, to conceal the deficiency, placed some of his companions behind the frame, so as to imitate the missing picture, and to deceive his father, who passed through the room without being conscious of his loss.

"A tableau vivant may be formed in two ways: it may consist of a group of persons, who take some well-known subject in history or fiction to illustrate, and who form a group to tell the story according to their own taste; or, it may be a copy, as exact as circumstances will permit, of some celebrated picture. The first plan, it may be easily imagined, is very rarely effective; since, as we find that even the best masters are often months, or even years, before they can arrange a group satisfactorily on canvas, it is not probable that persons who are not artists should succeed in making good impromptu pictures. Indeed, it has been observed that artists themselves, when they have to arrange a tableau vivant, always prefer copying a picture to composing one.

"Copying a real picture, by placing living persons in the positions of the figures indicated in the picture, appears, at first sight, an easy task enough; and the effect ought to be easily attained, as there can be no bad drawing, and no confused light and shade, to destroy the effect of the grouping.

There are, however, many difficulties to conquer, which it requires some knowledge of art to be aware of. Painting being on a flat surface, every means is taken to give round-ness and relief to the figures, which qualities of course are found naturally in a tableau vivant. In a picture the light is made effective by a dark shadow placed near it; diminished lights or demi-tints are introduced to prevent the principal light appears a spot; and these are linked together by art-ful shades, which show the outline in some places, and hide it in others. The colors must also be carefully arranged, so as to blend or harmonize with each other. A want of attention to these minute points will be sufficient to destroy the effect of the finest picture, even to those who are so unacquainted with art as to be incapable of explaining why they are dissatisfied, except by an involuntary liking or disliking of what they see.

"The best place for putting up a tableau vivant is in a door-way, with an equal space on each side; or, at least, some space on both sides is necessary; and if there is a room or a passage between the door selected for the picture and the room the company is to see it from, so much the better, as there should be a distance of at least four yards between the first row of the spectators and the picture. It must be remembered that, while the tableau is being shown, nearly all the lights must be put out in the room where the company is assembled; and, perhaps, only one single candle, properly placed, in the intervening space between the company and the tableau, must be left slightly to illuminate the frame. In the above-mentioned door- way a frame, somewhat smaller than the original picture, must be suspended, three, four, or even five feet from the floor, as may suit the height of the door; or, if the door is not very high, the frame may be put one or two feet behind, to gain space; but care must be taken to fill up the opening that would, in that case, show between the door-way and the frame; also a piece of dark cloth ought to be put from the bottom of the frame to the ground, to give the appearance of the picture hanging on the wall. The most important thing is, that the chairs or tables ought to be placed behind the frame, so that the persons who are to represent the tableau may sit or stand as nearly in the position, with regard to the frame, as the figures appear to do in the real picture they are trying to imitate, and at about two feet from the frame, so that the light which is attached to the back of the frame may fall properly on the figures.

In order to accomplish this, great study and contrivance are required, so that the shades may fall in precisely the same places as in the original picture; and sometimes the light is put on one side, sometimes on the other, and often on the top; and sometimes shades of tin or paper are put between the lights and the tableaux, to assist in throwing a shadow over any particular part. The background is one of the most important parts, and should be made to resemble that of the picture as nearly as possible; if it is dark, coarse cloth absorbs the light best; but whether it is to be black, blue, or brown, must depend on the tint of the picture; should the background be a light one, colored calico, turned on the wrong side, is generally used. If trees or flowers form the background, of course real branches or plants must be introduced to imitate those in the picture. Even rocks have been imitated; and spun glass has often successfully represented water. A thin, black gauze, black muslin, or tarlatan veil, should be fastened to the top of the frame, on the outside of it, through which the tableau is to be seen.

"Care ought to be taken to conceal the peculiarities of the different materials used in the draperies, and it is even sometimes necessary to cover the stuff used for the purpose with a gauze of a different color, so as to imitate the broken and transparent colors found in most good pictures.

This, carefully attended to, will give a quietness and simplicity to the whole, which will greatly add to the illusion."

The next subject upon the list of accomplishments, should be filled by some words upon fancy sewing. Under this head will come–Crochet, Knitting, Tapestry work, Embroidery, Chenille work, Netting, Canvas work, Berlin wool work, Frame work, Braiding, Bead work, etc.

Small social gatherings will be much more entertaining, the time will pass much more quickly, and the conversation flows more freely if the fingers are employed with some light work.

Pretty presents–nay, beautiful ones–may be made in this way, when the fingers would otherwise be idle, and these will have an additional value in being the work of your own hands.

From the most remote ages needlework has been not only a source of pecuniary advantage for poor women, but also of pleasant pastime for the rich. It is one of the most elegant of the imitative art, and from time immemorial it has been an amusement for otherwise idle fingers, from the cottage to the palace.

I have not space for a long disquisition upon the uses and pleasures of fancy work; every woman has moments when such pretty playwork will be a valuable recreation. The taste for fancy work increases daily, and can be made not only ornamental, but useful. A ladies' wardrobe consists of so many, and such varied objects, that the evenings of an entire winter may be spent in making various useful garments, which are, at the same time, suitable for company sewing. Opera hoods, wool shawls, sleeves, Sontags, and other ladies' articles, may be varied by embroidering smok-ing caps, slippers, or handkerchiefs for gentlemen.

Embroidering on canvas, or tapestry work, opens a large field for taste and skill in execution.

Beautiful articles for presents, chair covers, sofa cushions, slippers, may be worked in the otherwise idle moments spent in familiar society, and the fingers will soon acquire skill and astonishing rapidity.

The German ladies have constantly on hand a piece of netting or other fancy work, which they carry from place to place, and take out when conversing; and so far from entirely engrossing their thoughts, they chat more readily and freely with their fingers thus employed.

American ladies will find the custom worth imitating.

Many tedious hours will be smoothly, pleasantly passed, with the mind free, but the fingers pleasantly occupied.

An evening spent sewing or knitting, with one good reader to entertain the industrious workers, will be found very pleasant. I have known a circle of young people meet every week to work in this way, the reader being changed twice or three times in the course of the evening, and these meetings have proved so pleasant, that scarcely any member failed to plead "prior engagement" if invited out upon the evening appointed to read and sew.

It was formerly objected by the adversaries to mental cultivation in women, that the acquisition of book learning would make them neglect needlework; but so far from this being the case, the present, which is often called the age of learning, is preëminently a working age. Never were fingers more actively engaged than those of the rising female generation; braiding, embroidery, Berlin work, knitting, netting, and crochet, are all in full play. A long neglected work has been recently revived, called by the French "La Frivolité." It is very pretty evening work, partly because it does not impede conversation, for it may be carried on almost without looking at it, and partly because no other work shows to so much advantage the grace and delicacy of the hands. The simplest form of this work was anciently known under the name of Tatting, but that only consisted of a series of loops in a straight line, which were used for trimming linen articles, and which was not so pretty as La Frivolity, which has varieties which are a good imitation of point, and may be used for collars and sleeves.

I give a few specimens of pretty work for evening sewing, and refer the reader to "The Ladies' Handbook of Embroidery," published by G. G. Evans, for a full, complete description of every kind of fancy work, with specimens, patterns, and clear, plain directions.

NETTED CUFFS–These cuffs are very pretty, and easy to make. They are in plain netting, and will require white, and five shades of scarlet wool.

Set on thirty-five stitches of the white wool. Net five rows, then take a mesh a very little larger, and widen by netting two stitches in every stitch. Then net with the smallest mesh the two lightest shades, one row of each, and two rows of the other three shades. Then graduate the shades back again to white, narrowing the first row of white with the larger mesh. Net ten rows with the smaller mesh, widen again, repeat the shades of red, narrow again, and finish with the five rows of white.

KNITTED OPERA CAP.

MATERIALS REQUIRED–Half an ounce of white and half an an ounce of shaded Berlin wool will be sufficient.

Cast on a hundred stitches with white wool, and knit and pearl alternately for four rows.

Shaded wool–Knit one row plain; next row brings forward, and take two together to the end.

White wool–Knit and pearl alternately four rows. Shaded wool–Knit plain six rows.

White wool–Knit a row, decreasing it by taking the first two stitches together, and the last two. Pearl a row. Knit a row, decreasing it as before. Pearl a row.

Shaded wool–Knit a row, decreasing at the beginning and end. Next row, bring forward and take two together to the end.

White wool–Knit a row, decreasing at both ends. Pearl a row. Knit a row, decreasing as before. Pearl a row.

FOR THE PATTERN IN THE CENTRE OF THE CAP.

SHADED WOOL–1st row–Slip one.

Knit two plain stitches (a.) Wool forward. Knit one. Wool forward. Knit two together. Knit one. Knit two together. Repeat from (a.) 2nd row– Pearled.

3rd row–Slip one. Knit two plain stitches (b.) Wool forward. Knit three plain stitches. Wool forward. Slip one.

Knit two together. Pass the slipped stitch over the knitted ones. Repeat from (b.)

4th row–Pearled.

5th row–Slip one. Knit two plain stitches, (c.) Wool forward. Knit two together. Knit one. Knit two together. Wool forward. Knit one. Repeat from (c.) 6th row–Pearled.

7th row–Slip one. Knit two plain stitches (d.) Wool forward. Slip one. Knit two together. Pass the slipped stitch over the knitted ones. Wool forward. Knit three plain stitches. Repeat from (d.)

8th row–Pearled. Repeat the last eight rows.

White wool–Knit and pearl alternately for four rows; decrease at the beginning and ending of the two blank rows.

Shaded wool–Knit one blank row; decrease at the beginning and ending. Next row; bring the wool forward, knit two together to the end of the row.

White wool–Knit and pearl alternately for four rows; decrease at the beginning and ending of the two blank rows.

Knit eighteen plain stitches, run a piece of cotton through the remaining sixty-two stitches. Pearl and knit alternately, decreasing at the beginning and ending of every blank row, until you have four stitches remaining; cast them off; then take up eighteen stitches on the opposite sides, and work a piece to correspond; leaving forty-four centre stitches on the cotton.

Take up the centre stitches on a needle pointed at both ends, draw the cotton out; then pick up fourteen stitches at each end of the needle.

Shaded wool–Knit two plain rows.

White wool–Knit one plain row. Next row; wool forward, knit two together to the end of the row.

Shaded wool–Knit two plain rows and cast off. Join the two points together at the back of the cap. Fold the front at the first pattern row, and hem it to form the scallop at the edge.

Pick up eighty stitches at the back of the cap. AN ECONOMICAL POINT COLLAR.

It is well known that worked muslin collars, particularly if the work is good, very soon wear out; as the work is too heavy for the muslin, which, when it has been washed two or three times, becomes full of slits and holes, though the work is still as good as ever. When this is the case, cut the muslin off the work with a pair of sharp scissors, and lay the work on the pattern of a collar cut in paper, so as to fill the whole of the pattern. The work may be taken from two or three collars; the arrangement of it must depend upon taste. When the cut- out work is properly arranged, it must be tacked or basted to the paper pattern; and this is best done with colored thread, that no mistake may arise when the basting threads are to be drawn out. Four or six threads are then drawn from one piece of work to another, with a needle and cotton, so as to attach them together, and the loose threads are then overcast like button-holes, so as to imitate the uniting threads of point lace. When well done, with a sufficient quantity of the uniting threads, to make the work firm, these collars are handsome, and will wash and wear well.

KNITTED VEILS.

It is now customary to knit white veils of what is called Lady Betty's wool, for babies to put over their faces when they are carried out in cold weather, instead of pocket-handkerchiefs, which were formerly used for the purpose, though they were very unfit for it. Knitted veils in black silk or worsted are also worn by grown-up persons. The veils for babies are very simple in their construction; they consist of oblong pieces of knitting of any width and depth that may be required, with knitted lace at the bottom and sides, and a string case at the top. The following pattern is the most common:

Knit and pearl alternately four rows, so that there may be two of each; then bring forward and take two together an entire row. This pattern is repeated through the entire veil; and it must be observed that as many stitches must be cast on as will make it of the necessary width. The needles should be of the smallest size of bone. Any lace will do; but the following pattern, though not new, is both pretty and suitable; and has, besides, the important recomendation of being very easy.

Cast on eleven stitches and knit a row plain, then begin the pattern.

1st row–Knit three; bring forward and take two together; knit one, take two together; put the thread twice round the needle, take two together, and knit one.

2nd row–Knit two, pearl one, knit one, put the thread twice round the needle, take two together, bring forward, and knit five.

3rd row–Knit three, bring forward, take two together, knit one, bring forward, knit two, pearl one, bring forward, take two together, and knit two.

4th row–Knit two, bring forward, knit five, bring forward, take two together, knit five.

5th row–Knit three, bring forward, and take two together, knit the rest plain.

6th row–Cast off four, and knit the rest plain.

HINTS TO CROCHET-WORKERS.

Examine carefully the form of the needle, and try the hook, to ascertain that it is perfectly smooth. Some are so sharp and ill-made as to tear the cotton. Select those which are not of uniform thickness up to the hook; the best are those which are thinner there than an inch farther up.

Where the needle is not proportionally fine near the hook, it is almost impossible to keep the work even.

Chain stitch ought to be done rather loosely, as working on it afterwards contracts it, and is apt to give it a puckered appearance. It is often advisable to use a needle one size larger for making the chain than for the rest of the work, especially in edgings. It will be found much easier to work the succeeding rows when this precaution is taken. Crochet needles should be kept in a housewife similar to those used for ordinary needles. The slightest soil or rust should be effaced with fine sandpaper.

ORNAMENTAL NET FOR THE HAIR.

Take two pieces of fine silk braid, scarlet or royal blue, and a No. 3 bone crochet hook.

Make a chain of eight stitches, unite the ends, and then D.

C. the first round, putting two stitches into each loop; there will now be sixteen stitches and in the next round one long must be worked into every stitch, and two chain between each long; the round will now consist of forty-eight stitches, and we commence the pattern, or diamonds.

3rd round–Three long, two chain, four long with two chain after each, and these long put into every second loop; repeat.

4th round–Five long, two chain, five long with two chain after each, and these long put into every second loop with the exception of the fifth or last of them, which must skip two stitches instead of one; repeat.

5th round–Seven long, two chain, seven long with two chain after each, and each of these long put into every second stitch; repeat.

6th round–Five long, two chain, five long with two chain after each, and each of these long put into every other stitch, three long, two chain, five long again with two chain after each, and each put into every second stitch; repeat from beginning.

7th round–Three long, two chain, five long with two chain after each and worked in every third loop, five long, two chain, five long again with two chain after each, and these long worked as aforesaid in every third loop; repeat from beginning.

8th round–One long, two chain, five long with two chain after each and these long put into every third stitch, seven long, two chain, again five long, &c. &c.; repeat from beginning.

9th round–Six long with two chain after each and work in every third stitch, (five long, twelve long with two chain after each, these long put in every third stitch); repeat the pattern in brackets.

10th round–Nine long with two chain after them, these long being worked in every second loop, (three long, two chain, nineteen long with two chain after them, and the long worked in every second loop); repeat the pattern in brackets.

11th, 12th, and 13th rounds–A long and two chain all round, and the long being worked alternately in every second and third loop; care being taken to bring one into the position to complete each diamond as it is come to.

A crochet edging, begun with braid, and the last two or three rows worked with gold twist as nearly the size of the braid as may be, and a cord and tassels, finish off this elegant head-dress.

The cord should be run in and out through the thirteenth round. We, however, prefer a single-crochet band of some fifty stitches long and six or eight wide, worked in the same material as the net, to a cord, and this band may be finished off with a piece of gold fringe instead of tassels at the ends, or with a scallop of edging crocheted in gold twist.

DRESS GLOVE BANDS; FULL OR FRILLED SHAPE.

Take three pieces of fine embroidery chenille, and a No. 3

bone crochet hook.

Make a chain of about forty stitches, or one long enough to go round the wrist; Dc one row.

3rd row–Two long, one chain and miss a stitch–repeat this all along. Then one row Dc.

6th row–Long crochet worked very loosely, so much so as to leave these stitches at least half an inch high; two stitches to be put into every second or third loop and one in each of the others all the way along; fasten off.

Join the chenille now on to the first row, and work a similar row or frill to the one just directed, so that there be one on each side.

Run a narrow velvet through the holes of the third row and affix wider velvet ends, or chenille tassels to each extremity. Finish off with a button and loop, and flute the frill on each side over the finger to make it set.

We need scarcely say that the chenille used should be selected to match or agree with the evening dress, and that the velvet must match the chenille.

These bands may be made to look very handsome by working a row of Dc loosely and evenly along the edge of each frill with gold or silver twist, and running a band of gold or silver braid or trimming through the holes in the third row instead of velvet. Then small bullion tassels to match the twist will form a suitable and elegant finish.

These bands may be worked round and slid over the hand like muffatees, or made open as we have directed and buttoned, like the glove. The buttons should be covered with crochet, and the loops crocheted.

KNITTED UNDER HABIT SHIRT.

Three ounces of Three thread White Fleecy Wool. Pair of No. 10

Bone Knitting Pins. Cast on forty-five stitches.

Knit three rows.

4th row–Knit ten; × make two and knit two together; knit one; × knit the last six stitches.

5th row–Knit, dropping the second of each of the two made stitches all along.

Knit eight rows.

14th row–Knit ten; × make one and knit two together × repeat until six remain; knit three; make one; knit three. 15th row–Knit six; × make one and knit two together × repeat until ten remain, which knit.

Repeat these two rows three times more each, only not enlarging one (as in the end of row fourteen), every time, but only once in four rows, merely knitting the six in the intervening rows.

22nd row–Knit. Knit the next seven rows. 30th row–Same as 14th.

31st row–Same as 15th.

Keep on alternately knitting eight open, and then eight knitted rows, and enlarging one stitch at the end in every fourth row until there are a hundred and twenty-four rows.

Then decrease one stitch at the beginning or front in every other row for thirty-two rows, still continuing the pattern as before, and still enlarging one stitch in every fourth row, at the end or back. This shapes one side of the neck.

Now knit forty-eight rows without increase or decrease at either end, continuing the pattern or alternation of eight open and eight

plain knitted rows. This forms the back of the neck and the bottom of the back of the habit-shirt.

In the next thirty-two rows we diminish one in every fourth row, by knitting two together at the back, while at the same time in every fourth row, at the back, we knit two together, and make one in order to form a series of holes, or pattern parallel to that on the other side caused by enlarging in every fourth row. We also cast on one, at the opposite end, in every other row, to shape the second side of the neck. We then knit one hundred and twelve rows, having each ten knitted stitches in the front of the habit-shirt, as on the opposite side, and six at the back, and decreasing one in every fourth row, at the back, and continuing the pattern, and also the series of holes at the back.

Knit eight rows.

Knit ten stitches, × make two and knit two together; × knit six at end.

Knit all, dropping the second of each of the two made stitches. Knit two rows; cast off.

Now, with the same needles, pick up the stitches all along the right front of the habit-shirt; knit two rows and cast off. Do the same on the left front. Then pick up those of the neck, and do the same, shaping it, if necessary, by knitting two together occasionally. These finishing- off rows look pretty done in pale pink or blue wool. Button-holes may be made thus:–in the front or where the ten stitches are, and about once in thirty rows, knit three; cast off four; knit three instead of knitting the ten as usual. Next row, when we get back to the ten stitches, knit three; cast on four; knit three.

INFANT'S KNITTED SOCKS.

Half an ounce of White Lamb's Wool. Three No. 13 Knitting

Needles. Cast on Thirty stitches. 1st row–Knit.

2nd row–Knit two; make or enlarge one stitch by picking up one from the previous row and knitting it; knit all the rest.

3rd row–Knit. Repeat second and third rows alternately four times more each of them.

12th row–Knit two; make a stitch according to directions above given; knit rest until four remain; knit two together; knit two.

13th row–Knit. Repeat these two rows alternately three times more each.

20th row–Knit two; enlarge one as before directed; knit rest until two remain; enlarge one; knit two.

21st row–Knit. Repeat these two rows alternately three more times each.

28th row–Knit.

29th row–Knit fourteen stitches, and leave the other upon the needle. Take up the third needle and knit twenty rows more, of fourteen stitches each.

49th row–Knit two together; knit twelve; on the same needle, and with the same wool, cast on twenty-seven stitches.

50th row–Knit.

51st row–Knit two; knit two together; knit rest until four remain; knit two together; knit two.

52nd row–Knit. Repeat these two rows alternately twice more each.
57th row–Knit two; make one in manner directed; knit rest until four remain; knit two together; knit two.

58th row–Knit. Repeat these two rows alternately three times more each.65th row–Knit all until four remain; knit two together; knit two.

66th row–Knit. Repeat these two rows alternately four more times each.

75th row–Knit.

76th row–Cast off.

This completes the slipper portion of the sock. We now begin the instep-piece.

Take the wool and knit off ten stitches from the needle on which the twenty-seven stitches were left; knit these ten from the toe-end, or that where the twenty rows of fourteen stitches each has been made; leave the remaining seventeen stitches still on the same needle.

Knit twenty rows of ten stitches, and in every other one pick up the edge-stitch of the toe-piece and knit it with the tenth stitch, so as to unite these two portions, viz: the toe and the instep. With each stitch of the twentieth row, an edge-stitch of the side at the toe-end of the slipper must be picked up, knitted and cast off, and a neat and entire union of the toe of the slipper and the instep piece formed.

This instep piece is to be robbed in rows of four, viz: four rows in which the plain side is uppermost, and four rows in which the pearled side is uppermost.

We now commence the leg portion of the sock.

With the needle which has been left in the first side of the slipper carefully pick up the edge-stitches all along the instep-piece and side of the slipper; when this is done, there should be about fifty on the needle. Take the wool and knit all along, including the picked up stitches, and the seventeen originally on the needle. Knit two rows.

4th row–Knit two; × make two (not by picking up, but in the ordinary way, by passing the wool twice over the needle), and knit two together; knit one; × repeat.

5th row–Knit all; casting off one of each of the double made stitches. Now knit twenty rows ribbed like the instep-piece. 26th row–× Knit one; make one and knit two together; × repeat all round.

27th row–Knit.

28th row–Knit two; × make one and knit two together; knit one; × repeat.

29th, 30th, and 31st rows–Knit.

32nd row–Cast off.

Take a wool needle, thread it with wool, and sew up the sock neatly, stitch for stitch, from the top of the leg to the point of the sole; then sew the toe; turn it; put on a little rosette of raveled wool; run a ribbon in and out through the holes at rows 4 and 5, of the leg portion, and it is completed.

As this is intended for an Infant's Sock, we have ordered white wool, that being most useful; should it, however, be wished to knit socks for an older baby, the slipper may be made of Cerise, Scarlet, Pale Blue, Green, or Straw-colored wool; and the 26th, 27th, and 28th rows, of the leg portion, and the casting-off done in the color of the slipper; while the instep-piece and the rest of the sock are made in white wool.

The sock may also be enlarged by casting on extra stitches in the beginning, and adding a couple of rows to each of the divisions of the slipper part, and enough to the toe to preserve its form and symmetry.

Almost any of the open antimacassar patterns may be used for knitting the sock and instep-piece, if a light lace-like appearance is desired. The well-known rose-leaf pattern looks particularly pretty.

CHAPTER XXII

SERVANTS

An English writer, speaking of servants, says: –

"There is no question but that we should seek to perform all our duties without hope of recompense; and yet, as regards our treatment of servants, we should be especially careful that, in endeavoring to make their bodily comfort and mental improvement an object of consideration, we do not allow ourselves to dwell on the hope of gratitude or affection from them in return. Many have done so, and having, with that view, been tempted to accord unwise indulgences and to overlook serious faults, they have found that, far from gaining the love of their servants, they have incurred their contempt; and when they have perceived that their favors, unappreciated, have led but to new encroach-mends, they have hardened their hearts and rushed into an opposite extreme. Then they have considered their servants as mere machines, from which labor must be extorted by all available means.

"A man servant is rarely grateful, and seldom attached.

He is generally incapable of appreciating those advantages which, with your cultivated judgment, you know to be the most conducive to his welfare. Do you accord him regular hours, a stated allowance of work; do you refrain from sending him out because it is wet and he is unwell; do you serve yourself rather than ring for him at dinner time; he will rarely have the grace to thank you in his heart for your constant consideration. Hear him! He will thus describe a comfortable place: –'There were very few in the family; when they went out of a night, we made it up of a morning; we had nice hot suppers, and the cook made a good hash for breakfast, and we always got luncheon between that and dinner; and we were all very comfortable together, and had a friend in when we liked. Master swore at us sometimes, but often made us a present for it when he had been very violent; a good- hearted man as ever lived, and mistress was quite the lady, and never meddled with servants. It was a capital place!'

"Servants' sympathies are with their equals. They feel for a poor servant run off his legs, and moped to death; they have no feeling for a pains-taking mistress, economical both from principle and scanty means; they would (most of them) see her property wasted, and her confidence abused without compunction. It is the last effort of a virtue in a servant if, without any private reason, he should discharge his duty by informing you of the injury which you are enduring at the hands of his fellow servant. It is an effort of virtue, for it will bring down many a bitter taunt and hard work upon his faithful head. 'I never got a servant out of a place by telling tales on him,' will be said to him. Directly a servant departs, we all know, tongues, tied before, are loosed, to gain our favor by apparent candor. When it can avail us nothing, we are told. We all know this, and have said, 'Be silent now, you should have mentioned this at the time.' Supposing, then, you have the rara aviso, the servant that 'speaks at the time,' be chary of him, or let me say her, (the best servants are women.) Oh! as you value her, let her not suppose you cannot part with her. Treat her with confidence, but with strict impartiality; reprove, when necessary, mildly, but decidedly; lest she should presume (power is so tempting), and compel you, if you would retain your freedom, to let her go.

"There is one thing a man servant values beyond all that your kindness and your consideration can do for him–his liberty; liberty to eat, drink, and be merry, with your things in the company of his own friends; liberty to get the housemaid to clean his candlesticks, and bring up his coals; and the housemaid wishes for liberty to lie in bed in the morning, because she was up so late talking to John in the pantry; liberty to wear flounces and flowers. The cook desires liberty too. For this liberty, if you grant it, they will despise you; if you deny it, they will respect you. Aim at their esteem; despair of their love or gratitude; make your place what the best class of servants will value, and, though in their heart, they may not thank you for it, you will gain, perhaps, one servant out of twenty who will keep gross im- position and gross immorality at bay.

“These remarks can never be intended to deny the warm attachment of female servants to the children of their employers. Deep love, no doubt, is lavished by many women on the babe she has nursed. There is a great deal to be said on the chapter of nurses which would require to be dealt with by itself. Much wisdom is required in the administration of a nursery, to which few general rules would apply.

Cruel is the tyranny the nurse frequently practices on the parent, who often refrains from entering her nursery, not from want of love to her children, but positive dread of the sour looks which greet her. Let her be firm, let no shrinking from grieving her darling, who would ‘break his heart if his Nanna went,’ deter her from discharging the encroaching servant.

“I know a lady who was quietly informed by her nurse that she must have a ‘specified hour’ for visiting her children, for that her entering without ceremony was most inconvenient. The poor young lady, who was fully persuaded her delicate infant would die, if removed to a stranger’s hands, meekly obeyed, and though tortured by the cries of the poor sickly baby, never dared to intrude lest the nurse should abandon it. This is a true history, and the sequel may as well be given: that the nurse remained seven years, at the end of which time, having become insupportable, though really devoted to the children, she gave warning, and, though it cost her mistress bitter tears and much resolution, she was suffered to depart, and then peace entered that house.

“On the choice of servants much of the comfort of the young housekeeper depends. It often happens that her choice has been determined by appearance rather than the value of character. If such be the case, she will have many difficulties to encounter. It is, in the present day, hardly safe to take a servant if there be a single objection to character, however it may be glossed over by the person referred to on this point; for there is now an unhealthy disposition to pass over the failings of servants who have left their places, and to make them perfect in the eyes of others. In respect to sobriety, many people will not acknowledge that a servant had had the vice of drinking, but will cover the unpleasant truth in such gentle and plausible terms that it becomes difficult to comprehend how far the hint is grounded, or not.

Be assured when a lady or gentleman hesitates on this point, or on that of honesty, it is wiser not to engage a servant. Nor are you deviating from Christian charity in not overlooking a dereliction of so material a sort. The kindest plan to the vast community of domestic servants is to be rigid in all important points, and having, after a due experience, a just confidence in them, to be somewhat indulgent to errors of a more trivial nature.

"If all young housekeepers were strict upon the subject of dress, much misery to servants would be saved, much temptation avoided, and self-reproach prevented. Instead of this kind, and wise, and matronly particularity, a type of the good, old-fashioned common sense of our grandmothers, ladies now countenance their ladies'- maids in discontinuing caps, or, if they have caps, in wearing flowers and lace, flowered gowns, and other items of little apparent moment in detail, but of much importance to a community as serviceable to the public when well managed and respectable, as they are odious and noxious when immoral or insolent. After these cruel indulgences, ladies marvel when they find servants rise above their station and that they will not bear even a mild reproof; they wonder that a plain, useful servant is nowhere to be met with. There is now no medium between the fine lady with mittens and flowers who dresses your hair, and the dirty sloven of a lodging-house. All housemaids must now be upper housemaids; cooks must be cooks and housekeepers. The homely housemaid–that invaluable character in her way–is indeed difficult to be found; and, at a time when cleanliness is at its zenith, the rarity is to discover any one who will clean.

All, except the raw country girl, expect to have deputies; and, if we go on to perfection in this unhealthy system, we shall soon have no working servants above twenty years of age. The consequence is that a greater number of servants are kept in every household than formerly in similar families; many of these minerals are corrupted by congregating together and by idleness. The loud and crying complaints of the worthlessness of this class are but too justly founded.

That they are more mercenary than ever, is owing to the pernicious system which lifts them up above their condition, but fails to elevate them in the moral standard. In the scale of virtue, they sink lower and lower; in the outward attributes they are, as they consider it, raised in character and improved in appearance.

"But is it so? The beauty of everything is fitness. Is the half-fine, unlade-like, yet lady-like creature, who answers to your dressing-room bell, half so respectable as the old-fashioned, plainly dressed, careful, homely maiden of your young days? Is it not with a feeling of disgust that you turn from the attempted finery, and sign for plain collars, and caps undecked by flowers, again? I think, among the best-bred, the most sensible, and, indeed, the most highly born people of a superior stamp, this disgust is so strong that, in some families, a grave and suitable costume is introduced for the female servants, and the effect is satisfactory, both on the appearance and on the mode of thinking of these persons. But this wise, and therefore kind plan is far from being general; and I have heard that a lady's- maid complained to her mistress that she found herself the subject of ridicule, owing to her not wearing silks, and indeed satins, as the other ladies'-maids did.

"It becomes the duty of ladies of influence to rise above the silly vanity which, I fear, affects some of them, of seeing their ladies'-maids as smart as ladies, and to oppose innovations on the decencies of society, so pernicious to the class upon whom much of our comfort depends. In setting out in life, a young married lady ought to be more than ordinarily strict in these matters, for her inexperience will certainly be taken advantage of to some extent. If she is rich enough to have a housekeeper, let her endeavor to select one of strict religious faith, plain in attire, grave, but kind, and of good sense, and even intelligence; for cultivation of mind will never, whatever may be stated, detract from the utility of a servant. It is absurd to attribute to the diffusion of knowledge the deterioration of servants; it is rather owing to the scant amount of knowledge among them. Most superficial is the education about which so much is said and written; were servants more thoroughly grounded in many branches of knowledge, they would be wiser, less rapacious, more systematic, and better contented than they are. They are wretched reasoners, generally losing sight of their own true interest, and grasping at that which is unreal and visionray. If they were better educated, this would not be the case; they would be less vain, less credulous; they would know what qualities to respect; they would weigh the advantages of their lot; and they would work better as servants. They would give mind, where now they only give hands; and their acquirements, taken from school as they are in very early youth, are not ever likely to be such as to make the routine of their work distasteful to them, from over refinement or cultivation.

"It is always desirable to have, if possible, servants of one faith.

But if it so happens that you have a Roman Catholic servant and a Protestant in your service, you are bound to allow each the free exercise of her religion, and you ought not to respect them if, out of interest, they will conform to yours. An exercise of authority on this point amounts, in my opinion, to an act of tyranny, and it can only tend to promote insincerity, and, perhaps, engender skepticisms in its object.

Nothing is, indeed, so dangerous as to unsettle the faith of the lower classes, who have neither time nor opportunity of fairly considering subjects of religious controversy.

"While on the subject of servants, I must deprecate the over-indulgence of the present system towards them. Formerly they were treated with real kindness, but it was the kindness that exacted duty in return, and took a real interest in the welfare of each servant. The reciprocal tie in former times between servant and master was strong, now it is wholly gone. The easy rule of masters and mistresses proceeds far more from indifference than from kindness of heart; for the real charity is to keep servants steadily to their duties. They are a class of persons to whom much leisure is destruction; the pursuits of their idle hours are seldom advantageous to them, and theirs are not minds which can thrive in repose. Idleness, to them, is peculiarly the root of all evil, for, if their time is not spent in vicious amusements, it is often passed in slander, discontent, or vanity.

In writing thus, I do not recommend a hard or inconsiderate system to servants. They require, and in many instances, they merit, all that can be done to alleviate a situation of servitude. They ought not to be the slaves of caprice or the victims of temper. Their work should be measured out with a just hand; but it should be regularly exacted in as much perfection as can be expected in variable and erring human nature.

"Another point on which I would recommend firmness is that of early hours. In this respect example is as important as precept; but however uncertain you may be yourself; I would not relax a rule of that kind. For every comfort during the day depends upon the early rising of your servants. Without this, all their several departments are hurried through or neglected in some important respect.

"Your mode of address to servants must be decisive, yet mild. The authoritative tone I do not recommend. It is very unbecoming to any young person, and it rarely attains the end desired; but there is a quiet dignity of deportment which few servants ever can resist. This should be tempered with kindness, when circumstances call it forth, but should never descend to familiarity. For no caution is more truly kind than which confines servants strictly to their own sphere.

"Much evil results from the tendency, more especially of very young, or of very old mistresses of families, to partiality. Commonly, one servant becomes the almost avowed favorite; and it is difficult to say whether that display of partiality is more pernicious to the servant who is the object of it, or to the rankling and jealous minds of the rest of the household. It is true that it is quite impossible to avoid entertaining a greater degree of confidence in some servants than in others; but it should be shown with a due regard to the feelings of all. It is, of course, allowable towards those who take a decidedly responsible and confidential situation in a household. Still, never let such persons assume the reins of government; let them act the part of helmsman to the vessel, but not aspire to the control of the captain.

"It is generally wise and right, after a due experience of the principles and intentions of servants, to place confidence in their honesty, and to let them have the comfort of knowing that you do so. At the same time, never cease to exercise a system of supervision. The great principle of housekeeping is regularity; and without this (one of the most difficult of the minor virtues to practice) all efforts to promote order must be ineffectual. I have seen energetic women, clever and well-intentioned, fail in attaining a good method, owing to their being uncertain in hours, governed by impulse, and capricious. I have seen women, inferior in capacity, slow, and apathetic, make excellent heads of families, as far as their household was concerned, from their steadiness and regularity. Their very power of enduring monotony has been favorable to their success in this way, especially if they are not called upon to act in peculiar and difficult cases, in which their actual inferiority is traceable.

But these are not the ordinary circumstances of life.

"In closing these remarks on the management of servants, let me exhort you never to forget that they are fellow-laborers, in the life of probation, with ourselves; let us not embitter their lives by harshness, or proffer to them temptation from carelessness and over-indulgence. Since all that is given us of this world's goods is but in trust, let us regard our servants as beings for whose conduct, while under our control, we are more or less responsible. It is true that, if they come to us with morals wholly depraved, it is not likely that the most strenuous exertions can amend them; but many waver between good and evil. Let us endeavor to excite in their minds a respect for virtue, to give them motives for industry, inducements to save their wages. Those who have large households should not deem the morals of the meanest of their servants beneath their investigation, or too obscure for their influence to reach."

Some attention is absolutely necessary, in this country, to the training of servants, as they come here from the lowest ranks of English and Irish peasantry, with as much idea of politeness as the pig domesticated in the cabin of the latter.

Opening the door seems a simple act, yet few servants perform it in a proper, respectful manner. Let your servant understand that the door must be opened immediately after the bell rings. Visitors, from neglect of this rule, will often ring several times, and finally leave the door. I have known an instance when in a case of severe illness, the patient lost the visit of the doctor, who, after ringing some minutes, was obliged to pay other visits, and could not return to the sufferer's house until several hours later.

When opening the door some servants hold it ajar and hold a long parley with the person on the steps, as if afraid they wished to enter for the purpose of murder or theft.

Train them to answer the door promptly, speak politely to anyone who may be there, excuse you, if necessary, to visitors in courteous terms, or, if you are in, show the callers into the parlor, take their card, and come back quickly with your answer.

CHAPTER XXIII

ON AYOUNG LADY'S CONDUCT WHEN CONTEMPLATING MARRIAGE

THE following chapter, met with in a recent perusal of an English work for young ladies, strikes me as so admirable, and so appropriate in this place, that I quote the chapter entire:

"The difficulties and trials of life have only just begun when a young lady fancy herself to be of sufficient importance to become the theme of animadversion. She knows little of the true importance of self-control, until she experiences the first indications of preference shown her by the other sex.

"Such indications are often manifested, whilst she to whom they are directed, is wholly unprepared to analyze her own feelings, before her opinions upon what she has seen are by any means developed; before she has even considered adequately, on what her happiness depends; before she has discernment to reject what is frivolous, or wisdom to prefer what is good. This is more especially the case in the highest and lowest classes, in which, by a strange anal-logy, they either rush into the marriage state whilst children, or wait until the bloom and hopes of youth have forever passed away, in order to form interested matches. The matured period of five-and-twenty to thirty, is passed by the lower classes in the single state in labor to gain subsistence; after thirty, or even forty, we often find them marrying. But the majority have sealed their own fate before the age of twenty.

“In high life, the same haste to dispose of daughters prevails as among the lowest classes. At seventeen, most of our belles of fashion expect to receive proposals. If they do not marry within a few years after their introduction, they have a mortified sense of having lost time–that the expectations of friends and of parents have not been fulfilled; those others have ‘gone off’ before them. The next ten years are often a period of subdued vexation, and the sweetness and content- mend of the original character is impaired. About seven or eight and twenty, the views of life are sobered–the expectations chastened–a renovation takes place–women again become agreeable; their minds must in the lapse of time, even with a miserable store of observation, have improved. They then often marry–and, if the union be not a mere effort of despair, if it be based on sound and holy principles, and on good sense, there is, for both parties engaged, a great likelihood of happiness.

“But it may be naturally contended, that not to all young ladies the opportunities of which I write; those indications of preference arrive not to all. I am inclined to believe that, with good temper, pleasing manners, and respectable connections, there exists, in modern society, very few young ladies who have not received under various circumstances, some marks of preference, more or less decided. Beauty and plainness are arbitrary, not positive, terms. Unless there be any actual deformity, any great infirmity, in which case I think it were cruel to pre-suppose the likelihood of such indications, there is no one, that I hardly ever met with, who has not had, on some grounds, her par-titans and admirers. The plain is often particularized as elegant; tastes vary: even a sour look I have heard admired as sensible, cold manners eulogized as correct. Opinion, however it may generally verge to the correct, springs from so many sources, it is so governed by association of ideas, such trifles may guide it, that I am never surprised at the latitude given to personal encomium nor at the endless variety and incongruity of human judgment. It is well that all have a chance of being approved, admired, beloved, and it remains for them to avail themselves of those possibilities which contribute so much to happiness. For we are sympathizing beings, and a law of our nature makes us look for a return of sympathy. We are sent here to form ties, and to love, and to be loved, whether the term applies to parental, or filial, or fraternal love–or whether it respects the less sure and more fitful experiences of love, in its ordinary sense.

“I do not blame the parents who instill into their children of both sexes a desire to be married. I think those who teach the young a different lesson deceives them. Marriage, with all its chances, its infelicities, its sacrifices, is seldom so infelicitous, so uncertain, so full of sacrifice, as the single state.

Life must have some objects, and those objects must be progressive. The mind is happier and healthier with such interests, even if sorrow comes along with them, than in its solitude, its desolate freedom from care, when having, as the phrase is, no troubles of the conjugal sort to disturb its tranquility. I therefore do not censure those who desire to see their daughters happily and suitably established in life.

It is the indiscreet and vulgar haste, the indelicacy, the low mercenary views, and the equally low ambition to compass a splendid match, which is blamable and revolting in the parental conduct.

"Many are, however, blessed with guides and guardians of very different characters; with parents, whose lofty natures not only reject such unworthy notions, but somewhat incline to the extreme of repelling all advances for their daughters. In either case, the conduct of a young lady may be the same. It is she who must form her own destiny in points on which none can effectively aid her. It is she who is to be the happy wife, or the wretched victim; and it is to her that these observations of admonition and of warning are addressed. Let us suppose her young, of course, attractive in appearance, of good birth, and some fortune. I hear except heiresses, who, being anomalies, deserve a particular paragraph for themselves. But let us suppose that no obstacle of family or connection interferes to check the approach of a suitor.

"The eyes of her family and of her young friends are upon her, when a young lady receives the first indications of preference. She is generally ashamed of it. This is the first sentiment of a modest and ingenious mind, and it is one indication, in my opinion, of the impropriety of early marriages.

Nature seems still to wish to keep the young and blushing girl apart from that connection which entails grave and arduous duties. But Nature's voice is far less often heard than that of her adversary, expediency. I must, therefore, shape my injunctions to that which exists, not to that which we would wish to exist.

"Almost sinking under this painful sense of shame, this novel disturbance of her usual set of feelings, a young girl catches at the first reed to save herself from observation and detection. I mean detection of her perception of those which others may or may not see. She seizes upon ridicule. She pretends to laugh at one, whom sometimes her youthful romantic fancy dwells upon in a very different sense. She laughs at the foibles, supposed or real, of her admirer: she plays a dangerous game. If any of those to whom she imparts her witticisms are malevolently disposed or thought-less, she runs a risk either of wounding the feelings of a man whom she does not like, or of losing the regard of one whom she might in time not only esteem, but love.

"Another effect of such attentions as awakens a consciousness in a young lady's mind, is the gratification of vanity, perhaps until then latent in her heart. The first preference is apt to upset the reason of its object as of him who shows it. The word vanity does not seem to imply danger. Vanity is generally considered an innocent failing; but it is innocent only as some kinds of food are to a healthy subject. On a weak, or even on an inexperienced mind, it acts, sometimes, fatally for the vein. A girl is either carried away by admiration so as to be flippant and foolish, or she is blinded by her vanity to the failings of the man who first admires her. She is intoxicated with the notion of an offer of marriage; she imagines, in her simplicity, effervesced as it is by the infusion of flattered vanity, that she has inspired such an attachment as will never be recovered, should she prove averse to it. Many an engagement has been formed under this conviction, and fulfilled only to prove its fallacy, for the love which was supposed too strong to survive disappointment, has expired in the fruition of its hopes.

"To guard against either of these risks to happiness, a well-educated girl should endeavor, in this, to exercise her judgment.

She should be sincere.

She is blameable to ridicule the attentions which are meant as complimentary to her. They ought to be at least regarded with respect.

"Should they not be acceptable, she is inexcusable to requite them with levity and disdain. Let her reflect how she would like such conduct herself. Besides, she is often making a bitter enemy; perhaps she is exciting fierce and unamiable sentiments in one who otherwise might have been regarded as a mild and worthy individual. Let her be undeceived if she supposes that in doing, she is carrying herself with dignity, or acquiring any added admiration from others. She ceases, in thus acting, to support the character-istics of a gentlewoman, which are mildness, courtesy, and reserve. If she cherishes, in spite of her pretended disgust, a secret partiality for the individual who distinguishes her, if she is lowering the esteem of a man whom she prefers, she not only incurs the hazard of losing his regard, but she is scattering ridicule on one whom she afterwards avows as her choice. In that case, she is lowering herself, or she is sowing the seeds of distrust in the minds of those who know her–she is, perhaps, frustrating and delaying her own happiness. Let her act with candor, with consideration, with good sense, and all this web which her folly would weave around her will not embarrass her. Let her not madly and obstinately resist the advice of those on whose affection to her, and on whose good judgment, experience has taught her to rely. Let her be a child in nothing except humility; let her listen to counsels; yet her own heart must decide for her–none can know so well as herself its secret throbs, or the impression of dislike or of regard which has been made upon it.

"I am, I confess, an enemy to trying to like a person, as I have rarely seen such a mental process end in happiness to either party. If an advantageous proposal offer itself, it is wiser decidedly to refuse it, than to trust to the slow growth of affection, upon a foundation of original dislike. And the trials of married life are such, –its temptations to irritability and contention are so manifold, its anxieties so unforeseen and so complicated, that few can steer their difficult course safely and happily, unless there be a deep and true attachment, to contend with all the storms which may arise in the navigation.

"Deeply impressed with this conviction, should it be the lot of any young lady in whom I were interested to form a real, well-grounded attachment to a man whose circumstances were indifferent, I should counsel her, provided she can depend on the character and exertions of the object so beloved, to risk the event of an engagement–to trust to time and Providence, and to marry whenever means were afforded,– convinced as I am, that patience, and trust, and true affection, raise the character, and are acceptable in the eyes of our Heavenly Father. But in such a case, she must school her mind to meet the anxieties which attend limited means. She must prepare herself, by habits of diligence and economy, to become a poor man's wife. She must learn the difficult art of doing well upon a little. She must not, be she in any rank of life, think to indulge with impunity to herself in every refinement and luxury when she is single; and, upon her marriage, imagine that she can attain the practice of economy by wishing it. Such metamorphoses are out of reason–out of nature. She must endeavor before the bond which ties her to poverty is framed, to understand the duties of housekeeping, the mysteries of needle-work.

She must lay down to herself rules of expenditure suitable, in part, to her future condition in life. Many a wife, thus commencing, has laid the foundations of future fortune, at least independence, to her husband, by keeping his mind at peace, during his progress up the steep ascent to professional, or clerical, or literary fame. Many a home has been cheered by domestic forbearance, and placid submission to circumstances, even in the higher classes, during the life-time of a father, or in the course of those long expectancies, in which the fortitude and principle of many of the aristoc-racy are tried and proved. But the self-denial, the cheerfulness, the good management, the strict principle, are formed at an earlier period than that in which a young lady gives her hand to him whom she has chosen, in spite of the frown of fortune, as her husband.

"Of this let the young be assured; there are few situations in life, in which a man, young, and in health, cannot meliorate his circumstances, if he possess energy and if he be stimulated by a true affection. The clergyman, with humble stipend, often hopeless from want of interest, has leisure–he has had education. He may, if he desires to assist himself, have recourse to literary labor, or to tuition. If he make not such exertion, during the course of an engagement, what hope can there be of him in future life?

"The young lawyer, however tedious his advancement, however few his opportunities, may also distinguish himself in a literary career. Innumerable are the subjects open to one of such a profession. How few avail themselves of the chance! Upon this rely, the man truly in love will make the effort. To the military man, though perhaps he may be less qualified, the same course is open, in a degree. Some of our best travels, some of our most amusing literary productions, have been the compositions of military men. And the advantage of this mode of aiding a small fortune is, that a man not only does not lower, but he raises his position by it, if his works are moral, written in a gentlemanly spirit, and affording information. However deep the attachment, however agreeable the object, if a man be indisposed to help himself to independence and competence, I should counsel no woman to continue an engagement formed in the expectation of 'times mending.' When I advocate the indulgence of attachment, it is to worthy, not to unworthy, objects.

"I now come to speak of moral character. Hard is the contest between affection and expediency, when it is raised by the question of circumstances. But harder still is it, when its result is to be decided upon an inquiry into moral conduct. I know not a more cruel situation than that when the heart is bestowed on one whom the judgment could not approve. I know not one which should be more strictly guarded against, not only by parents and friends, but (for I would impress on very young lady how much she may prove the best guardian of her own happiness) by the female heart itself.

"With every vigilance, with little to blame, little to repent, such cases will occur in this world. The feelings are interested, but the judgment distrusts. Happy is it for those who know the combat between affection and principle only in single life, and have not the misery of encountering so severe a destiny when it can no longer be remedied–who know not how to fulfill the vow to honor what is proved to be unworthy–and yet still must love,–for the affections once given, are little in our own power.

"In such a case occurring to the young, in, perhaps, a first attachment, I think they must be guided by friends. I am not an advocate for the interference of friends: where it is much a question of a long and contingent engagement–a question of being married at once, or of waiting, in some uncertainty–a question of ease or discomfort, of limited means or luxury–in such instances, if the moral character be unexceptionable, it is the duty of parents to point out all the risk, all the disadvantages, but to leave the heart to form its own decisions. Let them not seek to wrench the affections from the channel in which they flowed, when fresh from their source. They cannot know how deep the channel is–they cannot know if ever those pure and beautiful waters will flow in peace again when once hastily turned aside. But in cases of moral character, of right or wrong, the affair is wholly different, and the strictest parental authority ought, upon due inquiry, to be exercised.

"Submission and self-control are then the duty of the young sufferer–for a sufferer she truly is;–no page of her after-history could unfold a bitterer pang. But peace and hope come at last–the struggle, though violent, leaves behind it none of that corroding sorrow, which would have accompanied the acquiescence of parents in a union un- blessed by a Providence, whose will is that all should be pure, even as He above is pure. Had your fond wishes been granted, young and trusting being, how fearful would have been your condition! For there is no suspicion so revolting to an innocent mind as that which unseats love from his throne in our affections, and places another in his stead. Be assured of this–little can you know of the moral conduct of the other sex; little is it desirable that you should know. But whenever improprieties are so flagrant as to be matters of conversation; when the good shun, and the pitying forbear to excuse; be assured some deeper cause than you can divine exists for the opprobrium. Think not that your empire over affections thus wasted can be a real one. It is transient, it will not last–it will not bring reformation–it will never be adequately requited. Throw yourself on the judgment of those whose interest in you has been life-long, or of such as you know truly regard your happiness; conquer the unhal-lowed preference; pray for support and guidance; trust in Him who 'catereth for the sparrow.'

"But, when the commencement of life is chilled by so cruel a sorrow–when the blight has fallen on the bud–we must not only look up to heavenly aid, we must take every means of care for an unfortunate, and, when once the judgment is convinced of the unworthiness of the object, a blameable attachment. How often, in the Psalms, in the Gospels, the word 'Help' is reiterated!

We are to help ourselves–we must work for our heavenly peace on earth–the mental discipline, to prosper, must be aided by divine grace, but its springs must be from our own hearts. And, to fulfill the will of God in this, as in the other events of life, let us take such means as may aid us in the work of self-government.

"In the first place, let employment be resorted to by the sorrowing, do not indulge in tears; do not sit alone: abstain, for a time, from music; abstain from the perusal of poetry, or works of imagination. They still soften the feelings and open up the sources of grief. Read works of fact–endeavor to occupy yourself with the passing events of the world. And, when the overburdened heart cannot be comforted, or its thoughts diverted–for there will be moments too mournful to be resisted–go forth into the fields, go to the houses of the poor–see the goodness and mercy of God–see too, the patience and long-suffering of the poor, who may often set the rich an example of fortitude. Occupy yourself, if you can, with children;

their freshness, their joyful unconsciousness, the elasticity of their spirits, will sustain and draw you from yourself, or have recourse to the soothing calmness of the aged. Hear them converse upon the affairs of life; how they appreciate the importance of each passing event, as a traveler does the ruts and inequalities of the road he has traversed. How their confidence in the effect of time sustains you! and you turn from them, reflecting on all that the happiest of them must necessarily have endured. Be assured of your own recovery, under an influence so certain.

"Avoid young persons of your own age. If possible, except to a sister, whose deep interest in you will probably teach her a superior lesson, never confide in young friends, a similar trial as that to which I have referred. In general, your resolution will be weakened, your feelings re-excited, your confidence in your best advisers will be shaken. For the young usually take the part of the rejected lover– they delight in that dangerous species of sympathy which flatters with hope. They are naturally incredulous as to the delinquencies of a man who is agreeable, and in love; they incline to the notion of the hard-heartedness of fathers, un-cles, and elder brothers; and even, if they happen to possess good sense, or to exercise the rare quality of prudence in such matters, the very communication of any sorrow, or the recital of any feelings, gives not only a merely temporary relief, but deadens that sorrow and strengthens those feelings, which grow every time they are imparted. If you wish to recover–and, if you have a sound and well-disposed mind, you will wish to recover–you must, after the first burst of grief is over, speak but rarely of a theme too painful and delicate to bear the contact of rude minds–too dangerous to dwell upon with those of a kindlier and loftier nature.

"To your female relations–to your mother, more especially, too great an openness cannot be practiced on these points, but openness does not imply a perpetual recurrence to a theme, which must wear out patience and exhaust all but maternal sympathy, in time. For maternal sympathy is exhaustless; be generous, and restrain, from that very reflection, the continual demand upon its flow. The first person to consult, the last to afflict–a mother–should not be the victim of her daughter's feelings. Her judgment should not be weakened by the incessant indulgence of a daughter's sorrows.

"I would, on many grounds, caution the young against hasty engagements. It seems extraordinary that the welfare of a life should often be determined upon the acquaintance of a few weeks. The principles, it is true, may be ascertained from the knowledge of others, the manners may please, the means and expectations may all be clearly understood.

But the temper–that word of unspeakable import–the daily habits, the power of constancy–these are not to be known without a long and severe examination of the motives, and a daily observation of the conduct, of others. Very little suffices to mar the happiness of married life, if that little proceed in the character of a man, from a rooted selfishness.

"It is true, in regard to this defect, that much may be done by a wife to meliorate a vice of character which is, in some, only the result of never having had their feelings developed.

But if there exist not this excuse–if, in spite of ties, which are dearer to an affectionate mind than existence; you find a man preferring his own comfort to that of those whom he professes to love–if you find him imperious to his servants, dictatorial to sisters, on cool terms with brothers, there is little hope that the mental disease will ever be rooted out, so as to leave a healthy character of mind. Examine well into this point; for a hasty temper may be remedied, and even endured–but the deep, slow, sullen course of a selfish nature wears away hope, imparts a cankering care, and, with it, often disgust. No defect is so little to be resisted as selfishness. It creeps into every detail; it infects the minutest affairs of life as well as the greatest concerns. It depresses the humble sufferer from its baneful effects; it irritates the passions of the unamiable. Study well the character in trifles; nor venture to risk your bark on the sea of matrimony, unless you know well how far this man, whom you might prefer, is free from this deadly infection. View him, if possible, in his home, before you pledge your faith with his–or, if that be not practicable, reflect upon the general course of his actions, of his sentiments, and endeavor dispassionately to judge them, as best you may."

CHAPTER XXIV

BRIDAL ETIQUETTE

IN preparing a bridal outfit, it is best to furnish the wardrobe for at least two years, in under-clothes, and one year in dresses, though the bonnet and cloak, suitable for the coming season, are all that are necessary, as the fash-ions in these articles change so rapidly. If you are going to travel, have a neat dress and cloak of some plain color, and a close bonnet and veil. Avoid, as intensely vulgar, any display of your position as a bride, whilst traveling.

Take, first, the weddings at church. In this case none are invited to the ceremony accepting the family, and the reception is at the house of the bride's mother, or nearest relative, either on the wedding-day or upon her return from the bridal tour.

In sending out the invitations, let the card of the bridegroom and that of the bride be tied together with a white ribbon, and folded in the note paper upon which is printed the name of the bride's mother, with the date of the reception-day, thus: –

MRS. JOHN SAUNDERS

At home, Thursday, Oct. 16th, from 11 till 2.

No. 218, —- St.of course, the hours and dates vary, but the form is the same.

If there is no bridal reception upon the wedding day, the cards are worded: –

MR. AND MRS. JAMES SMITH.

At home, Wednesdays, On, and after, June 6th. No. 17, —- St.

Tie the card with the bride's maiden name upon it to this one.

Enclose the invitation in a white envelope, and tie it with white satin ribbon. If you send cake, have it put in a white box, and place the note outside the cover, tying it fast with white satin ribbon.

The bride's dress must be of white entirely. If she is married in the morning, a plain white silk, white mantle, and white bonnet, full trimmed with orange flowers, with a plain veil, is the most suitable dress, and she may wear a richer one at her reception, when she returns from her bridal tour.

As soon as the carriages come, let the bridesmaids, and relatives set off first. –Last, the bride with her parents. The bride, her parents, and the bridesmaids go immediately to the vestry, where they meet the bridegroom, and the groomsmen. The father of the bride gives her his arm and escorts her to the altar, the bridegroom walking on the other side. Then follow the bridesmaids and groomsmen in couples.

When they reach the altar the bridegroom removes his right-hand glove, but the bride keeps hers on until the clergyman takes the ring. The first bridesmaid then removes the left-hand glove, and it is not resumed. The bridesmaids should wear white dresses, white mantles, and bonnets, but not veils or orange flowers.

The bride and groom leave the church first, after the ceremony is over, and take the carriage with the parents of the bride, and the others follow in the order in which they came.

If there is a breakfast or morning reception, the bride will not change her dress until she retires to put on her traveling attire. If the wedding takes place in the evening at church, to be followed by a full-dress reception at home, the bride should wear a white lace dress over satin, or any other material to suit her own taste, a veil, falling from her head to her feet, fastened to the hair by a coiffure of orange flowers; white kid gloves, and white satin slippers. A bouquet, if carried, should contain only white flowers.

The bridesmaids may wear white, or some thin, light-colored material over white, a head-dress of flowers, and carry bouquets of mixed flowers.

When the wedding takes place at home, let the company assemble in the front drawing-room, and close the doors between that and the back room. In the back room, let the bride, bridegroom, bridesmaids, and groomsmen, the parents of the bride, and the clergyman, assemble. The clergyman should stand in the center of the room, the bride and groom before him, the bridesmaids ranged beside the bride, the groomsmen beside the bridegroom. Then open the doors and let the ceremony begin. This arrangement saves that awkwardness attendant upon entering the room and taking the position before a large company.

After the ceremony is over, the parents of the bride speak to her first; then her near relatives, and not until then the other members of the company.

It is not usual now to have dancing, or even music, at a wedding, and the hour is named upon the cards, at which the guests are expected to retire.

A very pretty effect is produced in the wedding group, if the bride wears pure white, and the bridesmaids white, with flowers and trimmings of a different color. Thus, one in white, with a head-dress and trimming of green leaves; another, white, with blue ribbons and forget-me-nots; another, white, with pink roses and ribbons.

If the wedding is in the morning, the bride and family may wear full dress; in that case the shutters should be closed and the rooms lighted as in the evenings.

Let the supper be laid early, and ready when the ceremony is over, that the guests may pass into the dining-room, if they wish, as soon as they have spoken to the bride. If a morning wedding, let the table be set as for an evening wedding.

If the bride gives a reception at her own house, after her return from her bridal tour, she should not wear her wedding-dress. If in the evening, a supper should be set.

If a morning reception, let her wear a handsome light silk, collar and sleeves of lace. Wine and cake are sufficient to hand to each guest at a morning reception. At an evening reception let the bride wear full dress, but not her wedding-dress.

At parties given to a newly married couple, the bridesmaids and groomsmen are always invited, and the whole party is expected to wear the same dresses as at the wedding.

CHAPTER XXV

HINTS ON HEALTH

THE universal remark of travelers visiting America, as well as the universal complaint of Americans themselves, relates to the ill health of the fairer portion of the community. Look where you will, go to any city in the vast Union, the remark and complaint will be made everywhere.

With every natural advantage of climate, yet from North to South, East to West the cry resounds.

Foreigners, admiring the dark-eyed girls of the southern states or the blondes of the northern ones, will remark, with comments upon beauty: –

"But she looks delicate, poor thing! –Not strong? Ah! I thought not, none of the American women are, and how soon these young beauties fade!"

It seems to me, amongst the subjects treated in my present work, that a few words on health will not come amiss.

"Light and sunshine are needed for your health. Get all you can; keep your windows clean. Do not block them up with curtains, plants, or bunches of flowers; –these last poison the air, in small rooms.

"Fresh air is needful for your health. As often as you can, open all your windows, if only for a short time in bad weather; in fine weather, keep them open, but never sit in draughts. When you get up, open the windows wide, and throw down the bed-clothes, that they may be exposed to fresh air some hours, daily, before they are made up. Keep your bed-clothes clean; hang them to the fire when you can.

Avoid wearing at night what you wear in the day. Hang up your day-clothes at night. Except in the severest weather, in small, crowded sleeping-rooms, a little opening at the top of the window-sash is very important; or you will find one window pane of perforated zinc very useful. You will not catch cold half so easily by breathing pure air at night. Let not the beds be directly under the windows. Sleeping in exhausted air creates a desire for stimulants.

"Pure water is needful for your health. Wash your bodies as well as your faces, rubbing them all over with a coarse cloth. If you cannot wash thus every morning, pray do so once a week. Crying and cross children are often pacified by a gentle washing of their little hands and faces–it soothes them. Babies' heads should be washed carefully, every morning with soap. No scurf should be suffered to remain upon them. Get rid of all slops and dirty water at once. Disease, and even death, is often the consequence of our own negligence. Wash your rooms and passages at least once a week, use plenty of clean water; but do not let your children stay in them while they are wet, it may bring on croup or inflammation of the chest. If you read your Bibles, which it is earnestly hoped you do, you will find how cleanliness, both as to the person and habitation, was taught to the Jews by God himself; and we read in the 4th chapter of Nehemiah that when they were building their second temple, and defending their lives against their foes, having no time for rest, they contrived to put off their clothes for washing. It is a good old saying, that cleanliness is next to godliness.

"Wholesome food is needful for your health. Buy the most strengthening. Pieces of fresh beef and mutton go the farthest. Eat plenty of fresh salt with food; it prevents disease. Pray do not let your children waste their pennies in tarts, cakes, bull's eyes, hardbake, sour fruit, &c., they are very unwholesome, and hurt the digestion. People would often, at twenty years of age, have a nice little sum of money to help them on in the world, if they had put in the savings'

bank the money so wasted; Cocoa is cheaper and much more nourishing than tea. None of these liquids should be taken hot, but lukewarm; when hot they inflame the stomach, and produce indigestion.

“We are all made to breathe the pure air of heaven, and therefore much illness is caused by being constantly in-doors. Let all persons make a point, whenever it is possible, of taking exercise in the open air for at least an hour and a half daily. Time would be saved in the long run by the increased energy and strength gained, and by the warding off of disease.”

Let it not be supposed that it is not the duty of every young lady to take due care of her health, and to preserve in all its power of utility every portion of vigor which has been bestowed on her.

With many young ladies, it appears to be a maxim to do everything in their power to destroy the health which is so much wanted in the real business of life, and which forms so important a requisite to happiness. In the first place, as to hours–they never leave the ball-room until utterly exhausted, and scarcely fit to crawl to bed. The noon- day sleep, the scarcely touched breakfast, that most important meal, are followed by preparations for the succeeding night’s pleasures, or in head-aching morning calls, driving about in a close carriage, or lounging on a sofa, in an overheated room, reading novels.

Dressing follows; the warm wrapper or dress is thrown aside; over the tightly drawn corsets is fastened a flimsy dress, with an inch of sleeve; the neck laid bare; thin stockings drawn on, in place of thick ones, and the consumption-seeker goes forth to the ball-room again.

“At times, you miss from the gay assemblage some former ornament–you inquire about her–she has taken cold. Inflammation of the lungs, caught it in an accidental draught of air by one of these fair half-dressed beings, carried off, not long since, one of the gayest and fairest of the belles of the season–after an illness of three days.

“Preservation of the health ought, from an early stage of existence, to be enforced as a duty upon the young. To walk daily; to have daily recourse, in summer, even twice a day, to the sponging with cold water, or the shower-bath;–to eat sufficiently of plain, nutritious food; to keep the mind calm–these are duties; –they should be habitually exercised. Care should be taken not to come out heated, with a shawl just pinned across the shoulders, from a heated room. Where there is delicacy of the lungs or windpipe, yet not sufficient to render a withdrawal from evening parties necessary, the use of a respirator at night is desirable. It is usual to have recourse to this valuable invention only when disease is actually existing–as a preventive, it is neglected. Yet, preserving the temperature of a warm room, it is an excellent precaution, and can easily be assumed when the shawl or cloak is put on. The atmosphere of a city is destructive where there is any pulmonary delicacy, and who shall say, where there is not pulmonary delicacy? In this climate, there is a tendency to it, more or less, in almost every family, –at all events, it is too easily induced in our predisposed constitutions, by cold, aided by the debilitating effect of heated rooms and an artificial mode of existence, and accelerated also, most decidedly, by bared shoulders. For, in this climate, it is scarcely ever safe to lay bare that portion of the frame, the back and chest in which the lungs are seated; and, although custom may greatly lead to diminish the injurious effects, the sudden chill may strike, and may never be recovered.

"During every season, certain people have 'head colds,' coughs, and 'feverish colds.' These are produced by certain states of climate acting on certain states of constitution. At particular seasons such complaints abound–at others they abound still more; and again, from some singularity, they prevail so much that people say, there is an Influenza.

"Influenza has been long known in the world. It has often visited Europe; and made its appearance on our shores with greater severity than at present. It has sometimes been very severe, and left many persons ill for a year or two.

"The symptoms of influenza need not be dwelt on, as they have been so generally felt by our readers or their friends.

It varies in different people, to be sure, both in kind and in degree. Considering the number of people it attacks, it may be looked on as an innocent disease; but, on the other hand, looking at the increase it has made in the number of deaths, it is an exceedingly serious one after all.

"In simple cases–confinement to a pure and temperate air, warm drinks, and a warm bath, or, at least, a warm foot-bath, with an extra blanket, and a little more rest than usual, keeping to mild food, and toast and water, and taking, if necessary, a dose of aperient medicine,–is all that is required. In serious cases, the domestic treatment must become professional. Mustard plasters to the back relieve the headache. Squills find other medicines 'loosen' the out- standing cough. Bark and wine, and even cold baths are sometimes requisite for the weakness left behind. But these things can only be used with discrimination by a regular professional man.

"Supposing that the seeds of disease have not been laid in childhood, and that there is no particular predisposition to any malady in the constitution, a young woman enters life with every fair prospect of enjoying tolerable health;–yet, how variable, and delicate, and complaining, do the majority of women become! What a vast expense is incurred, during the course of their lives, in physicians, medicine, change of air, baths abroad and at home, and journeys! How few women can walk,–or can suppress nervous feelings,–or can eat like reasonable beings: how many suffer, or say they suffer from debility, headaches, dyspepsia, a tendency to colds, eternal sore throats, rheumatic attacks, and the whole list of polite complaints! With all our modern wisdom, with all our books on health, our smatterings of physiological science, our open carriages, sponging baths, and attention to diet, women now are a far more feeble race than our grandmothers, or even our mothers, were. What daughter can walk half as far as her mother can? What young woman can take the active part that her mother did? In most families, the order of things is reversed. It is not a child trembling for her mother's health, and fearing, lest her parent, no longer young, should be fatigued; but it is the mother who is always striving to spare her child exertions which she can herself perfectly well undergo, but which the enfeebled child of modern self-indulgence dares not encounter.

"Yes! we are a self-indulgent race, this present generation. Witness our easily excited feelings; witness our late hours of rising, our sofas and easy chairs, our useless days and dissipated nights! Witness our pallid faces, our forms, sometimes attenuated and repulsive while yet in early life, age marching, not creeping, on before his time; or witness our over-fed and over-expanded forms, enfeebled by indolence, and suffering the worst species of debility–the debility of fat. Witness our doing those things by deputy which our grandmothers did themselves; witness our host of scents and perfumed waters on our dressing-tables; our over-refinement, which amounts to an enervating puerility, and our incapacity of parting with one accustomed indulgence, even at the bidding of the learned and disinterested adviser?

"'In the education of women,' writes a modern physician,'too little attention is given to subdue the imaginative faculty, and to moderate sensibility; on the contrary, they are generally fostered; and, instead of a vigorous intellect and healthy condition of mind, we find imagination and sentiment predominant over the reasoning faculties, and laying the foundation of hysterical, hypochondriacal, and even maniacal diseases.' It is, in fact, this want of judgment in the management of early life that produces so much misery when women are called upon to perform an important part in society, and when all that exertion can do is required at their hands.

"The Sick-Room," by Dr. A. T. Thomson.

"The duration of sleep should not, in the adult, exceed six or eight hours; women injure their health greatly by excess in this respect. On rising, all women should use some mode of cold or tepid bath; and, indeed, in this respect the practice of the present day is admirable; there is every facility for the bath. To some, the use of the shower-bath is deleterious, and to all inconvenient, and not likely to be resorted to except when positively ordered. Dr. Combe recommends for general use the tepid or warm bath, as being much more suitable than the cold bath, 'especially in the winter for those who are not robust, and full of animal heat.' When the constitution is not sufficiently vigorous to ensure reaction after the cold bath, by producing a warm glow over the surface, 'its use,' observes the same admirable writer, 'inevitably does harm.' But he enforces, that 'in order to promote a due exhalation from the skin, the warm, the tepid, or the shower- bath, as a means of preserving health, ought to be in as common use as a change of apparel, for it is equally a measure of necessary cleanliness.' He inclines to the use of the tepid bath, as likely to be the most generally efficacious.

"I have known the most beneficial effects from a modification of this advice, namely, from using a sponging-bath, into which you pour a jug of warm water, and in which you stand, whilst you sponge the body and limbs profusely with cold water. A strong friction should be employed after this process, either with horsehair gloves or with a large coarse towel, and few persons will find the use of the sponging- bath disagree with them when thus employed. It is, indeed, incredible, when we consider the importance of the exhalation performed by the skin, to what extent ablution is neglected, not only, as Dr. Combe specifies, in charitable institutions and seminaries for the young, but by ladies, in ordinary circumstances, to whom the use of the bath could be productive of no inconvenience. In nervous complaints, which are more or less the besetting evil of womankind, the bath, in its various forms, becomes an invaluable aid.

"In the formation of those habits which are necessary for the preservation of health, another circumstance, which, from its importance to health, cannot be deemed trifling should be mentioned. It is a general practice that beds should be made as soon as the occupants have left their rooms, and before the air has been freely admitted to play upon the recent depositary of the human frame; but this should be avoided. The bed-linen and blankets should be taken off, and the windows opened, so that, for an hour or more, a thorough ventilation should be procured.

"Upon another point, the inconsistency and mental blind-ness of women are almost inconceivable–the insufficiency of their dress to resist the attacks of our variable climate.

How few women clothe themselves like rational beings! Although, in latter years, they have wisely adopted the use of warm dresses, and, more especially, of the valuable Scottish plaid, yet how commonly they neglect the aid of flannel in preserving them not only from cold, but in securing a necessary circulation of vitality in the skin! 'The necessary effect of deficient circulation in the skin,' remarks Dr. Combe,'is to throw a disproportionate mass of blood inwards; and when this condition exists, insufficient clothing perpetuates the evil, until internal disease is generated, and health is irrecoverably lost.' How common is the complaint among young women, especially those of sedentary habits, of chilliness, cold feet, and other symptoms of deficient circulation! and yet how impossible would it often be–for women are usually obstinate on this head–to induce them to exchange the thin silk stocking for a warm merino one, or to substitute a proper walking shoe for the paper-like articles which they designate by that name! Hence arise many diseases, which are, by insensible degrees, fostered in the system by the unequal distribution of the blood oppressing the internal organs. The habitual tendency to that chilliness which has been referred to should never be disregarded, 'laying, as it does,' says Dr. Combe, 'the foundation of tubercles in the lungs, and other maladies, which show themselves only when arrived at an incurable stage.' 'All those who value health, and have common sense, will therefore take warning from signs like these, and never rest until equilibrium of action be restored.' Warm clothing, exercise in the open air, sponging with tepid water and vinegar, or the warm bath, the use of a flesh-brush or hair-glove, are adapted to remedy these serious and threatening evils.

"But, whilst insufficiency of clothing is to be deprecated, excessive wrapping up should also be avoided. Great differences exist between the power of generating heat and resisting cold in individuals, and it is therefore impossible to prescribe general rules upon the subject of clothing. The best maxim is, not to dress in an invariable way in all cases, but to put on clothing sufficient in the individual case, to protect the body effectively against the sensation of cold Dr. Combe.

"The insufficiency of warmth in the clothing of females constitutes only one part of its injurious effects. The tight-ness of dress obstructs the insensible perspiration hurtfully, and produces an irregular circulation. Every part and function of the human frame are linked together so closely, that we cannot act wrongly towards one organ without all suffering, nor act rightly without all sharing the benefit of our judgment and good sense.

"The mischief arising from cold or wet feet is admitted by all persons who have given the subject of health even the most casual consideration. In conversing with very aged people, you will generally find a disregard of diet, and very different notions and practices upon the subject of exercise and ablution; but they all agree in the necessity of keeping the feet dry. I remember inquiring of a venerable clergyman, who, up to the age of ninety-six, had enjoyed a fair proportion of health, after a youth of delicacy. I asked him what system he pursued. 'Now,' was his reply, 'I never took much care of what I ate; I have always been temperate. I never minded the weather; but I always took care to keep my feet dry and well shod.' Wet and damp are, indeed, more un-wholsome when applied to the feet than when they affect other parts; 'because they receive a greater supply of blood to carry on a high degree of perspiration, and because their distance from the heart, or centre of circulation, diminishes the force with which this is carried on, and thus leaves them more susceptible from external causes.' Dr. Combe.

"God, in his infinite benevolence, has given to his creatures other means of acquiring a healthy warmth than by clothing; he has endowed us with the power of exercise–that blessing which women of weak judgment and indolent natures are so prone to neglect and disparage. Most ladies appear to think that the privilege of walking is only intended for persons of inferior condition. They busy themselves, in their in-door occupations all the morning, take a hearty luncheon, and drive out in their carriages until dinner-time. It is partly owing to such customs as these that a rapid deterioration takes place in the physical state of our sex, in their looks, and in their power of utility, and enjoyment of happiness. God never intended us to be inactive.

“The chief purpose of the muscles with which we are endowed, is to enable us to carry into effect the volitions of the mind; and, whilst fulfilling this grand object, the active exercise of the muscles is conducive to the well-being of many other important functions. The processes of digestion, respiration, secretion, absorption, and nutrition, are promoted, and the healthful condition of the whole body influenced.

The mind also is depressed or exhilarated by the proper or improper use of muscular exercise; for man is intended for a life of activity: nor can his functions ever go on so properly as when he duly exercises those organs with which Nature has endowed him. The evils arising from want of exercise are numerous: –the circulation, from the absence of due stimulus, becomes languid, the appetite and digestion are weakened, the respiration is imperfect, and the blood becomes so ill-conditioned, that when distributed through the body it is inadequate to communicate the necessary stimulus to healthy and vigorous action. These points being established, it now becomes a consideration in what mode, or at what periods, ladies, in society, can most advantageously avail themselves of that privilege which is granted to so many, denied, comparatively, to so few.

“Much is said on the benefits of walking before breakfast, and to a person in full vigor it may, there is no doubt, be highly salutary; whilst, to the delicate, it will prove more hurtful than beneficial, producing a sense of weariness which destroys all the future pleasures of the day. I am disposed to think, however, from observation, that walking before breakfast may be rendered beneficial almost to any one by degrees. Most persons walk too far the first day; they are proud of the effort, become, nevertheless, exhausted, and dare not repeat it. A first walk before breakfast should not exceed a quarter of a mile; it should be extended, very gradually, and, in delicate women, with great care, lest over-fatigue should ensue. It is, however, so valuable a habit, such a saving of time, so refreshing, so soothing, that many sacrifices of inclination should be made to procure it; in a gay season the freshness and seclusion of a morning’s walk is peculiarly needed, and when it becomes so difficult to take exercise in the subsequent part of the day, the afternoon being too short, and the evening too much occupied.

And the morning's walk, stolen from the hour given to a species of repose which seldom rests, may be, without the reproach of indolence, followed by the afternoon's siesta–a practice much to be commended, and greatly conducive to rest of nerves and invigoration of the frame, when used in moderation.

"Exercise may be taken, by the robust, at any time, even after eating heartily, but the delicate ought to avoid that risk; they should resort to it only when the frame is vigorous enough to bear it, and this is usually from one to four or five hours after eating. The morning is, therefore, the best time; but exercise ought not to be delayed until some degree of exhaustion has taken place from want of food, as in that case it dissipates rather than renovates the remaining strength, and impairs digestion. Exercise immediately before meals is therefore, unless very gentle, injurious; if it has been violent, before eating rest should intervene. 'Appetite,' says Dr. Combe, 'revives after repose.'

"Of all modes of exercise, that which nature has bestowed upon us, walking, is decidedly the most salutary; and the prevailing system of substituting horse and carriage exercise almost entirely for it, is far from being advantageous to the present generation. Walking, which has for its aim some pleasing pursuit, and, therefore, animates the mind, is efficacious to the majority. Gardening, which is a modification of walking, offers many advantages both to the delicate and the strong, and it is a species of exercise which we can adjust to our powers. In a continued walk you must go on–you must return; there is no appeal, even if you have gone too far, and would willingly give up any further exertion.

But, while gardening, you are still at home–your exertions are devoted to objects the most interesting, because progressive; hope and faith form a part of your stimulus. The happy future, when flowers shall bloom around you, super-sides in your thoughts the vexatious present or the mournful past. About you are the budding treasures of spring, or the gorgeous productions of summer, or the rich hues of those beauties which autumn pours forth most lavishly before it departs,–and is succeeded by winter. Above you are the gay warblers, who seem to hail you as you mingle in the sylvan scenes which are not all theirs, but which you share and appropriate. The ruffled temper, the harassed mind, may find a solace in the occupation of gardening, which aids the effect of exercise and the benign influence of fresh air.

Stores of future and never-dying interest are buried in the earth with every seed, only to spring up again redoubled in their value. A lady, as a writer in the 'Quarterly Re-view' observes, should 'not only have but know her plants.'

And her enjoyment of those delights is truly enhanced by that personal care, without which few gardens, however superintended by the scientific gardener, can prosper, and which bless as they thrive; her plants bestow health on the frame which is bowed down to train them–they give to her the blessing of a calm and rational pleasure– they relieve her from the necessity of excitement–they promote alike, in the wealthy and the poor, these gentle exertions which are coupled with the most poetical and the sweetest of associations.

"Exercise on horseback is not equally attainable with the two modes which I have just specified; when it is, the accelerated circulation, the change of scene and of ideas, are highly beneficial. Where the lungs are weak, it is thought by the learned to possess a great advantage over walking, as it does not hurry the breathing. The gentleness of the exercise enables a delicate person to enjoy the advantage of open air and motion for a much longer period than could be endured in the action of walking. From the tendency of horse exercise to equalize the circulation and stimulate the skin, it is invaluable, too, for the nervous and dyspeptic portion of young women, among whom, unhappily, such complaints are but too prevalent.

"Dancing, which is the most frequent mode of exercise with ladies in great cities, practiced, as it is, in heated rooms, and exhausting from its violence, often does more harm than good, from producing languor and over-fatigue.

Unhappily there are but few modes of exercise in-doors adapted for women. If, from any circumstances, they are confined to their homes, and they become feverish and languid from want of exercise, it never occurs to them to throw open the windows and to walk about, or to make use of battledore and shuttlecock, or any other mode of exertion.

They continue sitting, reading, or walking, or lounging, or sleeping, or gossiping,–whilst the bloom of health is rapidly giving place to the wanness and debility of the imprisoned frame.

"It is often the custom of young women to declare that they cannot walk, sometimes from indolence, no doubt, and want of habit, occasionally from real inability. But if we in-vestigate the causes of this real inability, we shall often find it to proceed from an improper choice of time in taking exercise, or from a defective judgment in the manner of taking it. Many women exhaust and fatigue themselves with the duties of their house, and by a thousand trying occupations, including that which forms a serious item in the day's work, namely, running up and down stairs, and then discover that they cannot walk. Others go to extremes, and walk for a certain distance, whether they feel fatigued or not by such exertions. 'It is only,' observes Dr. Combe, 'by a diffusion of the laws of exercise as a part of useful education, that individuals can be enabled to avoid such mistakes,' To be beneficial, exercise should always be proportioned to the strength and to the constitution of an individual. When it causes extreme fatigue or exhaustion, it is hurtful; it ought to be resumed always after a period of rest, and adopted regularly, not, as too many people are in the habit of doing, once in four or five days. The average walk which a young woman in good health and in ordinary circumstances, may take, without undue and injurious fatigue, is from four to five miles a-day. From this rule I accept the very young. It has been found by experience that until twenty-two or three the strength is not completely matured. The rate of mortality, as it has been proved by statistical tables, increases in all classes of society from fourteen until the age of twenty-three, when it begins to decrease.

"Another precaution which I would recommend to those who have the regulation of families under their care, relates to the subject of ventilation. The heated state of our rooms in ordinary occupation is one great source of all those mischiefs which arise from catching cold, a subject on which Mr. Abernethy was wont to declare, that 'a very useful book might be written.' There are some houses into which one can never enter with impunity, from the want of due ventilation. Housemaids, more especially, have an insupportable objection to opening windows, on account of the dust which flies in and settles upon the furniture. This evil–for the soiling of furniture certainly may be called an evil–may easily be obviated by fastening a muslin blind against the open window, or by pinning a large piece of coarse muslin against it, so that the dusty particles will be excluded.

"Generally, our ordinary sitting-rooms are tolerably well ventilated by the opening and shutting of doors, the size of the fire-place,

&c., but in our bed-rooms the vitiation of the air is far greater, owing to these rooms being wholly closed during the seven or eight hours in which we sleep in them, and, also, owing to the mass of curtains with which we usually take care to surround our beds. In this respect we are, indeed, improved, by the introduction of French bedsteads, which are among the most valuable of modern suggestions.

But, notwithstanding this improvement, and many others which reflection and science have contributed to introduce, we incur much suffering from our ignorance and prejudice on the subject of ventilation. For generations, society has experienced the evil effects of the want of ventilation, and has felt in towns its results in the form of fevers, general ill-health, cutaneous and nervous diseases; and yet the most direful ignorance continues on this subject. Hospitals are among the few well-ventilated buildings which are erected, because an idea prevails that ventilation is essential for the sick, but it seems to have been forgotten that what is essential for the recovery of health is equally necessary for its preservation. 'Were,' says Dr. Combe, 'a general knowledge of the structure of man to constitute a regular part of a liberal education, such inconsistencies as this would soon disappear, and the scientific architect would speedily devise the best means for supplying our houses with pure air, as he has already supplied them with pure water."'

CHAPTER XXVI

MISCELLANEOUS

THERE are many little pieces of rudeness, only too common, which, while they evince ill-breeding, and are many of them extremely annoying, yet they are met with every day, and in persons otherwise well-bred.

As they come under no particular head, they will merely be mentioned here, as habits carefully to avoid.

It is rude to look over the shoulder of a person who is either reading or writing, yet it is done every day.

To stand with the arms a-kimbo, the hands on the hips, or with the arms crossed, while conversing, is exceedingly unlady-like.

Avoid restless movements either with the hands, or feet; to sit perfectly quiet, without stiffness, easily, yet at the same time almost motionless, is one of the surest proofs of high-breeding.

If you wish to make yourself agreeable to any one, talk as much as you please about his or her affairs, and as little as possible about your own.

Avoid passing before persons seated in the same room with yourself. If you must rise to move from place to place, endeavor to pass behind the chairs of your companions.

Above all, never pass between two persons who are conversing together.

Avoid personal remarks; they evince a want of judgment, good taste, kindness, and politeness. To exchange glances or significant smiles with a third person, whilst engaged in a conversation with a second, is a proof of low-breeding. Suppressed laughter, shrugging of the shoulders, rolling of the eyes, and significant glances are all marks of ill-breeding.

If you meet a gentleman at the foot of a flight of stairs, do not go up before him. Stop, bow, and motion to him to precede you. He will return your bow, and run up, leaving you to follow him.

Never whisper, or make any confidential communication in company. Keep private remarks for private occasions.

Accepting presents from gentlemen is a dangerous thing.

It is better to avoid any such obligations, and, if you make it a rule never to accept such presents, you will avoid hurting any one's feelings, and save yourself from all further perplexity.

In meeting your elderly friends in the street, look at them long enough to give them an opportunity of recognizing you; and if they do so, return their salutations respectfully, not with the familiar nod you would give to one of your own age.

Never remain seated, whilst a person older than yourself is standing before you, talking to you.

Never lounge on a sofa, while there are those in the room, whose years give them a better claim to this sort of indulgence.

Never tease a person to do what she has once declined.

Never refuse a request or invitation in order to be urged, and accept afterwards. Comply at once. If the request is sincere, you will thus afford gratification; if not, the individual making it deserves to be punished for insincerity, by being taken at her word.

It is not polite when asked what part of a dish you will have, to say, "Any part–it is quite indifferent to me;" it is hard enough to carve for one's friends, without choosing for them.

It is not polite to entertain a visitor with your own family history, or the events of your own household.

It is not polite for married ladies to talk, in the presence of gentlemen, of the difficulty they have in procuring domestics, and how good-for-nothing they are when procured.

It is not polite to put food upon the plate of a guest without asking leave, or to press her to eat more than she wants.

It is not polite to stare under ladies' bonnets, as if you suspected they had stolen the linings from you, or wore something that was not their own.

Never affect a foolish reserve in a mixed company, keeping aloof from others as if in a state of mental abstraction. If your brain is so full and so busy that you cannot attend to the little civilities, cheerful chit-chat, and light amusements of society, keep out of it.

Never read in company. You may open a book to look over the engravings, if you will, but do not attend to the letter-press until you are alone.

Never jest upon serious subjects. Avoid scandal. If another person attempts to open a conversation upon scandalous matters, check her. Say gravely that it is painful for you to hear of the faults or misfortunes of others, where your counsel and assistance can be of no service.

Many persons, whose tongues never utter a scandalous word, will, by a significant glance, a shrug of the shoulders, a sneer, or curl of the lip, really make more mischief, and suggest harder thoughts than if they used the severest language. This is utterly detestable. If you have your tongue under perfect control, you can also control your looks, and you are cowardly, contemptible, and wicked, when you encourage and countenance slander by a look or gesture.

Never speak of gentlemen by their first name unless you are related to them. It is very unlady-like to use the sur-name, without the prefix, Mr. To hear a lady speak of Smith, Brown, Anderson, instead of Mr. Anderson or Mr. Smith sounds extremely vulgar, and is a mark of low breeding.

Avoid eccentricity either in dress, conversation, or manner. It is a form of vanity, as it will attract attention, and is therefore in bad taste.

Never act as if in a hurry. Ease of action need not imply laziness, but simply polite self-possession.

Never laugh at your own wit. That is the part of those who hear you, and if you take their duty from them, they may omit to join you in your laugh.

Do not indulge in ridicule. It is coarse and unlady-like as well as unfeeling. Like every other personality, it should be carefully avoided.

Never handle any ornament or article of furniture in the room in which you are a visitor.

Do not lean your head against the wall. You leave an indelible mark upon the paper, or, if the wall is whitewashed, you give your hair a dingy, dusty look, by bringing it into contact with the lime.

Never lean forward upon a table. Let neither hands nor arms rest there heavily.

To bestow flattery upon a person to his face, betrays a want of delicacy; yet, not less so, rudely to rebuke his errors or mention his faults, and not have a tender regard for his feelings. It is not improper, and may sometimes be very kind to mention to an individual what yourself and others think of his conduct or performances, when it is for his interest or usefulness to know it. To express to a friend deserved approbation is generally proper.

Nothing but a quick perception of the feelings of others, and a ready sympathy with them, can regulate the thousand little proprieties that belong to visits of condolence and congratulation. There is one hint, however, as regards the former, which may perhaps be useful, and that is, not to touch upon the cause of affliction, unless the mourner leads the way to it; and if a painful effort is made to appear cheerful, and to keep aloof from the subject, do not make the slightest allusion that could increase this feeling.

When at table to press your guests to take more than they have inclination for, is antiquated and rude. This does not, however, prevent your recommending particular dishes to their attention. Everything like compulsion is quite exploded.

It is a great mistake to suppose that the best music is the most difficult of execution. The very reverse, generally speaking, is the case. Music of a high order certainly demands high gifts and attainments on the part of the performer. But the gifts of nature may be possessed by the amateur as well as by the professor; and the attainments of art may be the result of moderate study and application.

A young lady possessed of a sweet and tunable voice, a good ear, intelligence, and feeling, may cultivate music in its grandest and most beautiful forms, and may render its practice a source of the purest enjoyment, not only to herself but to her domestic and social circle.

The various ceremonies observed in refined society are very useful in settling little points, on which there might otherwise be much doubt and perplexity; but they should never be so strenuously insisted upon as to make an accidental omission of them a ground of resentment, and an apology should always be accepted in their place.

Your enjoyment of a party depends far less on what you find there, than on what you carry with you. The vain, ambitious, the designing, will be full of anxiety when they go, and of disappointment when they return. A short triumph will be followed by a deep mortification, and the selfishness of their aims defeats itself. If you go to see, and to hear, and to make the best of whatever occurs, with a disposition to admire all that is beautiful, and to sympathize in the pleasures of others, you can hardly fail to spend the time pleasantly. The less you think of yourself and your claims to attention, the better. If you are much attended to, receive it modestly, and consider it as a happy accident; if you are little noticed, use your leisure in observing others.

It was unjust and ungrateful to conceive that the amusements of life are altogether forbidden by its beneficent Author. They serve, on the contrary, important purposes in the economy of human life, and are destined to produce important effects both upon our happiness and character. They are, in the first place, in the language of the Psalmist, “the wells of the desert;” the kind resting-places in which toil may relax, in which the weary spirit may recover its tone, and where the desponding mind may resume its strength and its hopes. It is not, therefore, the use of the innocent amusements of life which is dangerous, but the abuse of them; it is not when they are occasionally, but when they are constantly pursued; and when, from being an occasional indulgence, it becomes an habitual desire.

Women in the middle rank are brought up with the idea that if they engage in some occupations, they shall lose “their position in society.” Suppose it to be so; surely it is wiser to quit a position we cannot honestly maintain, than to live dependent upon the bounty and caprice of others; better to labor with our hands, than eat the bread of idleness; or submit to feel that we must not give utterance to our real opinions, or express our honest indignation at being required to act a base or unworthy part. And in all cases, however situated, every female ought to learn how all household affairs are managed, were it only for the purpose of being able to direct others. There cannot be any disgrace in learning how to make the bread we eat, to cook our dinners, to mend our clothes, or even to clean the house. Better to be found busily engaged in removing the dust from the furniture, than to let it accumulate there until a visitor leaves palpable traces where his hat or his arm have been laid upon a table.

Never put temptation in a servant's way; never be severe for trifling offences, such as accidentally breaking anything, but reserve your severity for those offences which are moral evils, such as a want of truth, general laxity of principle, &c.

The orders given to servants should be clear and definite; and they should be trained as much as possible to perform their duties regularly, so that every morning they may know pretty nearly what will be expected of them during the day.

It is a great point to live, when you are alone, as if you expected company; that is to say, to have everything so neat and orderly that you need not be ashamed of anyone seeing your table. It is very little trouble, and certainly no more expense; and the advantages in comfort are unspeakable.

If a foolish girl, by dint of squeezing and bracing with busk and bones, secures the conventional beauty of a wasp waist, she is tolerably certain to gain an addition she by no means bargained for, a red nose, which, in numberless instances, is produced by no other cause than the unnatural girth, obstructing circulation, and causing stagnation of the blood, in that prominent and important feature. Often, in assemblages of the fair, we have seen noses faultless in form, but tinged with the abhorred hue, to which washes and cosmetics have been applied in wild despair; but in vain! If the lovely owners had known the cause, how speedily the effect would have vanished! for surely the most per-verse admirer of a distorted spine and compressed lungs, would deem the acquisition of a dram-drinker's nose, too heavy a condition to be complied with.

A well-bred woman will not demand as a right what she may have a claim to expect from the politeness of the other sex, nor show dissatisfaction and resentment if she fancies herself neglected. For want of good breeding some females are exorbitant in their expectations, and appear unthank-ful even when everything is done which true politeness demands. Young women should guard against this unamiable defect.

A well-bred person will take care not to use slang words and expressions. There never has been a time, at least in late years, when there have not been some two or three cant vul-garisms in vogue among all the blackguards of the country.

Sometimes these phrases have been caught up from some popular song or farce; sometimes, we believe, they have had their origin "where assembles the collective wisdom of the country." A dozen of these terse but meaningless sayings now dance before our recollection, for who has not heard them, even to loathing? But from Whatever source they may have been drawn, or whatever wit there might be in their original position, the obtrusion of them into decent society is an unwarrantable piece of impertinence.

A habit of inserting into familiar conversation such phrases as "You know," "You perceive," "You understand," "Says he," "Says she," is, so far as those matters extend, a sign of a want of good breeding.

With regard to any specific rules for dressing, we do not pretend to arbitrate in such matters. Let a true sense of propriety, of the fitness of things, regulate all your habits of living and dressing, and it will produce such a beautiful harmony and consistency of character as will throw a charm around you that all will feel, though few may comprehend.

Always consider well whether the articles of dress, which you wish to purchase, are suited to your age, your condition, your means; to the climate, to the particular use to which you mean to put them; and let the principles of good taste keep you from the extremes of the fashion, and regulate the form, so as to combine utility and beauty, whilst the known rules of harmony in colors save you from shocking the eye of the artist by incongruous mixtures.

"Manners," says the eloquent Edmund Burke, "are of more importance than laws. Upon them, in a great measure, the laws depend. The law can touch us here and there, now and then. Manners are what vex or sooth, corrupt or purify, exalt or debase, barbarize or refine, by a constant, steady, uniform, insensible operation, like that of the air we breathe in. They give their whole form and colors to our lives. According to their quality they aid morals, they supply them, or they totally destroy them."

FOUR IMPORTANT RULES.

"Order is heaven's first law."

A suitable place for everything, and everything in its place.

A proper time for everything, and everything done in its time.

A distinct name for everything, and everything called by its name.

A certain use for everything, and everything put to its use.

Much time would be saved; many disputes avoided; numerousarticles kept from being lost or injured, and constant confusion and disorder prevented, by the strict observance of these four important rules.

Dispense with ornaments altogether rather than wear mock jewelry.

Depending upon it, silvery hair is better adapted to the faded cheeks of middle age, than are tresses of nut-brown or coal-black, or any of the mysterious shades produced by a dirty decoction called Hair-dye.

The habitual use of very thin shoes invariably makes the feet tender, and a host of other inconveniences arise there-from. If you are tempted to purchase tight shoes, don't, for several reasons; but one may suffice–you will not wear them more than twice.

If you are not quite certain of the line between neatness and the reverse, be over-scrupulous about your undergarments. The edge of a soiled petticoat, or the glimpse of a rent stocking is singularly disenchanting.

Men of sense–I speak not of boys of eighteen to five and twenty, during their age of detestability–men who are worth the trouble of falling in love with, and the fuss and inconvenience, of being married to, and to whom one might, after some inward conflicts, and a course perhaps of fast-ing and self-humiliation, submit to fulfil those ill- contrived vows of obedience which are exacted at the altar, such men want, for their wives, companions, not dolls; and women who would suit such men are just as capable of loving fer-vently, deeply, as the Ringlettina, full of song and sentiment, who cannot walk, cannot rise in the morning, cannot tie her bonnet-strings, faints if she has to lace her boots, never in her life brushed out her beautiful hair, would not for the world prick her delicate finger with plain sewing; but who can work harder than a factory girl upon a lamb's-wool shepherdess, dance like a dervise at balls, ride like a fox-hunter, and, whilst every breath of air gives her cold in her father's house, and she cannot think how people can endure this climate, she can go out to parties in February and

March, with an inch of sleeve and half-a-quarter of boddice.

All circumstances well examined, there can be no doubt Providence has willed that man should be the head of the human race, even as woman is its heart; that he should be its strength, as she is its solace; that he should be its wisdom, as she is its grace; that he should be its mind, its impetus, and its courage, as she is its sentiment, its charm, and its consolation. Too great an amelioration could not be affected, in our opinion, in the system generally adopted, which, far from correcting or even compensating the presumed intellectual inequality of the two sexes, generally serves only to increase it. By placing, for example, dancing and needle-work at the extreme poles of female study, the one for its attraction and the other for its utility, and by not filling the immense interval with anything more valuable than mere monotonous, imperfect, superficial, and totally unphilosophical notions, this system has made of the greater number of female seminaries, establishments which may be compared alike to nursery- grounds for coquettes and seamstresses. It is never remembered that in domestic life conversation is of more importance than the needle or choreography; that a husband is neither a pacha nor a lazzarone, who must be perpetually intoxicated or unceasingly patched; that there are upon the conjugal dial many long hours of calm intimacy, of cool contemplation, of cold tenderness; and that the husband makes another home elsewhere if his own hearth offers him only silence; or what is a hundred times worse, merely frivolous and monotonous discourse. Let the woman play the gossip at a given moment, that is all very well; let her supervise the laundry or the kitchen at another, that is also very well; but these duties only comprise two-thirds of her mission. Ought care not to be taken that during the rest of her time she could also be capable of becoming to her husband a rational friend, a cheerful partner, an interesting companion, or, at least, an efficient listener, whose natural intelligence, even if originally inferior to his own, shall, by the help of education, have been raised to the same level!

Pascal says: “Kind words do not cost much. They never blister the tongue or lips. And we have never heard of any mental trouble arising from this quarter. Though they do not cost much. 1. They help one’s own good nature. Soft words soften our own soul. Angry words are fuel to the flame of wrath, and make it blaze more fiercely. 2. Kind words make other people good natured. Cold words freeze people, and hot words scorch them, and bitter words make them bitter, and wrathful words make them wrathful. There is such a rush of all other kinds of words in our days, that it seems desirable to give kind words a change among them.

There are vain words, and idle words, and hasty words, and spiteful words, and silly words, and empty words, and pro-fane words, and boisterous words, and warlike words. Kind words also produce their own image on men's souls. And a beautiful image it is. They are smooth, and quiet, and comfort the hearer. They shame him out of his sour, morose, unkind feelings. We have not yet begun to use kind words in such abundance as they ought to be used."

A writer in the New York Observer, speaking of the necessity of guarding the tongue, says:–

"It is always best to avoid saying everything that is improper; but it is especially so before children. And here parents, as well as others, are often in fault. Children have as many ears as grown persons, and they are generally more attentive to what is said before them. What they hear, they are very apt to repeat; and, as they have no discretion, and not sufficient knowledge of the world to disguise anything, it is generally found that 'children and fools speak the truth.' See that boy's eyes glisten while you are speaking of a neighbor in a language you would not wish to have repeated. He does not fully understand what you mean, but he will remember every word; and it will be strange if he does not cause you to blush by the repetition.

"A gentleman was in the habit of calling at a neighbor's house, and the lady had always expressed to him great pleasure from his calls. One day, just after she had remarked to him, as usual, her happiness from his visit, her little boy entered the room. The gentleman took him on his knee, and asked, 'Are you not glad to see me, George?' 'No, sir,' replied the boy. 'Why not, my little man?' he continued.

'Because mother doesn't want you to come,' said George. 'Indeed! how do you know that, George?' Here the mother became crimson, and looked daggers at her little son. But he saw nothing, and therefore replied, 'Because, she said yes-terday, she wished that old bore would not call here again.'

That was enough. The gentleman's hat was soon in requisition, and he left with the impression that 'great is the truth, and it will prevail.'

"Another little child looked sharply in the face of a visitor, and being asked what she meant by it, replied, 'I wanted to see if you had a drop in your eye; I heard mother say you had frequently.'

"A boy once asked one of his father's guests who it was that lived next door to him, and when he heard his name, inquired if he was not a fool. 'No, my little friend,' replied the guest, 'he is not a fool, but a very sensible man. But why did you ask that question?' 'Because,' replied the boy, 'Mother said the other day, that you were next door to a fool; and I wanted to know who lived next door to you.'"

The best way to overcome the selfishness and rudeness you sometimes meet with on public occasions, is, by great politeness and disinterestedness on your part; overcome evil with good, and you will satisfy your own conscience, and, perhaps, touch theirs. Contending for your rights stirs up the selfish feelings in others; but a readiness to yield them awakens generous sentiments, and leads to mutual accommodation. The more refined you are, and the greater have been your advantages, the more polite and considerate you should be toward others, the more ready to give place to some poor, uneducated girl, who knows no better than to push herself directly in your way.

Politeness is as necessary to a happy intercourse with the inhabitants of the kitchen, as with those of the parlor; it lessens the pains of service, promotes kind feelings on both sides, and checks unbecoming familiarity; always thank them for what they do for you, and always ask rather than command their services.

In later years, the wearing of jewelry, in season and out of season, both by matrons and unmarried females, has increased vastly. It is an indication that the growing wealth of the people is not accompanied by a corresponding refinement; but that the love of vulgar show, the low pride of ostentation, takes the place of a pure and elevated taste. The emulation with fashionable dames, now-a-days, so far from being, as with the Spartan women, to excel each other in household virtues, is to wear the largest diamonds. And, in this ambition, they forget fitness, beauty, taste, everything but the mere vulgar desire to shine. To be gracefully and elegantly attired, in short, is secondary to the desire to be a sort of jeweler's walking show-card. We do not oppose the use of diamonds and pearls altogether, as some people might imagine from these remarks. A few diamonds, judiciously worn, look well, on proper occasions, on married women.

But young girls rarely, or never, improve their appearance by the use of these dazzling jewels; and, as a general rule, the simpler the costume of a woman in her teens, the better.

Women are usually pretty, up to the age of twenty, at least. Consequently, at this period of life, there are few whom an elaborate attire does not injure; a simple dress, or a rose-bud in the hair, is frequently all that is required; and more only spoils that combination of youthfulness, grace, and modesty, which it should be the highest ambition of the girl to attain; because, if she did but know it, it is her highest charm.

Instead of this, however, we see gay females, scarcely freed from the nursery, wearing enormous jeweled ear-drops, or sporting on the finger, a diamond ring as large as a sixpence.

Sometimes, too, ladies pretending to be well-bred, descend to receive a morning visitor of their own sex, glittering like a jeweler's case, with costly gems. In all this, we repeat, there is neither refinement or elegance, but simply vulgar ostentation. Female dress has ceased to be a means of beautifying the person or displaying the wearer's taste, and has become instead, a mere brag of the husband's or father's wealth.

A knowledge of domestic duties is beyond all price to a woman. Every one of the sex ought to know how to sew, and knit, and mend, and cook, and superintend a household. In every situation of life, high or low, this sort of knowledge is of great advantage. There is no necessity that the gaining of such information should interfere with intellectual acquisition or even elegant accomplishment. A well- regulated mind can find time to attend to all. When a girl is nine or ten years old, she should be accustomed to take some regular share in household duties, and to feel responsible for the manner in which her part is performed–such as her own mending, washing the cups and putting them in place, cleaning silver, or dusting and arranging the parlor. This should not be done occasionally, and neglected whenever she finds it convenient–she should consider it her department. When older than twelve, girls should begin to take turns in superintending the household–making puddings, pies, cakes, &c. To learn effectively, they should actually do these themselves, and not stand by and see others do them. Many husbands have been ruined for want of these domestic qualities in a wife–and many a husband has been saved from ruin by his wife being able to manage the household concerns.

It is a mark, not only of ill-breeding, but of positive want of feeling and judgment, to speak disparagingly of a physician to one of his patients. Many persons, visiting an invalid friend, will exclaim loudly against the treatment pursued, recommend a different doctor, and add to the sufferings of the patient by their injudicious remarks upon the medicines or practice used.

It is too much the fashion, in conversation, to use exaggerated expressions which are opposed to truth, without the person employing them being aware of it, from the mere force of habit. Why need we say splendid for pretty, magnificent for handsome, horrid for unpleasant, immense for large, thousands, or myriads, for any number more than two? This practice is pernicious, for the effect is to deprive the person who is guilty of it, from being believed, when she is in earnest. No one can trust the testimony of an individual who, in common conversation, is indifferent to the import, and regardless of the value of words.

Politeness is very essential to the right transaction of that great business of woman's life, shopping. The variety afforded by the shops of a city renders people difficult to please; and the latitude they take in examining and asking the price of goods, which they have no thought of buying, is so trying to the patience of those who attend upon them, that nothing but the most perfect courtesy of demeanor can reconcile them to it. Some persons behave, in shopping, as if no one had any rights, or any feelings, but the purchasers; as if the sellers of goods were mere automatons, put behind the counter to do their bidding; they keep them waiting, whilst they talk of other things, with a friend; they call for various goods, ask the price, and try to cheapen them, without any real intention of buying. A lady who wants decision of character, after hesitating and debating, till the poor trader's patience is almost exhausted, will beg him to send the article to her house, for her to examine it there; and, after giving him all this trouble, she will refuse to purchase it, without any scruple or apology. Some think they have a right to exchange articles at the place where they were bought; whereas that privilege should be asked as a favor, only by a good customer,–and then but rarely.

RECEIPTS.

FOR THE COMPLEXION.

COLD CREAM, 1.–Take 2 1 ounces of sweet oil of almonds, 2 3 drachms of white wax, and the same of spermaceti, 2 12 ounces of rose-water, 1 drachm of oil of bergamot, and 15 drops each of oil of lavender, and otto of roses. Melt the wax and spermaceti in the oil of almonds, by placing them together in a jar, which should be plunged into boiling water.

Heat a mortar (which should, if possible, be marble) by pouring boiling water into it, and letting it remain there until the mortar is uniformly heated; the water is to be poured away, and the mortar dried well. Pour the melted wax and spermaceti into the warm mortar, and add rose-water gradually, while the mixture is constantly stirred or whisked with an egg-wisp, until the whole is cold, and, when nearly finished, add the oils and otto of roses.

In the absence of a mortar, a basin plunged into another containing boiling water will answer the purpose.

COLD CREAM, 2.–Take 10 drachms of spermaceti, 4 drachms of white wax, half a pound of prepared lard, 15 grains of sub carbonate of potash, 4 ounces of rose-water, 2 ounces of spirits of wine, and ten drops of otto of roses.

Proceed as above. Some persons prefer orange-flower-water instead of rose-water, in which case use the same proportions.

Cold cream is a useful local application to hard and dry parts of the skin, to abrasions and cracks. When spread thickly upon rag, it is an excellent application to blistered surfaces or burns, or may be used to protect exposed parts from the influence of the sun.

GRANULATED COLD CREAM. –Take white wax and spermaceti, of each one ounce; almond oil 3 ounces, otto of rose, as much as you please. Dissolve the wax and spermaceti in the almond oil, by means of heat, and when a little cool, pour the mixture into a large wedgwood mortar previously warmed, and containing about a pint of warm water. Stir briskly until the cream is well divided, add the otto, and suddenly pour the whole into a clean vessel containing 8 or 12 pints of cold water. Separate the cream by straining through muslin, and shake out as much water as possible.

WHITE CAMPHORATED OINTMENT, 1.–Take 3 ounces 2 drachms of powdered carbonate of lead (ceruse), 45 grains of powdered camphor. Mix, and then stir into 5 ounces of melted lard.

This is applied to burns and contusions with very good effect, and is much used in Austria. The surface must not be abraded when it is applied.

WHITE CAMPHORATED OINTMENT, 2.–Take 4 ounces of olive oil,

1 ounce of white wax, 22 grains of camphor, and 6 drachms of spermaceti. Melt the wax and spermaceti with the oil, and when they have cooled rub the ointment with the camphor, dissolved in a little oil. Sometimes the white wax is omitted, and lard substituted for it.

It is useful in chaps, fissures, abrasions, and roughness of the skin.

PITCH POMADE, 1.–Take 1 drachm of pitch, and 1 ounce of lard. Mix well, and apply twice a day to the affected parts. This is used for ringworm, and scald head.

TO SOFTEN THE SKIN, AND IMPROVE THE COMPLEXION.–If flowers of sulphur are mixed in a little milk, and, after standing for an hour or two, the milk (without disturbing the sulphur) is rubbed into the skin, it will keep it soft, and make the complexion clear. It is to be used before washing.

TO REMOVE BLACK STAINS FROM THE SKIN.–Ladies those who wear mourning clothes in warm weather are much inured by the blackness it leaves on the arms and neck, and which cannot easily be removed, even by soap and warm water. To have a remedy always at hand, keep, in the drawer of your wash-stand, a box, containing a mixture in equal portions of cream of tartar, and oxalic acid (POISON). Get, at a druggist's, half an ounce of each of these articles, and have them mixed and pounded together in a mortar. Put some of this mixture into a cup that has a cover, and if, afterwards, it becomes hard, you may keep it slightly moistened with water. See that it is always closely covered.

To use it, wet the black stains on your skin with the corner of a towel, dipped in water (warm water is best, but is not always at hand). Then, with your finger, rub on a little of the mixture. Then immediately wash it off with water, and afterwards with soap and water, and the black stains will be visible no longer. This mixture will also remove ink, and all other stains from the fingers, and from white clothes. It is more speedy in its effects if applied with warm water. No family should be without it, but care must be taken to keep it out of the way of young children, as, if swallowed, it is poisonous.

PASTES.

ALMOND.–Take 1 ounce of bitter almonds, blanch and pound them to a fine powder, then add 1 ounce of barley flour, and make it into a smooth paste by the addition of a little honey. When this paste is laid over the skin, particularly where there are freckles, it makes it smooth and soft.

PALATINE.–Take 8 ounces of soft-soap, of olive oil, and spirits of wine, each 4 ounces, 1 1 ounce of lemon-juice, suf-2ficient silver-sand to form into a thick paste, and any perfume that is grateful to the person. Boil the oil and soap together in a pipkin, and then gradually stir in the sand and lemon-juice. When nearly cool add the spirit of wine, and lastly the perfume. Make into a paste with the hands, and place in jars or pots for use.

This paste is used instead of soap, and is a valuable addition to the toilette, as it preserves the skin from chapping, and renders it smooth and soft.

AMERICAN COSMETIC POWDER.–Calcined magnesia applied the same as ordinary toilette powders, by means of a swan's-down ball, usually called a "puff."

MALOINE.–Take 4 ounces of powdered marsh-mallow roots, 2 ounces of powdered white starch, 3 drachms of powdered orris-root, and 20 drops of essence of jasmine.Mix well, and sift through fine muslin.

This is one of the most agreeable and elegant cosmetics yet known for softening and whitening the skin, preserving it from chapping, and being so simple that it may be applied to the most delicate or irritable skin.

This receipt has never before been published, and we know that only six bottles of it have been made.

OXIDE OF ZINC is sprinkled into chaps and fissures to promote their cure.

YAOULTA.–Take 1 ounce of white starch, powdered and sifted, 1 a drachm of rose pink, 10 drops of essence of jas-2 mine, and 2 drops of otto of roses. Mix and keep in a fine muslin bag.

This exquisite powder is to be dusted over the face, and, being perfectly harmless, may be used as often as necessity requires. It also imparts a delicate rosy tinge to the skin preferable to rouge.

CRÈME DE L'ENCLOS.–Take 4 ounces of milk, 1 ounce of lemon-juice, and 2 drachms of spirit wine. Simmer over a slow fire, and then bring it to the boil, skim off the scum, and when cold apply it to the skin.

It is much used by some persons to remove freckles and sun-burnings.

WASHES AND LOTIONS.

MILK OF ROSES, 1.–Take 2 ounces of blanched almonds; 12 ounces of rose-water; white soft-soap, or Windsor soap; white wax; and oil of almonds, of each 2 drachms; rectified spirit, 3 ounces; oil of bergamot, 1 drachm; oil of lavender, 15 drops; otto of roses, 8 drops. Beat the almonds well, and then add the rose-water gradually so as to form an emulsion, mix the soap, white wax, and oil together, by placing them in a covered jar upon the edge of the fire-place, then rub this mixture in a mortar with the emulsion. Strain the whole through very fine muslin, and add the essential oils, previously mixed with the spirit.

This is an excellent wash for "sunburns," freckles, or for cooling the face and neck, or any part of the skin to which it is applied.

MILK OF ROSES, 2.–This is not quite as expensive a receipt as the last; and, at the same time, is not so good.

Take 1 ounce of Jordan almonds; 5 ounces of distilled rose-water; 1 ounce of spirit of wine; 1 a drachm of Venetian 2

soap, and 2 drops of otto of roses. Beat the almonds (previously blanched and well dried with a cloth) in a mortar, until they become a complete paste, then beat the soap and mix with the almonds, and afterwards add the rose-water and spirit. Strain through a very fine muslin or linen, and add the otto of roses.

The common milk of roses sold in the shops frequently contains salt of tartar, or pearlash, combined with olive oil and rose-water, and therefore it is better to make it yourself to ensure it being good.

FRENCH MILK OF ROSES.–Mix 2 1 pints of rose-water 2 with 1 a pint of rosemary-water, then add tincture of storax 2 and tincture of benzoin, of each 2 ounces; and esprit de rose, 1 an ounce. This is a useful wash for freckles.

2GERMAN MILK OF ROSES. -- Take rose-water and milk of almonds, each 3 ounces; water 8 ounces; rosemary-water 2 ounces; and spirit of lavender 1 an ounce. Mix well, and 2 then add 1 ounce of sugar or lead. 2

This is a dangerous form to leave about where there are children, and should never be applied when there are any abrasions, or chaps on the surface.

MILK OF ALMONDS.–Blanch 4 ounces of Jordan almonds, dry them with a towel, and then pound them in a mortar; add 2 drachms of white or curd soap, and rub it up with the almonds for about ten minutes or rather more, gradually adding one quart of rose-water, until the whole is well mixed, then strain through a fine piece of muslin, and bottle for use.

This is an excellent remedy for freckles and sunburns, and may be used as a general cosmetic, being applied to the skin after washing by means of the corner of a soft towel.

ANTI-FRECKLE LOTION, 1.–Take tincture of benzoin, 2 ounces; tincture of tolu, 1 ounce; oil of rosemary, 1 a 2 drachm. Mix well and bottle. When required to be used, add a teaspoonful of the mixture to about a wine-glassful of water, and apply the lotion to the face or hands, &c., night and morning, carefully rubbing it in with a soft towel.

ANTI-FRECKLE LOTION, 2.–Take 1 ounce of rectified spirit of wine; 1 drachm of hydrochloric acid (spirit of salt); and 7 ounces of water. Mix the acid gradually with the water, and then add the spirit of wine; apply by means of a camel's-hair brush, or a piece of flannel.

GOWLAND'S LOTION.–Take 1 1 grains of bichloride of 2 mercury, and 1 ounce of emulsion of bitter almonds; mix well. Be careful of the bichloride of mercury, because it is a poison.

This is one of the best cosmetics for imparting a delicate appearance and softness to the skin, and is a useful lotion in acne, ringworm, hard and dry skin, and sun-blistering.

COLD CREAM.–Sweet almond oil, 7 lbs. by weight, white wax, 3 lb., spermaceti, 3 lb., clarified mutton suet, 1 lb., 4 rose-water, 7 pints, spirits of wine, 1 pint. Directions to mix the above:–Place the oil, wax, spermaceti, and suet in a large jar; cover it over tightly, then place it in a saucepan of boiling water, (having previously placed two or more pieces of fire-wood at the bottom of the saucepan, to allow the water to get underneath the jar, and to prevent its breaking) keep the water boiling round the jar till all the ingredients are dissolved; take it out of the water, and pour it into a large pan previously warmed and capable of holding 21 pints; then, with a wooden spatula, stir in the rose-water, cold, as quickly as possible, (dividing it into three or four parts, at most,) the stirring in of which should not occupy above five minutes, as after a certain heat the water will not mix.

When all the water is in, stir unremittingly for thirty minutes longer, to prevent its separating, then add the spirits of wine, and the scent, and it is finished. Keep it in a cold place, in a white glazed jar, and do not cut it with a steel knife, as it causes blackness at the parts of contact. Scent with otto of roses and essential oil of bergamot to fancy. For smaller quantities, make ounces instead of pounds.

PALM SOAP.–I make it in the following manner:–Cut thin two pounds of yellow soap into a double saucepan, occasionally stirring it till it is melted, which will be in a few minutes if the water is kept boiling around it; then add quarter of a pound of palm oil, quarter of a pound of honey, three pennyworth of true oil of cinnamon; let all boil together another six or eight minutes; pour out and stand it by till next day; it is then fit for immediate use. If made in these directions it will be found to be a very superior soap.

CURE FOR CHAPPED HANDS.–Take 3 drachms of gum camphor, 3 drachms of white beeswax, 3 drachms of spermaceti, 2 ounces of olive oil,–put them together in a cup upon the stove, where they will melt slowly and form a white ointment in a few minutes. If the hands are affected, anoint them on going to bed, and put on a pair of gloves. A day or two will suffice to heal them.

TO WHITEN THE NAILS.–Diluted sulphuric acid, 2 drachms; tincture of myrrh, 1 drachm; spring water, 4 ounces. Mix. First cleanse with white soap, and then dip the fingers into the mixture.

TO WHITEN THE HANDS.–Take a wine-glassful of eau de Cologne, and another of lemon-juice; then scrape two cakes of brown Windsor soap to a powder, and mix well in a mould. When hard, it will be an excellent soap for whitening the hands.

FOR THE TEETH.

TO REMOVE TARTAR FROM THE TEETH.–1st. The use of the tooth-brush night and morning, and, at least, rinsing the mouth after every meal at which animal food is taken.

2nd. Once daily run the brush lightly two or three times over soap, then dip it in salt, and with it clean the teeth, working the brush up and down rather than–or as well as–backwards and forwards. This is a cheap, safe, and effectual dentifrice. 3rd. Eat freely of common cress, the sort used with mustard, under the name of small salad; it must be eaten with salt only. If thus used two or three days in succession it will effectually loosen tartar, even of long standing. The same effect is produced, though perhaps not in an equal degree, by eating strawberries and raspberries, especially the former. A leaf of common green sage rubbed on the teeth is useful both in cleansing and polishing, and probably many other common vegetable productions also.

CARE OF THE TEETH. –The water with which the teeth are cleansed should be what is called lukewarm. They should be well but gently brushed both night and morning; the brush should be neither too hard nor too soft. The best tooth-powders are made from cuttle- fish, prepared chalk, and orris-root commingled together in equal quantities.

SIMPLE MEANS OF REMOVING TARTAR FROM THE TEETH. –In these summer months, tartar may be effectually removed from the teeth, by partaking daily of strawberries.

TOOTH POWDER.–Powdered orris-root, 1 an ounce; pow-2 dread charcoal, 2 ounces, powdered Peruvian bark, 1 ounce; prepared chalk, 1 an ounce; oil of bergamot, or lavender, 20 2 drops. These ingredients must be well worked up in a mortar, until thoroughly incorporated. This celebrated tooth-powder possesses three essential virtues, giving an odorous breath, cleansing and purifying the gums, and preserving the enamel; the last rarely found in popular tooth-powders.

TOOTH-POWDER.–One of the best tooth-powders that can be used may be made by mixing together 1 1 ounces pre-2 pared chalk, 1 ounce powder of bark, and 1 ounce of camphor.

A CHEAP BUT GOOD TOOTH-POWDER.–Cut a slice of bread as thick as may be, into squares, and burn in the fire until it becomes charcoal, after which pound in a mortar, and sift through a fine muslin; it is then ready for use.

CHEAP AND INVALUABLE DENTIFRICE.–Dissolve 2 ounces of borax in three pints of water; before quite cold, add thereto one tea-spoonful of tincture of myrh, and one table-spoonful of spirits of camphor; bottle the mixture for use. One wine-glass of the solution, added to half a pint of tepid water, is sufficient for each application. This solution, applied daily, preserves and beautifies the teeth, extirpates all tartarus adhesion, produces a pearl-like whiteness, ar- rests decay, and induces a healthy action in the gums.

INVALUABLE DENTIFRICE.–Dissolve two ounces of borax in three pints of boiling water; before quite cold, add one tea-spoonful of tincture of myrrh, and one table-spoonful of spirits of camphor; bottle the mixture for use. One wine-glassful of this solution, added to half a pint of tepid water, is sufficient for each application.

FOR THE HAIR.

LOSS OF HAIR.–The most simple remedy for loss of hair is friction to the scalp of the head, using for the purpose an old tooth- brush, or one of which the bristles have been softened by soaking in boiling water. The shape of the instrument adapts it to be inserted readily and effectually between the hair, where it should be rubbed backwards and forwards over the space of an inch or so at a time. In addition to the friction, which should be used once or twice a day, the head may be showered once a day with cold water, carefully drying it with soft, spongy towels.

POMATUM.–Take of white mutton suet 4 pounds, well boiled in hot water, (3 quarts) and wash it to free it from salt. Melt the suet, when dried, with 1 1 pounds of fresh 2

lard, and 2 pounds of yellow wax. Pour into an earthen vessel, and stir till it is cold; then beat into it 30 drops of oil of cloves, or any other essential oil whose scent you prefer.

If this kind of pomatum is too hard, use less wax.

At times numbers of loose hairs come away in the brushing or combing. Such cases as these will generally be found remedial. Wilson recommends women with short hair to dip their heads into cold water every morning, and afterwards apply the brush until a glow of warmth is felt all over the scalp. Those who have long hair are to brush it till the skin beneath becomes red, when a lotion is to be applied, as specified here.

Eau de Cologne 2 oz. Tincture of Cantharides 1 oz. 2 Oil of Nutmegs 1 drachm.

2 Oil of Lavender 10 drops. To be well mixed together. Another is composed of:–

Mezereon bark in small pieces 1 oz. Horse-Radish root in small pieces 1 oz. Boiling distilled Vinegar 1 pint.

Let this infusion stand for a week, and then strain through muslin for use.

If irritating to the skin, these lotions can be made weaker, or less frequently applied than might otherwise be necessary. Either of them, or distilled vinegar alone, may be rubbed into a bald patch with a tooth-brush. The same lotions may also be used if the hair is disposed to become gray too early; as they invigorate the apparatus situated beneath the skin, and enable it to take up coloring matter. Dyeing of the hair is a practice which ought never to be resorted to.

Those who are unwilling or unable to discontinue the practice of applying some kind of dressing to the hair, should, at least, content themselves with a simple, yet good material.

The best olive oil is most suitable for the purpose, scented with otto of roses or bergamot; the latter, as many people know, is the essence of a species of mint. The same scents may also be used for pomatum, which should be made of perfectly pure lard, or marrow.

HAIR OILS, &c.–When used moderately, oils, ointments, &c., tend to strengthen the hair, especially when it is naturally dry. When used in excess, however, they clog the pores, prevent the escape of the natural secretions, and cause the hair to wither and fall off. The varieties of "oils,"

"Greases," "ointments," rivaling each-other in their high sounding pretensions, which are daily imposed upon public credulity, are interminable. We add one or two of the most simple.

FOR THICKENING THE HAIR.–To one ounce of Palma Christi oil, add a sufficient quantity of bergamot or lavender to scent it. Apply it to the parts where it is most needed, brushing it well into the hair.

AN OINTMENT FOR THE HAIR.–Mix two ounces of bear's grease, half an ounce of honey, one drachm of lau-danum, three drachms of the powder of southernwood, three drachms of the balsam of Peru, one and a half drachms of the ashes of the roots of bulrushes, and a small quantity of the oil of sweet almonds.

MACASSAR OIL.–It is said to be composed of the following ingredients:–To three quarts of common oil, add half-a-pint of spirits of wine, three ounces of cinnamon powder, and two ounces of bergamot; heat the whole in a large pipkin. On removing from the fire, add three or four small pieces of alkanet root, and keep the vessel closely covered for several hours. When cool, it may be filtered through a funnel lined with filtering paper.

Whether oils are used or not, the hair ought night and morning to be carefully and elaborately brushed. This is one of the best preservatives of its beauty.

The following is recommended as an excellent Hair Oil:–

Boil together half-a-pint of port wine, one pint and a-half of sweet oil, and half-a-pound of green southernwood. Strain the mixture through a linen rag several times; adding, at the last operation, two ounces of bear's grease. If fresh southernwood is added each time it passes through the linen, the composition will be improved.

POMADE VICTORIA.–This highly-praised and excellent pomade is made in the following way–and if so made, will be found to give a beautiful gloss and softness to the hair:–

Quarter of a-pound of honey and half-an-ounce of bees' wax simmered together for a few minutes and then strain.

Add oil of almonds, lavender, and thyme, half-a-drachm each. Be sure to continue stirring till quite cold, or the honey and wax will separate.

LEMON POMATUM.–Best lard, two pounds; suet, half-a-pound; dissolve with a gentle heat, and mix them well together. Then add four ounces of orange-flower water, and four ounces of rose-water, and mix them well together before adding, or they will separate. Having done this, add a quarter of an ounce of essence of lemon; half-a-drachm of musk, and half-a-drachm of oil of thyme.

TO COLOR POMATUM.–Yellow, by palm oil or annatto; red, by alkanet root; and green, by guaiacum, or the green leaves of parsley.

BANDOLINE FOR THE HAIR, (A FRENCH RECEIPT).–To one quart of water, put 1 ounce of quince pips, boil it nearly 2 an hour, stirring it well, strain it through a fine muslin, let it stand twenty-four hours, and then add fourteen drops of the essential oil of almonds. A dessert-spoonful of brandy may be added, if required to keep for a long time.

BANDOLINE FOR THE HAIR.–Take of castor oil, two ounces; spermaceti, one drachm; oil of bergamot, one drachm; mix with heat and strain; then beat in six drops of roses. If wished colored, add half-a-drachm of annatto.

ANOTHER.–I furnish you with an excellent form of Bandoline, much more quickly made than others. Have a small packet of powdered gum dragon by you, and when you require any fresh bandoline, take a tea-spoonful of the powder, and pour enough boiling water on it to make a small bottle full. Scent with otto of roses.

CURLING FLUID.–Place two pounds of common soap, cut small, into three pints of spirits of wine, with eight ounces of potash, and melt the whole, stirring it with a clean piece of wood. Add, on cooling, essence of amber, vanilla, and neroli, of each quarter of an ounce. The best method of keeping ringlets in curl, is the occasional application of the yolk of an egg, and the hair, afterwards, well washed in lukewarm water. Apply the egg with a tooth or hair-brush.

FOR THE LIPS.

VERY EXCELLENT LIP-SALVE.–Take four ounces of butter, fresh from the churn, cut it small, put it into a jar, cover it with good rose-water, and let it remain for four or five days; then drain it well, and put it into a small and very clean saucepan, with one ounce of spermaceti, and one of yellow beeswax sliced thin, a quarter of an ounce of bruised alkanet root, two drachms of gum benzoin, and one of storax, beaten to powder, half an ounce of loaf sugar, and the strained juice of a moderate sized lemon. Simmer these gently, keeping them stirred all the time, until the mixture looks very clear, and sends forth a fine aromatic odor; then strain it through a thin doubled muslin, and stir to it from twelve to twenty drops of essential oil of roses, and pour it into small gallipots, from which it can easily be turned out when cold, and then be rubbed against the lips, which is the most pleasant way of using it, as it is much firmer than common lip-salve, and will be found more healing and infinitely more agreeable. When butter cannot be had direct from the churn, any which is quite fresh may be substituted for it, after the salt has been well washed and soaked out of it, by working it with a strong spoon in cold water, in which it should remain for a couple of days or more, the water being frequently changed during the time.

ROSE LIP-SALVE. –8 ounces sweet almond oil, 4 ounces prepared mutton suet, 1 1 ounce's white wax, 2 ounces sper-2 machete, 20 drops otto; steep a small quantity of alkanet root in the oil, and strain before using. Melt the suet, wax, and spermaceti together, then add the coloric oil and otto.

LIP-SALVES.–A good lip-salve may be made as follows:–

Take an ounce of the oil of sweet almonds, cold drawn; a drachm of fresh mutton suet; and a little bruised alkanet root: and simmer the whole together in an earthen pipkin.

Instead of the oil of sweet almonds you may use oil of Jasmin, or oil of any other flower, if you intend the lip-salve to have a fragrant odour.–2. Take a pound of fresh butter; a quarter of a pound of beeswax; four or five ounces of cleansed black grapes, and about an ounce of bruised alkanet root. Simmer them together over a slow fire till the wax is wholly dissolved, and the mixture becomes of a bright red color; strain, and put it by for use. 3. Oil of almonds, spermaceti, white wax, and white sugar-candy, equal parts, form a good white lip-salve.

SUPERIOR LIP-SALVE.–White wax, two and a half ounces; spermaceti, three quarters of an ounce; oil of almonds, four ounces.

Mix well together, and apply a little to the lips at night.

ANOTHER.–A dessert spoonful of salad oil in a saucer, hold it over a candle, and drop melted wax over it till the oil is thinly covered, when they are incorporated, pour it into boxes.–(Wax taper will do.)

FOR CORNS.

CURE FOR CORNS.–Place the feet for half an hour, two or three nights successively, in a pretty strong solution of common soda. The alkali dissolves the indurated cuticle, and the corn falls out spontaneously, leaving a small excavation, which soon fills up.

TO REMOVE CORNS.–Get four ounces of white diachylon plaster, four ounces of shoemaker's wax, and sixty drops of muriatic acid or spirits of salt. Boil them for a few minutes in an earthen pipkin, and when cold, roll the mass between the hands and apply a little on a piece of white leather.

A CERTAIN CURE FOR SOFT CORNS.–Dip a piece of soft linen rag in turpentine, and wrap it round the toe on which the soft corn is, night and morning; in a few days the corn will disappear; but the relief is instantaneous.

PERFUMES.

TO MAKE EAU DE COLOGNE.–Rectified spirits of wine, four pints; oil of bergamot, one ounce; oil of lemon, half an ounce; oil of rosemary, half a drachm; oil of Neroli, three quarters of a drachm; oil of English lavender, one drachm; oil of oranges, one drachm.

Mix well and then filter. If these proportions are too large, smaller ones may be used.

EAU DE COLOGNE.–Oil of neroli, citron, bergamot, orange, and rosemary, of each twelve drops; cardamom seeds, one drachm; spirits of wine, one pint. Let it stand for a week.

LAVENDER WATER.–Oil of lavender, 2 drachms; oil of bergamot, 1 drachm; essence of musk, 1 drachm; spirits of 2

wine, 13 ounces; water, 5 ounces. Let it stand for a week. FOR KEEPING THE WARDROBE IN ORDER.

TO CLEAN KID GLOVES.–Make a strong lather with curd soap and warm water, in which steep a small piece of new flannel. Place the glove on a flat, clean, and unyielding surface–such as the bottom of a dish, and having thoroughly soaped the flannel (when squeezed from the lather), rub the kid till all dirt be removed, cleaning and recouping the flannel from time to time. Care must be taken to omit no part of the glove, by turning the fingers, &c. The gloves must be dried in the sun, or before a moderate fire, and will present the appearance of old parchment. When quite dry, they must be gradually "pulled out," and will look new.

ANOTHER. –First see that your hands are clean, then put on the gloves and wash them, as though you were washing your hands, in a basin of spirits of turpentine, until quite clean; then hang them up in a warm place, or where there is a good current of air, which will carry off all smell of the turpentine. This method was brought from Paris, and thousands of dollars have been made by it.

TO CLEAN COLORED KID GLOVES. –Have ready on a table a clean towel, folded three or four times, a saucer of new milk, and another saucer with a piece of brown soap. Take one glove at a time, and spread it smoothly on the folded towel. Then dip in the milk a piece of clean flannel, rub it on the soap till you get off a tolerable quantity, and then, with the wet flannel, commence rubbing the glove. Begin at the wrist, and rub lengthways towards the end of the fingers, holding the glove firmly in your right-hand. Continue this process until the glove is well cleaned all over with the milk and soap. When done, spread them out, and pin them on a line to dry gradually. When nearly dry, pull them out evenly, the crossway of the leather. When quite dry, stretch them on your hands. White kid gloves may also be washed in this manner, provided they have never been cleaned with India-rubber.

TO CLEAN WHITE OR COLORED KID GLOVES.–Put the glove on your hand, then take a small piece of flannel, dip it in camphene, and well, but gently, rub it over the glove, taking care not to make it too wet, when the dirt is removed, dip the flannel (or another piece if that is become too dirty) into pipe-clay and rub it over the glove; take it off, and hang it up in a room to dry, and in a day or two very little smell will remain; and if done carefully they will be almost as good as new. In colored ones, if yellow, use gamboge after the pipe-clay, and for other colors match it in dry paint.

TO CLEAN WHITE KID GLOVES.–Stretch the gloves on a clean board, and rub all the soiled or grease-spots with cream of tartar or magnesia. Let them rest for an hour. Then have ready a mixture of alum and Fuller's earth (both powdered), and rub it all over the gloves with a brush (a clean tooth-brush or something similar), and let them rest for an hour or two. Then sweep it all off, and go over them with a flannel dipped in a mixture of bran and finely powdered whiting. Let them rest another hour; then brush off the powder, and you will find them clean.

TO CLEAN LIGHT KID GLOVES.–Put on one glove, and having made a strong lather with common brown soap, apply it with a shaving brush, wipe it off immediately with a clean towel, then blow into the glove, and leave it to dry.

AN EXCELLENT PASTE FOR GLOVES.–Liquor of ammonia half an ounce, chloride of potash ten ounces, curd soap one pound, water half a pint; dissolve the soap in the water, with a gentle heat, then as the mixture cools, stir in the other ingredients. Use it, by rubbing it over the gloves until the dirt is removed.

TO WASH THREAD LACE.–Rip off the lace, carefully pick out the loose bits of thread, and roll the lace very smoothly and securely round a clean black bottle, previously covered with old white linen, sewed tightly on. Tack each end of the lace with a needle and thread, to keep it smooth; and be careful in wrapping not to crumple or fold in any of the scallops or pearlings. After it is on the bottle, take some of the best sweet oil and with a clean sponge wet the lace thoroughly to the inmost folds. Have ready in a wash-kettle, a strong cold lather of clear water and white Castile soap. Fill the bottle with cold water, to prevent its bursting, cork it well, and stand it upright in the suds, with a string round the neck secured to the ears or handle of the kettle, to prevent its knocking about and breaking while over the fire.

Let it boil in the suds for an hour or more, till the lace is clean and white all through. Drain off the suds, and dry it on the bottle in the sun. When dry, remove the lace from the bottle and roll it round a wide ribbon-block; or lay it in long folds, place it within a sheet of smooth, white, paper, and press it in a large book for a few days.

TO WASH A WHITE LACE VEIL.–Put the veil into a strong lather of white soap and very clear water, and let it simmer slowly for a quarter of an hour. Take it out and squeeze it well, but be sure not to rub it. Rinse it in two cold waters, with a drop or two of liquid blue in the last. Have ready some very clear and weak gum-arabic water, or some thin starch, or rice-water. Pass the veil through it, and clear it by clapping. Then stretch it out evenly, and pin it to dry on a linen cloth, making the edge as straight as possible, opening out all the scallops, and fastening each with pins. When dry, lay a piece of thin muslin smoothly over it, and iron it on the wrong side.

TO WASH A BLACK LACE VEIL.–Mix bullock's gall with sufficient hot water to make it as warm as you can bear your hand in. Then pass the veil through it. It must be squeezed, and not rubbed. It will be good to perfume the gall with a little musk. Next rinse the veil through two cold waters, tinging the last with indigo. Then dry it. Have ready in a pan some stiffening made by pouring boiling water on a very small piece of glue. Pat the veil into it, squeeze it out, stretch it, and clap it. Afterwards pin it out to dry on a linen cloth, making it very straight and even, and taking care to open and pin the edge very nicely. When dry, iron it on the wrong side, having laid a linen cloth over the ironing-blanket. Any article of black lace may be washed in this manner.

TO CLEAN WHITE SATIN AND FLOWERED SILKS.–1.Mix sifted stale bread crumbs with powder blue, and rub it thoroughly all over, then shake it well, and dust it with clean, soft cloths. Afterwards, where there are any gold or silver flowers, take a piece of crimson ingrain velvet, rub the flowers with it, which will restore them to their original lustre. 2. Pass them through a solution of fine hard soap, at a hand heat, drawing them through the hand. Rinse in lukewarm water, dry and finish by pinning out. Brush the flossy or bright side with a clean clothes-brush, the way of the nap. Finish them by dipping a sponge into a size, made by boiling isinglass in water, and rub the wrong side. Rinse out a second time, and brush, and dry near a fire, or in a warm room. Silks may be treated in the same way, but not brushed.

TO CLEAN WHITE SILK.–Dissolve some of the best curd soap in boiling water, and when the solution is as hot as the hand can bear, pass the silk through it thoroughly, handling it gently, not to injure the texture. If there are any spots, these may be rubbed carefully until they disappear. The article must then be rinsed in lukewarm water.

TO IRON SILK.–Silk cannot be ironed smoothly, so as to press out all the creases, without first sprinkling it with water, and rolling it up tightly in a towel, letting it rest for an hour or two. If the iron is in the least too hot, it will injure the color, and it should first be tried on an old piece of the same silk.

TO WASH SILK. –Half a pint of gin, four ounces of soft soap, and two ounces of honey, well shaken; then rub the silk, with a sponge (wetted with the above mixture), upon a table, and wash through two waters, in which first put two or three spoonful of ox gall, which will brighten the colors, and prevent their running. The silks should not be wrung, but well shaken and hung up smoothly to dry, and mangled while damp. The writer has had green silk dresses washed by this receipt, and they have looked as good as new.

TO RENOVATE BLACK SILK. –Slice some uncooked pot-toes, pour boiling water on them; when cold, sponge the right side of the silk with it, and iron on the wrong.

TO KEEP SILK. –Silk articles should not be kept folded in white paper, as the chloride of lime used in bleaching the paper will probably impair the color of the silk. Brown or blue paper is better– the yellowish smooth India paper is best of all. Silk intended for a dress should not be kept in the house long before it is made up, as lying in the folds will have a tendency to impair its durability by causing it to cut or split, particularly if the silk has been thickened by gum.

We knew of an instance of a very elegant and costly thread-lace veil being found, on its arrival from France, cut into squares (and therefore destroyed) by being folded over a pasteboard card. A white satin dress should be pinned up in blue paper, with coarse brown paper outside, sewed together at the edges.

TO RESTORE VELVET.–When velvet gets plushed from pressure, holding the reverse side over a basin of boiling water will raise the pile, and perhaps it may also succeed in the case of wet from rain.

TO IRON VELVET.–Having ripped the velvet apart, damp each piece separately, and holding it tightly in both hands, stretch it before the fire, the wrong side of the velvet being towards the fire. This will remove the creases, and give the surface of the material a fresh and new appearance. Velvet cannot be ironed on a table, for, when spread out on a hard substance, the iron will not go smoothly over the pile.

TO CLEAN ERMINE AND MINIVAR FUR.–Take a piece of soft flannel, and rub the fur well with it (but remember that the rubbing must be always against the grain); then rub the fur with common flour until clean. Shake it well, and rub again with the flannel till all the flour is out of it. I have had a Minivar boa for four years. It has never been cleaned with anything but flour, and is not in the least injured by the rubbing. It was a school companion who told me that her aunt (a Russian lady) always cleaned her white furs with flour, and that they looked quite beautiful. It has one advantage–

the lining does not require to be taken out, and it only requires a little trouble. Ermine takes longer than Minivar.

The latter is very easily done.

TO PERFUME LINEN.–Rose-leaves dried in the shade, or at about four feet from a stove, one pound; cloves, caraway-seeds, and allspice, of each one ounce; pound in a mortar, or grind in a mill; dried salt, a quarter of a pound; mix all these together, and put the compound into little bags.

TO RESTORE SCORCHED LINEN.–Take two onions, peel and slice them, and extract the juice by squeezing or pound-ing. Then cut up half an ounce of white soap, and two ounces of fuller's earth; mix with them the onion juice, and half a pint of vinegar. Boil this composition well, and spread it, when cool, over the scorched part of the linen, leaving it to dry thereon. Afterwards wash out the linen.

TO WHITEN LINEN THAT HAS TURNED YELLOW.–Cut up a pound of fine white soap into a gallon of milk, and hang it over the fire in a wash-kettle. When the soap has entirely melted, put in the linen, and boil it half an hour.

Then take it out; have ready a lather of soap and warm water; wash the linen in it, and then rinse it through two cold waters, with a very little blue in the last.

TO WASH CHINA CRAPE SCARFS, &c.–If the fabric be good, these articles of dress can be washed as frequently as may be required, and no diminution of their beauty will be discoverable, even when the various shades of green have been employed among other colors in the patterns. In cleaning them, make a strong lather of boiling water– suffer it to cool; when cold, or nearly so, wash the scarf quickly and thoroughly, dip it immediately in cold hard water, in which a little salt has been thrown (to preserve the colors), rinse, squeeze, and hang it out to dry in the open air; pin it at its extreme edge to the line, so that it may not in any part be folded together; the more rapidly it dries, the clearer it will be.

TO CLEAN EMBROIDERY AND GOLD LACE.–For this purpose no alkaline liquors are to be used; for while they clean the gold, they corrode the silk, and change its color.

Soap also alters the shade, and even the species of certain colors. But spirit of wine may be used without any danger of its injuring either color or quality; and, in many cases, proves as effective for restoring the luster of the gold as the corrosive detergents. But, though spirits of wine is the most innocent material employed for this purpose, it is not in all cases proper. The golden covering may be in some parts worn off; or the base metal with which it has been alloyed may be corroded by the air, so as to leave the particles of the gold disunited; while the silver underneath, tarnished to a yellow hue, may continue a tolerable color to the whole, so it is apparent that the removal of the tarnish would be prej-udicial, and make the lace or embroidery less like gold than it was before. It is necessary that care should be taken.

TO REMOVE STAINS OF WINE OR FRUIT FROM TABLE LINEN.– A wine stain may sometimes be removed by rubbing it, while wet, with common salt. It is said, also, that sherry wine poured immediately on a place where port wine has been spilled, will prevent its leaving a stain. A certain way of extracting fruit or wine stains from table-linen is to tie up some cream of tartar in the stained part (so as to form a sort of bag), and then to put the linen into a lather of soap and cold water, and boil it awhile. Then transfer it wet to a lukewarm suds, wash and rinse it well, and dry and iron it. The stains will disappear during the process.

Another way is to mix, in equal quantities, soft soap, slack-ened lime, and pearl-ash. Rub the stain with this preparation, and expose the linen to the sun with the mixture plastered on it. If necessary, repeat the application. As soon as the stain has disappeared, wash out the linen immediately, as it will be injured if the mixture is left in it.

STAIN MIXTURE.–Take an ounce of sal-ammoniac (or hartshorn) and an ounce of salt of tartar–mix them well, put them into a pint of soft water, and bottle it for use, keeping it very tightly corked. Pour a little of this liquid into a saucer, and wash in it those parts of a white article that have been stained with ink, mildew, fruit, or red wine. When the stains have, by this process, been removed, wash the article in the usual manner.

CHEMICAL RENOVATING BALLS–for taking out grease, paint, pitch, tar, from silks, stuffs, linen, woolen, carpets, hats, coats, &c., without fading the color or injuring the cloth:– 1 ounce of fuller's earth, 1 ounce of pipe-clay, 4 ounce salt of tartar, 1 ounce beef gall, 1 ounce spirits of wine.

Pound the hard parts and mix the ingredients well together.

Wet the stain with cold water, rub it well with this ball, then sponge it with a wet sponge and the stain will disappear.

TO PREVENT COLORED THINGS FROM RUNNING.–

Boil 1 pound of soap till nearly dissolved, then add a small 4 piece of alum and boil with it. Wash the things in this lather, but do not soap them. If they require a second water put alum to that also as well as to the rinsing and blue water.

This will preserve them.

TO REMOVE STAINS FROM MOURNING DRESSES.–Take a good handful of fig-leaves, and boil them in two quarts of water until reduced to a pint. Squeeze the leaves and put the liquor into a bottle for use. The articles, whether of bom-basin, crape, cloth, &c., need only be rubbed with a sponge dipped in the liquor, when the effect will be instantly produced. If any reason exists to prevent the substance from being wetted, then apply French chalk, which will absorb the grease from the finest texture without injury.

TO SHRINK NEW FLANNEL.–New flannel should always be shrunk or washed before it is made up, that it may be cut out more accurately, and that the grease which is used in manufacturing it may be extracted. First, cut off the list along the selvage edges of the whole piece. Then put it into warm (not boiling) water, without soap. Begin at one end of the piece, and rub it with both hands till you come to the other end; this is to get out the grease and the blue with which new white flannel is always tinged. Then do the same through another water. Rinse it through a clean, lukewarm water; wring it lengthways, and stretch it well.

In hanging it out on a line do not suspend it in festoons, but spread it along the line straight and lengthways. If dried in festoons, the edges will be in great scollops, making it very difficult to cut out. It must be dried in the sun. When dry let it be stretched even, clapped with the hands, and rolled up tight and smoothly, till wanted.

GUM ARABIC STARCH.–Get two ounces of fine, white gum arabic, and pound it to powder. Next, put it into a pitcher, and pour on it a pint or more of boiling water (according to the degree of strength you desire), and then, having covered it, let it set all night. In the morning, pour it carefully from the dregs into a clean bottle, cork it, and keep it for use. A table-spoonful of gum water stirred into a pint of starch that has been made in the usual manner, will give to lawns (either white or printed) a look of newness to which nothing else can restore them after washing. It is also good (much diluted) for thin white muslin and bobinet.

TO WASH WHITE THREAD GLOVES AND STOCKINGS.–

These articles are so delicate as to require great care in washing, and they must not on any account be rubbed. Make a lather of white soap and cold water, and put it into a saucepan.

Soap the gloves or stockings well, put them in, and set the saucepan over the fire. When they have come to a hard boil, take them off, and when cool enough for your hand, squeeze them in the water. Having prepared a fresh cold lather, boil them again in that. Then take the pan off the fire, and squeeze them well again, after which they can be stretched, dried, and then ironed on the wrong side.

TO CLEAN SILK STOCKINGS.–First wash the stockings in the usual manner, to take out the rough dirt. After rinsing them in clean water, wash them well in a fresh soap liquor. Then make a third soap liquor, which is colored with a little stone-blue; then wash the stockings once more, take them out, wring them, and particularly dry them. Now stove them with brimstone, and draw on a wooden leg two stockings, one upon the other, observing that the two fronts or outsides are face to face. Polish with a glass bottle. The two first liquors should be only lukewarm, but the third as hot as you can bear your hand in. Blondes and gauzes may be whitened in the same manner, but there should be a little gum put in the last liquor before they are stoved.

TO TAKE OUT MILDEW FROM CLOTHES.–Mix some soft soap with powdered starch, half as much salt, and the juice of a lemon, lay it on the part with a brush, let it be exposed in the air day and night, until the stain disappears. Iron-moulds may be removed by the salt of lemons. Many stains in linen may be taken out by dipping linen in sour butter-milk, and then drying it in the sun; afterwards wash it in cold water several times. Stains caused by acids may be removed by tying some pearlash up in the stained part; scrape some soap in cold, soft water, and boil the linen till the stain is out.

BLEACHING STRAW.–Straw is bleached, and straw bonnets cleaned, by putting them into a cask into which a few brimstone matches are placed. The fumes of the sulphur have the effect of destroying the color, or whitening the straw. The same effect may be produced by dipping the straw into the chloride of lime dissolved in water.

TO WASH MOUSELINE-DE-LAINE.–Boil a pound of rice in five quarts of water, and, when cool enough, wash in this, using the rice for soap. Have another quantity ready, but strain the rice from this and use it with warm water, keeping the rice strained off for a third washing which, at the same time, stiffens and also brightens the colors.

TO BLEACH A FADED DRESS.–Wash the dress in hot suds, and boil it until the color appears to be gone; then rinse it and dry it in the sun. Should it not be rendered white by these means, lay the dress in the open air, and bleach it for several days. If still not quite white, repeat the boiling.

INDELIBLE MARKING INK, WITHOUT PREPARATION.– 1 1 drachms nitrate of silver (lunar caustic), 1 ounce distilled 2 water, 1 ounce strong mucilage of gum arabic, 3 drachm 2 liquid ammonia; mix the above in a clean glass bottle, cork tightly, and keep in a dark place till dissolved, and ever afterwards. Directions for use:–Shake the bottle, then dip a clean quill pen in the ink, and write or draw what you require on the article; immediately hold it close to the fire, (without scorching) or pass a hot iron over it, and it will become a deep and indelible black, indestructible by either time or acids of any description.

MIXTURE FOR REMOVING INK STAINS AND IRON-MOULDS.– Cream of tartar and salts of sorrel, one ounce each; mix well, and keep in a stoppered bottle.

TO WASH HAIR-BRUSHES.–Never use soap. Take a piece of soda, dissolve it in warm water, stand the brush in it, taking care that the water only covers the bristles; it will almost immediately become white and clean; stand it to dry in the open air with the bristles downwards, and it will be found to be as firm as a new brush.

TO CLEAN HEAD AND CLOTHES-BRUSHES.–Put a table-spoonful of pearl-ash into a pint of boiling water. Having fastened a bit of sponge to the end of a stick, dip it into the solution, and wash the brush with it; carefully going in among the bristles. Next pour over some clean hot water, and let it lie a little while. Then drain it, wipe it with a cloth, and dry it before the fire. Lola Montez in her “Arts of Beauty” gives the following receipts for complexion, hair, &c:–

FOR THE COMPLEXION.–“Infuse wheat-bran, well sifted, for four hours in white wine vinegar, add to it five yolks of eggs and two grains of ambergris, and distill the whole. It should be carefully corked for twelve or fifteen days, when it will be fit for use.

“Distill two handfuls of jessamine flowers in a quart of rose-water and a quart of orange-water. Strain through porous paper, and add a scruple of musk and a scruple of ambergris.”

TO GIVE ELASTICITY OF FORM.–“Fat of the stag or deer 8 oz. Florence oil (or olive oil) 6 oz. Virgin wax 3 oz. Musk 1 grain. White brandy 1 pint. Rose-water 4 oz.

“Put the fat, oil, and wax into a well glazed earthen vessel, and let them simmer over a slow fire until they are as-similated; then pour in the other ingredients, and let the whole gradually cool, when it will be fit for use. There is no doubt that this mixture, frequently and thoroughly rubbed upon the body on going to bed, will impart a remarkable degree of elasticity to the muscles. In the morning, after this preparation has been used, the body should be thoroughly wiped with a sponge, dampened with cold water.”

FOR THE COMPLEXION.–“Take equal parts of the seeds of the melon, pumpkin, gourd, and cucumber, pounded till they are reduced to powder; add to it sufficient fresh cream to dilute the flour, and then add milk enough to reduce the whole to a thin paste. Add a grain of musk, and a few drops of the oil of lemon. Anoint the face with this, leave it on twenty or thirty minutes, or overnight if convenient, and wash off with warm water. It gives a remarkable purity and brightness to the complexion.

"Infuse a handful of well sifted wheat bran for four hours in white wine vinegar; add to it five yolks of eggs and two grains of musk, and distill the whole. Bottle it, keep carefully corked for fifteen days, when it will be fit for use. Apply it overnight, and wash in the morning with tepid water."

TOOTH-POWDER.–

"Prepared chalk 6 oz. Cassia powder 1 oz. 2 Orris-root 1 oz.

"These should be thoroughly mixed and used once a day with a firm brush.

"A simple mixture of charcoal and cream of tartar is an excellent tooth-powder."

TO WHITEN THE HAND.–"Both Spanish and French women–those, at least, who are very particular to make the most of these charms–are in the habit of sleeping in gloves which are lined or plastered over with a kind of pomade to improve the delicacy and complexion of their hands. This paste is generally made of the following ingredients:–

"Take half a pound of soft soap, a gill of salad oil, an ounce of mutton tallow, and boil them till they are thoroughly mixed. After the boiling has ceased, but before it is cold, add one gill of spirits of wine, and a grain of musk.

"If any lady wishes to try this, she can buy a pair of gloves three or four sizes larger than the hand, rip them open and spread on a thin layer of the paste, and then sew the gloves up again. There is no doubt that by wearing them every night they will give smoothness and a fine complexion to the hands. Those who have the means, can send them to Paris and purchase them ready made.

"If the hands are inclined to be rough and to chop, the following wash will remedy the evil.

Lemon-juice 3 oz.

White wine vinegar 3 oz. White brandy 1 pint." 2 FOR THE HAIR.–

"Beat up the white of four eggs into a froth, and rub that thoroughly close to the roots of the hair. Leave it to dry. Then wash the head and hair clean with a mixture of equal parts of rum and rose-water."

"HONEY-WATER.–

"Essence of ambergris 1 dr. Essence of musk 1 dr.

Essence of bergamot 2 drs. Oil of cloves 15 drops.

Orange-flower water 4 oz.

Spirits of wine 5 oz. Distilled water 4 oz.

"All these ingredients should be mixed together, and left for about fourteen days, then the whole to be filtered through porous paper, and bottled for use.

"This is a good hair-wash and an excellent perfume." "TO REMOVE PIMPLES.

There are many kinds of pimples, some of which partake almost of the nature of ulcers, which require medical treatment; but the small red pimple, which is most common, may be removed by applying the following twice a-day:–

"Sulphur water 1 oz.

Acetated liquor of ammonia 1 oz. 4 Liquor of potassa 1 gr.

White wine vinegar 2 oz. Distilled water 2 oz."

"TO REMOVE BLACK SPECKS OR 'FLESHWORMS.'

Sometimes little black specks appear about the base of the nose, or on the forehead, or in the hollow of the chin which are called 'fleshworms,' and are occasioned by coag-ulated lymph that obstructs the pores of the skin. They may be squeezed out by pressing the skin, and ignorant persons suppose them to be little worms. They are permanently removed by washing with warm water, and severe friction with a towel, and then applying a little of the following preparation:–

"Liquor of potassa 1 oz. Cologne 2 oz.

White brandy. 4 oz.

"The warm water and friction alone are sometimes sufficient."

"TO REMOVE FRECKLES.

The most celebrated compound ever used for the removal of freckles was called Unction de Maintenon, after the celebrated Madame de Maintenon, mistress and wife of Louis XIV. It is made as follows:–

"Venice soap 1 oz. Lemon-juice 1 oz.

Oil of bitter almonds 1 oz. Deliquiated oil of tartar 1 oz.

Oil of rhodium 3 drops

"First dissolve the soap in the lemon-juice, then add the two oils, and place the whole in the sun till it acquires the consistency of ointment, and then add the oil of rhodium. Anoint the freckled face at night with this function, and wash in the morning with pure water, or, if convenient, with a mixture of elder-flower and rose-water.

"TO REMOVE TAN.

An excellent wash to remove tan is called Crème de l'Enclos, and is made thus:

"New milk 1 pint. Lemon-juice 1 oz. White brandy 1 oz.

"Boil the whole, and skim it clear from all scum. Use it night and morning.

"A famous preparation with the Spanish ladies for removing the effects of the sun and making the complexion bright, is composed simply of equal parts of lemon-juice and the white of eggs. The the whole is beaten together in a var-nished earthen pot, and set over a slow fire, and stirred with a wooden spoon till it acquires the consistency of soft pomatum. This compound is called Pommade de Seville. If the face is well washed with rice-water before it is applied, it will remove freckles, and give a fine lustre to the complexion.``

9 789358 486339

Printed at Repro India Ltd.